LITERATURE, RELIGION, AND POSTSECULAR STUDIES
Lori Branch, Series Editor

A THEOLOGY OF SENSE

John Updike, Embodiment,
and Late Twentieth-Century
American Literature

SCOTT DILL

THE OHIO STATE UNIVERSITY PRESS
COLUMBUS

Copyright © 2018 by The Ohio State University.
All rights reserved.

Library of Congress Cataloging-in-Publication Data is available online at https://catalog.loc.gov

Cover image: Barracoon (c) PacificSunTradingCompany. Courtesy of Warren Adelson and Frank E. Fowler.

Cover design by Angela Moody
Text design by Juliet Williams
Type set in Adobe Minion Pro

♾ The paper used in this publication meets the minimum requirements of the American National Standard for Information Sciences—Permanence of Paper for Printed Library Materials. ANSI Z39.48-1992.

for Janette

CONTENTS

Acknowledgments		*ix*
Preface		*xi*
INTRODUCTION	A Theology of Sense	1
CHAPTER 1	Touching	31
CHAPTER 2	Seeing	61
CHAPTER 3	Tasting	91
CHAPTER 4	Hearing	119
CHAPTER 5	Smelling	149
EPILOGUE	The Aesthetics of Easter	173
Works Cited		*187*
Index		*195*

ACKNOWLEDGMENTS

A WORD OF THANKS to everyone who helped me with this book along the way. Mark Eaton and James Schiff provided much-needed encouragement and thoughtful advice from start to finish. Lindsay Martin and Kristen Elias Rowley smoothly guided the process of getting it into print. Michelle Bard suggested significant changes to the introduction. Mark Pruitt, Matthew Phelps, Brian Hollan, Scott Waalkes, Jim Brownlee, Steve Jenson, Jay Case, Jacci Welling, David Beer, Steve Pinkerton, Brie Parkin, Ray Horton, and Daniel Luttrull all offered helpful feedback on different chapters. Peter Whiting and the SAGES program at Case Western Reserve University gave helpful support and funding. Some parts of this book first appeared in different versions elsewhere. Portions of the introduction and chapter 1 appeared online at *Books & Culture* and in *Critique* (54, no. 4, 2013); a significantly altered version of chapter 2 in *The John Updike Review* (4.2 2016); and a version of chapter 3 in *Religion & Literature* (48, no. 3, 2016). A special note of gratitude to Janette Dill for her patience, love, and joy: This book is dedicated to her—in every sense.

PREFACE

THIS BOOK began with a confusing experience. Despite John Updike's reputation for misogynistic, self-obsessed characters, I found myself feeling not only more thoughtful toward others but generally more pleasant to live with when I was deep into reading one of his books. From St. Augustine to René Girard, the aesthetic theorists of Updike's own Christian tradition have long argued that literary representations affect the reader mimetically. According to that logic, reading about narcissists who see others as sex objects should have incited either total disgust or similarly selfish, objectifying thoughts and feelings. Yet I felt little of either. Whatever self-centered thoughts or actions Updike's characters had, there was something in the way Updike's prose described his characters' sense experiences that ignited a very different set of emotions in me. Why? Did I really think reading John Updike—*John Updike!*—was making me a more thoughtful person?

A Theology of Sense is an attempt to answer that question. It does not offer a comprehensive introduction to all of Updike's work or a thorough interpretation of any single aspect of it. Instead, this book argues that Updike's work provides a profound way to address a much broader set of aesthetic questions: Can certain kinds of literature create uniquely *religious* affects? How would you define such affects as religious? Is there something in the nature of such affects that should influence the way we think about the secularity of literature more generally? These questions are being addressed in the emerging field of postsecular studies, and especially where that field is theorizing affect and aesthetic experience. For example, Talal Asad has pointed out the need to understand how and why we might assume affects "secular" in the first place. He argues for the need to

> start with a curiosity about the doctrine and practice of secularism regardless of where they have originated, and [. . .] ask: How do attitudes to the human body (to pain, physical damage, decay, and death, to physical integrity, bodily growth, and sexual enjoyment) differ in various forms of life? What structures of the senses—hearing, seeing, touching—do these attitudes depend on? (17)

Empirical inquiry is not first and foremost a patently secular fact but an attitude, and a "structure of the senses." Attitudes both drive human action and derive from the sense experiences of human action. Asad's anthropological approach to these structures of the senses is part of a number of social, philosophical, and historical inquiries into the practices and theoretical assumptions that inform our understanding of sense experience. *A Theology of Sense* enters that conversation to demonstrate how theological concepts expressed in literary "forms of life" can inform the most basic sense perceptions. My ultimate goal—and I'm convinced this is the gift Updike's work gives us—is a fuller understanding of how literature shapes our sense experiences.

While the field of postsecular studies is rich in historicist and sociological readings of literature and culture, I focus on the models Updike provides us for theorizing the religious components of aesthetic experience. My concern here is largely with literature and theological aesthetics, though I do draw on aesthetic theory more generally as well as work that addresses painting and music specifically. A renewed interest in the importance of aesthetics for literary study, as demonstrated by the impact of Rita Felski's work and the number of other attempts to develop alternatives to secular critique, has naturally complemented the rise of postsecular studies. John Updike's sense-drenched prose deserves a role in these.

Toward that end, I explain Updike's "theology of sense" in the introduction while laying out the stakes, scope, and resources of my main argument. Gratitude, lyricism, and love are foundational aspects of Updike's approach to the senses, and I compare the unique aesthetic they compose to his contemporaries' and the contribution of that aesthetic to the field of postsecular studies. After that, each of the following chapters addresses how Updike portrays one of the five senses. For centuries past, writers and critics who work on the five senses have pointed out that it is impossible to truly isolate any one sense from the others. While I don't disagree, each chapter takes up a single sense experience to isolate one aspect of Updike's understanding of embodiment and aesthetics. This approach allows me to show how his writing immerses specific instances of sense experience in the sense of God's good creation. It also enables me to compare Updike's representations of that individual sense alongside his contemporaries' treatment of embodiment.

Chapter 1 addresses how Updike's theology of sense approaches affect theory and the meaning of embodiment. I show how the sense of touch is one of Updike's primary ways of exploring how humans relate to their environment. I argue that Updike's portrayal of the relationship between touching and talking requires reconsidering trends in contemporary affect theory from a postsecular standpoint. Though it refers to a few of Updike's novels, the chapter relies most heavily on Updike's autobiographical writings to explain how touch orients his sense of self. It also argues that Don DeLillo's later work, in particular *The Body Artist,* reveals a surprising rapport with Updike's association of touch and identity. Finally, it turns to John Dewey's aesthetics to demonstrate the importance of Updike's correlation of words and hands for aesthetic theory.

Chapter 2 turns from touch to sight in order to explain how images can often be less—not more—realistic than words in faithfully representing bodies. This chapter uses Updike's essays in art criticism, alongside his novel *In the Beauty of the Lilies* (1996), to reevaluate the relationship between the written word, the visual image, and the ontological dimensions of Updike's moral assumptions. Plenitude, a concept more associated with medieval philosophy than American painting and literature, guides his critical sensibility and names the reality his fiction envisions. Ending with Updike's affinity to Susan Sontag's writing about visual culture, this chapter argues that the ways of seeing expressed in his art criticism and his novel about American cinema revise the concept of plenitude for a contemporary society awash in privative images.

Chapter 3 treats the aesthetic problem of good taste. The notions of beauty that the phrase "good taste" invokes are at odds with Updike's cruder moments, yet taste also refers to the educational dynamic of aesthetic perception. This chapter shows how attending to the physical act of tasting, as Updike does, offers a theologically sensitive pedagogy of desire. In order to show how, I look at three of his short stories—"The Music School" (1964), "The Gun Shop" (1972), and "The Full Glass" (2008)—and how all three stories promote literature as a way of cultivating a taste for the given world as such. It includes a reading of Flannery O'Connor's "The Crop" (1947/1971) and shows how O'Connor's sacramental writing largely shares Updike's concerns, but without his emphasis on the aesthetic implications of creaturehood.

Chapter 4 argues that postsecular aesthetics should question the increasing importance of empathy in ethical treatments of the novel genre. Popular music, car stereos, and civic and familial responsibility are interlinked presences that help imagine social space throughout Updike's *Rabbit Angstrom* tetralogy (1960–90). Yet the sounds Rabbit hears inspire a desire deep within him quite different from the desire that music inspires in Patricia Highsmith's Tom Ripley, the protagonist of another tetralogy published in the same period (1955–91). The chapter uses Rabbit's and Ripley's aural experiences to explain how Updike and Highsmith question the validity of ethical arguments for the novel genre's virtual experiences of empathetic feeling and instead recast the ethics of novel reading as a question of "the good" instead of "the right."

Chapter 5 explores how Updike's portrayal of the sense of smell launches a parallel version of the agrarian writer Wendell Berry's critique of American culture. Updike forces the question, Why does a good creation so often smell bad? I argue that including the sense of smell in aesthetics—a sense usually excluded from accounts of the beautiful—exhibits Updike's Christian conception of beauty. The chapter begins with how *Villages* (2004), an update on Updike's earlier, more sociological *Couples* (1968), depicts the sour smells of sex. Then I discuss how the unsparing descriptions of the scents of the human body in *The Coup* (1978) revalue what counts as good through smell. From *The Coup* I turn to Updike's *Complete Henry Bech* (2001) and how Bech's sense of smell persistently associates life with the smell of rot and decay and what that has to teach us about the aesthetic relationship between literature and life.

The book's closing epilogue, "The Aesthetics of Easter," considers how Updike's work as a poet thinks about the dying body. Death not only is a fundamental part of life but is affirmed as good because of its natural—and theological—relationship to life. Updike's Christian belief in the Resurrection frees him to pay attention to the good in death without succumbing to the disingenuous consolation of literary metaphors. Updike's poetry about death, dying, and the Resurrection makes a case for the central role of embodiment in postsecular aesthetics. Thus, the book finishes with a final argument for the aesthetic consequences of Updike's theology of sense and its theory of the body's intrinsic beauty.

INTRODUCTION

A Theology of Sense

"PLATO WAS WRONG," John Updike contends; "what is is absolute. Ideas pale" (*The Collected Later Stories* [hereafter *CLS*] 188). Updike's disciplined, grateful attention to the embodied experience of "what is" constitutes a profound affirmation of creation's goodness. Unlike Plato's idealism, Updike's writing celebrates the experiences of specific things more than generalizing ideas. In doing so, it captures a resplendent vision of the given world's astonishing singularities. Furthermore, the distinctive way that Updike's writing lingers over the peculiarities of human experience portrays a robust response to Plato's famous denigration of material reality. Updike once wrote that the body painted in the Andrew Wyeth image on the cover of this book "is as graceful as its pose is perennial and more delicate, in its hippy rhythm" (*Just Looking* 186). If the pose is generic enough, the body's "hippy rhythm" curves in time to the beat of a distinct, substantial body. "Ideas pale" before the absolute reality of such surprising facts. For Updike, beauty begins with bodies.

Yet Updike's lush, sensory style is often maligned for its lack of ideas. Though Lawrence Buell's recent study of the "Great American

Novel" calls Updike "the late twentieth century's most prominent voice," Updike's contribution to intellectual culture rarely receives the same consideration as his near contemporaries Thomas Pynchon or Toni Morrison (Buell 60). Alongside Pynchon's diffuse, international plots or Morrison's stark genealogies of race and culture, Updike's work appears innocuously parochial, if naively realist. In addition, Updike's detractors complain that whereas Pynchon and Morrison raise difficult questions about history, the conditions of modernity, and the possibility of human freedom, Updike has "nothing to say" (De Bellis, *Encyclopedia* 207). Updike's novels may not overtly address philosophical theories, but his subtle rendering of embodied experience expresses its own ambitious intellectual content. As he wrote in a preface he later added to his first novel, *The Poorhouse Fair* (1958), "There is, then, a philosophical ambition here; an attempt, no less, to present the meaning of being alive, as conveyed by its sensations" (xvi). This philosophical ambition permeates nearly everything he wrote. Moreover, it is because Updike so assiduously avoids abstract ideas in favor of distinct impressions, as his early model Marcel Proust once advised, that Updike's work is worthy of continued reading (Proust 450). Revisiting Updike's attention to the details of sense experience can revise our understanding of how late twentieth-century American literature thinks about embodiment—in particular because of his postsecular aesthetics.

While Updike is often celebrated as the chronicler of the American middle class (Batchelor ix), his work is unparalleled in its exploration of the body's sensory knowledge. Instead of using his novels to argue for the logical viability of his lifelong Christian faith, Updike's characters live ostensibly secular lives that nevertheless express what it feels like to be immersed in the awareness of God's goodness and blessing. Even in the midst of chaotic impulses and desires, their perceptions shimmer with the ubiquitous propinquity of what Plato called "the Good." Contra Plato's idealist conception of that Good, however, Updike's writing imagines for the reader a lived theology of sense experience—what it both *means* and *feels like* to be in love with the gift of a good creation. However secular his stories might seem, a theological conviction inspires their attention to the body.

Updike became famous to the American public for the annals of adulterous affairs in his 1968 novel, *Couples,* but this apparently salacious content shouldn't distract from Updike's robust theology of embodiment. His novels, stories, essays, poems—even his lone attempt at drama—sought to identify the complex aesthetic relationship among the body, its loves, and their effect on the soul. Christina Bieber Lake recently asserted the need for more literary criticism to begin "to ask what kind of lovers we are becoming" (*Prophets* 11). My present book explains how Updike's writing (over sixty books' worth) can help answer that question through its portrayals of sense experience. He is less a lascivious provocateur than a patient archeologist, polishing each fragment of human desire for the reader's reconsideration—how *do* we come to love what we love? What makes it beautiful? Under his spell, sexuality is less a corridor of shameful fantasies than an airy comedy of marvels.

Yet his fascination with love at its moral limits is a function of what we might call, with all due respect, Updike's shallowness. In one of the short stories a man tells his lover, as they end an affair, "For me it was wonderful to become a partner in your response to textures. Your shallowness, as my wife calls it [. . .] broke a new dimension into my hitherto inadequately superficial world" (*The Collected Early Stories* [hereafter cited as *CES*] 453). Such superficiality has not lent itself to portraying very deep characters. His male characters tend to see little beyond the surface of a woman's body. Yet this shallowness is not only intentional but the key to his theology of sense. In this introduction I want, first, to connect the gratitude evident in Updike's prose style to his theology of Creation; second, to place his sexual descriptions within the context of Christianity's view of love and the body; and, finally, to show how what I will call his "secular parables" and their theology of sense can reframe a broader range of problems in postsecular aesthetics.

IN PRAISE OF SUPERFICIALITY

It is Updike's shallow sensuousness, his description of the "superficial world," that makes him worth reading deeply. His superficiality—

using sensation to present the meaning of being alive—is actually quite profound. If his writing at first appears to lack big ideas, it nonetheless contains one abiding ambition: a theology of sense. As empirically grounded in the secular world of the senses as Updike's writing may be, it is imbued with an overarching sense of God, one that enlivens the senses with eager sensitivity. The English noun and verb forms of *sense* have several meanings, though I will draw on two of its broader uses: (1) an intuitive grasp of the whole and (2) the body's means of perception, the five senses. These two different senses of sense are inextricable in Updike's work. Updike's sense of God's goodness animates his characters' eyes, ears, mouths, noses, and hands. They sense individual phenomena in their concreteness because of this holistic, intuited sense of meaning—the two forms of sense enable each other. His theology of sense cultivates a healthy respect for the fundamental ambivalence in such different definitions of the word *sense* and exploits that ambivalence to illuminate the goodness, truth, and beauty of creation's particularity.

It may seem strange to some of Updike's readers to claim he has something profound to say about philosophical issues or Christian theology. Other than a smattering of early book reviews for a general readership, Updike rarely wrote anything explicitly philosophical or theological. Perhaps even more unfavorable to my argument is that Updike's occasional comments on faith could sound uncommonly listless. He denied being a "Christian author" and referred to himself as a "kind of a lackadaisical Christian" (Plath 202). Before his death some critics had even begun wondering if he had lost the faith he had previously claimed (Boswell, "Review" 191). Updike's early work referenced Christian ideas whereas his later only seemed to reference the loss of faith—albeit elegiacally (Bailey, *Rabbit Unredeemed* 26). This trajectory seemed to confirm what Charles Taylor has called the "subtraction story" of secular modernity, where the secular, empirical truth was all that was left once Updike was liberated from the misguided assumptions of his religious superstitions (Taylor, *Secular Age* 22).

Updike's faith was strong throughout his life, however, and his theological acumen sharper than his idiosyncratic combination of rural Pennsylvania humility and urbane *New Yorker* insouciance usually let on (Begley 482–83). More than any apologetic for Christian belief, though, it is precisely Updike's shallowness, his unexpected descriptions of sense perceptions, which makes his work theologically valuable. They offer delicately tinged examples of the color of Christian faith, of what it smells and tastes like to live within the Christian story of Creation, Fall, and Redemption. Jeff Campbell got it right when he asked Updike, "Do you see your sensibility as specifically Christian?" When asked about his "sensibility"—the whole aesthetic context of his work—Updike admits, "I think Christianity is the only world-frame that I've been exposed to that I can actually look through" (Plath 94). Note his wording: The sense of Christianity's "world-frame" enables him to sense the world. Christianity is not an ideology that drives him to seek converts through writing. No, for Updike, Christianity makes sense *make sense.*

Even more so—Christianity provides the very reason for writing the way he does. In a frequently cited passage from his memoirs, *Self-Consciousness* (1989), Updike argues that his writing portrays all of life, since "God is the God of the living":

> Imitation is praise. Description expresses love. [. . .] I have felt free to describe life as accurately as I could, with especial attention to human erosions and betrayals. What small faith I have has given me what artistic courage I have. My theory was that God already knows everything and cannot be shocked. And only truth is useful. Only truth can be built upon. From a higher, inhuman point of view, only truth, however harsh, is holy. (*Self-Consciousness* 231)

With just the faith of a mustard seed Updike has the assurance that his art must praise the Creator, love the creation, and speak truly. His representations of the senses derive all significance from this theological sensibility. Truth is not what you get when you subtract the religion; truth is what Updike's religion commanded him to seek and value as holy.

Am I overstating the case here? Let me be clear that I do not think his Protestant Christianity offers the single interpretive key for a body of work as fecund as Updike's. That would be ridiculous. Furthermore, my argument in this book extracts theological and aesthetic claims from Updike's writing that might surprise him. Updike once good-naturedly grumbled that the dexterous criticism of Alice and Kenneth Hamilton, whose work he lauded, could co-opt his writing for their "Sunday school a little too quickly and efficiently" (Plath 92). Updike saw himself as posing—rather than answering—questions about the meaning of human experience. Recall, too, that his penultimate novel, *Terrorist* (2006), uses an epigraph from Gabriel García Márquez that seems to directly contradict my point: "Disbelief is more resistant than faith because it is sustained by the senses." For Márquez, belief concerns the intelligible, not visible, world.

Yet the effect of this radical dichotomy between the sensory and the spiritual is *Terrorist*'s tempering theme (Naydan 100). When the young protagonist of the novel, Ahmad, tells a classmate, "The human spirit asks for self-denial. It longs to say 'No' to the physical world," she responds by arguing, "The spirit is what comes out of the body, like flowers come out of the earth. Hating your body is like hating yourself, the bones and blood and skin and shit that make you you" (*Terrorist* 72). This view of the physical and spiritual worlds' relationship resounds throughout the novel. And yet, to his credit, rather than set up this Christian teaching as somehow more world-affirming than Ahmad's Muslim faith, Updike is at pains to convey Islam's own this-worldliness in his work. Ahmad clings to a verse from the Koran—perhaps Updike's favorite since another Muslim protagonist, Colonel Ellelloû from *The Coup* (1978), also quotes it: It asserts God is "closer to him than his neck-vein" (*Terrorist* 145). That vivid physical detail aptly captures Updike's way of representing the spiritual as the most intense plane of physical reality. Not beyond or above the real world but somehow within it. "Reality transcends itself within," he wrote in his 1969 autobiographical poem, "Midpoint" (*Midpoint* 38). The spiritual world is not opposed to the material world; rather, "spirit is what comes out of the body." In a word, no, I don't think I'm overstating my point. Though I don't think it a typical "Sunday school" lesson, either.

Nevertheless, theologians continue to condemn Updike's sensory orientation as pejoratively "superficial." Peter Leithart claims Updike's writing won't "endure" because its God doesn't judge and it fails to penetrate beyond the surface (Leithart). To borrow Updike's own term: It's too lackadaisical. And two of our most astute critics of religion and literature, Ralph Wood and James Wood, have made similarly disparaging claims. Yet Updike repeatedly demonstrates the truth of David Bentley Hart's contention that "theology should take its lead from the 'inauthenticity' of beauty, its superficiality, its exclusive dwelling in the intensity of surfaces, the particularity of form, and the splendor of created things" (24). In dwelling on the surfaces of created things, Christian theology can best articulate God's passion for the unrepeatable singularities of his handiwork. If Sunday school theology is too reductionist for Updike's sense of his art, then perhaps a good dose of his writing could help theology escape its Sunday school associations. From Emily Dickinson's domestic panorama to Flannery O'Connor's incarnational affirmation of the body, I'm not sure that any other American author offers more sensuous, theologically driven descriptions of what it feels like to dwell in the surfaces of Christian experience.

One reason is that Updike's work insists with a tenacious consistency that adequate superficiality requires a three-dimensional body. His portrayals of bodies are neither ideological mouthpieces nor the clichéd images of the beauty industry. They taste and touch and stink. Their downy-coated limbs end in boxy digits; they wobble and go gnarly; they pulse with moist warmth, smell faintly sour, intone habitual phrases with accompanying gestures, and glisten with sweaty vitality. Their place matters, too; more often than not the rural Pennsylvania of his youth leaves its trace somewhere on those bodies. "The Happiest I've Been" (1959), a story about driving across Updike's birth state, includes a detailed description of a girl at a party playing Ping-Pong. As she "lunged forward toward the net the stiff neckline of her semi-formal dress dropped away and the white arcs of her brassiere could be glimpsed cupping fat, and when she reached high her shaved armpit gleamed like a bit of chicken skin" (*CES* 176). A gleaming bit of chicken skin. As D. Quentin Miller has noted, "Details are the core substance of Updike's artistry" (Miller 15). Detailed descriptions like this celebrate fully imagined bodies made visible not by lustful caricature but by grateful curiosity.

And yet some readers have argued that Updike's writing is too autobiographical, too self-obsessed. Updike himself was somewhat taken aback by the charge since his sentences so often carry outward-directed descriptions (*Self-Consciousness* 103). Yet the truth in this criticism is that Updike's fiction lacks any examples of genuine friendship. Like Philip Roth's and Don DeLillo's, his characters have little interest in friendship. He has no Sula and Nel like Toni Morrison, or any Mason and Dixon like Thomas Pynchon. So thoroughly does sensation drive his prose that even his very few children characters are not at play with others as much as cherishing some new discovery. This lack of what Aristotle thought absolutely necessary for any full experience of a good life can make Updike's fiction feel solipsistic, despite its immersion in the wonder of created things. Furthermore, without any non-erotic forms of friendship, occasions for empathy are few and far between. My point, then, is not to argue that Updike's work provides convincing models of good people but to show how his writing values the inherent goodness of embodied experience.

How his prose describes such experiences is what makes all the difference. Unlike many of his post-Hemingway contemporaries, Updike does not shy from piling on the similes and adjectives. He dispenses them freely. In one story a typical Updike stand-in character looking to describe the ocean muses, "It is a chronic question, whether to say simply 'the sea' and trust to people's imaginations, or whether to put in the adjectives. I have had only fair luck with people's imaginations; hence tend to trust adjectives" (*CES* 301). Updike's ability to burnish everyday experiences with those carefully chosen adjectives invests his representations of perception with a basic emotional predisposition that is also a theological conviction: creaturely gratitude. Creaturely gratitude, the core assumption of Updike's theology of sense, is a way of knowing that is also a way of feeling. The senses sense differently—more distinctly—under the overarching sense of the goodness of creation.

Updike shared the theologian Karl Barth's belief that human experience flourishes, becomes most fully *human,* in expressing gratitude to the Creator (*Church Dogmatics* III.2 166). He wrote accordingly, and a humble responsibility flows throughout his writing. It focuses on how to receive the good gifts of life in faithfulness instead of striving for inventive genius. He has said as much in interviews, but his fiction makes the point as fully as only a story can. The Reverend Tom Marshfield, the main character of Updike's 1975 novel *A Month of Sundays,* reminds us, "Our task is to love not what might be but *is* given" (*Sundays* 135). Do not create an ideal but instead idealize the particularities of creation. A better life will come not through a new idea but through more faithful, loving attention to what is already there. This command is at the center of the novel's thematic unity—the given world better satisfies us than the "might be" of misbegotten fantasy. Tom Marshfield calls this realization of the world's givenness, "gratitude": "Gratitude is the way [God] gets us, when we have gnawed off a leg to escape His other snares" (56). Gratitude is how Updike gets us too, for the literary secret to Updike's theology of sense is in *how* his prose performs that gratitude: He uses specific forms of phrasing, pacing, nouns, and adjectives to convey love for what his prose describes.

Before turning to an example of how this works in *A Month of Sundays,* first a word about this particular novel's structure since it provides a vivid example of Updike's thinking about aesthetics. The novel is part of Updike's three-volume homage to the love triangle of *The Scarlet Letter* (the other two volumes being *Roger's Version* and *S.*) and is written from the perspective of an Arthur Dimmesdale-like character. This series is, as James Schiff has remarked, "trickier and more multi-layered than the more conventionally realistic Rabbit tetralogy" (*Updike's Version* 2). *A Month of Sundays*' epistolary form demonstrates those layers insofar as it takes its inspiration beyond *The Scarlet Letter* to Søren Kierkegaard's "Seducer's Diary" section from *Either/Or.* "Ethical passion," Tom Marshfield reflects, is "the hobgoblin of trivial minds" (192). Like Kierkegaard, Updike was suspicious of the sanctimonious prescriptions of secular ethics for a variety of reasons, some theological. He once quoted Karl Barth to an interviewer, "A drowning man cannot pull himself up by his own hair," and then explained his view of secular ethical prescriptions: "There is no help from within—without the supernatural the natural is a pit of horror. I believe that all problems are basically insoluble and that faith is a leap out of total despair" (Plath 14). Instead of ethical passion, Tom's diary entries convey a sense of love. This affective quality is crucial because it allows the novel's aesthetic achievements to open the door to religious forms of transformation. Tom Marshfield selfishly desires adulterous sexual gratification, but the reader is lured into something else—a more complicated attention to surfaces and textures.

A Month of Sundays' true theological content lies not in any dense ideas but in its own lyrical surprises. If gratitude "is the way [God] gets us," as Marshfield reflects, the same is true of Updike's novels (*Sundays* 56). This particular novel's emphasis on that gratitude offers a good example of how Updike paints the fallen world in all its suffering while at the same time showing, without pedantry, what it feels like to be the loving "new creature" of the New Testament (2 Cor. 5:17). For Updike, novels don't make arguments; they imagine ways of feeling. Instead of proofs for God's existence, his work is riddled throughout with the overwhelming *sense* of God's goodness. Yet his theology of sense goes beyond providing the feeling of such a context insofar as it also provides a means to cultivate the sense of God's goodness through revaluing what is worthy of our desire, and why. The moment in the novel when Marshfield recalls his father's basement workshop provides an example of the way Updike's style conveys its theological content. Pay attention to how the pacing of the first sentence intensifies the evident pleasure Marshfield has in recalling this image of his father at work in the basement. The scene's details add up to an homage imbued with patient, forgiving love.

> He was at his best [. . .] in his basement, in the succession of our basements, where he would establish a workbench of phenomenal neatness, the hammers and pliers and calipers placed upon their outlines painted on pegboard, the well-oiled tablesaw (its absolutely level metal top my first vision of rectitude) established on the right, and the cans of paint and putty and solvent shelved on the left, and the jars of nails and screws of progressive and labeled sizes nailed by their lids to a board above; and there my father would spend part of most afternoons, performing, in the warmth of the proximate furnace, small tasks of mending and manufacture that, to my childish sense, were meaningless but for the meaning the shavings breathed, and the cleansing aroma of the turpentine, and the inner peace emanating from my puttering, pipe-smoking, fussy, oblivious father. I

would sit on a sawhorse and love my upward view of his cleft chin, his vital nostrils, his wavy gray hair—its brushed luxuriance his one overt vanity. (21–22)

To "love my upward view"—the sentence subtlety conveys a contagious affection that urges the reader to love that view, too. Not only does it enumerate the organized objects and the father's appearance with reverential patience, it also conveys the serendipitous delight of a child's fascination with this orderly underworld where shavings breathe out meaning. Here is a world full of things and people worth attending to, rendered in prose that coaxes the reader into delighting in its rapt attention. But there is no inspiring vista or gorgeous body here; it's an old man fussing about in a small-town basement. As such, this passage is fairly representative of Updike's prose and the kinds of perceptions his writing can cultivate. Throughout the course of an essay, story, or novel, sentences like this add up to a transformative pedagogy of desire, where the reader goes beyond learning *in* delight (Sir Philip Sidney's classic defense of poetry's educational use) to learning *to* delight in the world, "to love, not what might be, but what *is* given."

Fostering an "attitude of gratitude" is no tired cliché for Updike. David Foster Wallace memorably included such virtue-celebrating clichés in his novel *Infinite Jest* and wrote what is perhaps the most famous pan of Updike's writing. While Wallace's fiction lucubrates over the possible wisdom such clichés about gratitude might contain, Updike puts gratitude at the cornerstone of his sumptuous style. In its lyricism Updike's theology of sense shows us the superiority of the physical world to any of our idealizations of it while simultaneously exhibiting how a Christian love of the physical world enhances our experience of it. The passage quoted above from *A Month of Sundays* amiably charms as it continues, moving up from the basement to the furniture upstairs. He renders faith not as a mental certitude concerning some argument or idea but as a sensual experience of surfaces:

> But it was, somehow, [. . .] in the *furniture* I awoke among, and learned to walk among, and fell asleep amid—it was the moldings of

> the doorways and the sashes of the windows and the turnings of the balusters—it was the carpets each furry strand of which partook in a pattern and the ceilings whose random cracks and faint discolorations I would never grow to reach, that convinced me, that *told me,* God was, and was here, even as the furnace came on, and breathed gaseous warmth upon my bare, buttonshoed legs. Something invisible had cared to make these things. There was a mantel clock, with a face of silver scrolls, that ticked and gonged time which would at the last gong end, and the dead would awake, and a new time would begin. Beyond the stairs, there were invisible stairs leading unimaginably upward. There was a sofa where I would, older, lie and eat raisins and read O. Henry and John Tunis and Admiral Byrd and dream; the sofa itself felt to be dreaming; it was stuffed with the substance of the spirit. Though we had moved, following my father's call, from one city of inland America to another, this sofa was a constant island, and the furniture a constant proof of, as it were, a teleological bias in things, a temporary slant as of an envelope halfway down the darkness inside a mailbox. (22–23)

Updike is reflexively linking the patient panegyric of his enumerations here with the experience of faith. Objects made God an objective truth for Marshfield. This is no watertight proof for the truth of Christianity, but Marshfield's conviction of a "teleological bias in things" is perhaps the most succinct way of summarizing Updike's theology of sense: Our sense of the world is determined by distinct sense experiences of the world as God's gift. When received as the gifts they were given to be, things testify to God's activity in creation. We sense a larger sense of meaning, their "teleological bias," their "temporary slant."

This "superficial" theology is a result of the fact that Updike is writing as a novelist, not a theologian. Theology couldn't give lived experience the same "sense" that Updike's descriptive prose does. To make that comparison clear, Marshfield steps out of his pastoral trappings for a moment to differentiate his view—that inanimate, material things express God's presence—to another novelist's way of thinking. Alain Robbe-Grillet's *nouveau roman* sought out the purest objectivity in its disorienting realism. His antihumanist writing sought to empty itself of all previous novels' naive anthropomorphisms and religious teleology. In a transparent moment of Updike-the-author peeking through, Marshfield identifies the values of his own realism: "My intuition about objects is thus the exact opposite of Robbe-Grillet, who intuits [. . .] in tables, rooms, corners, knives, etc., an emptiness resounding with the universal nullity. He has only to describe a chair for us to know that God is absent. Whereas for me, puttying a window sash, bending my face close in, awakens a plain suspicion that someone in the immediate vicinity immensely, discreetly cares. God" (25). When we care enough to attend to the otherwise unheralded kitchenware of life, we find an infinitely scrupulous God. This kind of argument, more or less circular reasoning if you press on it very hard, is the closest thing to a theological proof you will find in Updike's fiction. Yet it is everywhere in that fiction. Especially in the sex.

ORDO AMORIS

If, as I have argued, Updike's writing affirms sense experience as the very sense of God, and even kindles the reader's desire to begin to love and cherish those sense experiences, what about the infamous, descriptive sex scenes that landed him on the cover of the magazine *Time* not once but twice? It is not an idle or prudish question. It is, rather, at the heart of what Updike can show us in a new way: the old Augustinian theological anthropology that humans are first and foremost lovers. Updike once remarked that the *New Yorker* asked him to review "all the religious [books] or the dirty ones. Somehow the two go together: they are the ultimates of life" (Plath 19). While I will discuss the anthropology that connects these "ultimates of life" throughout the book, let me say two things about Updike's Christianity and his frank descriptions of sex. First, the sex is not merely some scintillating window dressing used to sell more books; far from being beside the point, the sex in Updike's writing is very much the point. Second, contemporary American culture—as awash in objectifying images as it is—could use more of Updike's sex scenes.

Why? Because, as Tom Marshfield puts it, "Generalizations belong to the devil; particulars to the Lord" (*Sundays* 138). Updike's sex scenes describe bodies in their obdurate, human singularity. To borrow a distinction from Herbert Marcuse, they are more sensuous than sensual; rather than arouse genital-directed desire, they express the panoply of sensuous pleasures available to embodied beings (175). The sex in *A Month of Sundays,* for example, portrays the human body *in itself* as intrinsically desirable not because this particular, flawed body tries to fit into the role of some pornographic cliché but because it does just the opposite—it smells, it's oddly shaped, and it subverts and surprises our too dreary desires with variety and detail.

One of the more memorable ways Updike upends fantasy with the full physical presence of bodies is Harry "Rabbit" Angstrom's sexual escapades. The novels have several vivid sexual encounters. In *Rabbit Is Rich* (1981), his attempt to sell a car to a girl who Rabbit thinks could be his daughter reminds him of an old, adulterous liaison. While he and the girl are out for a test drive, his thoughts are never far from his senses, as the "inside of the Corolla is warming with a mingled human smell. Harry thinks of the girl's long thigh as she stretched her way into the back seat and imagines he smells vanilla. Cunt would be a good flavor of ice cream, Sealtest out to work on it" (*Rabbit Angstrom* 639). Rabbit does not smell an attractive perfume but a "human smell" that reminds him not of sex but of ice cream, and his thoughts go from the smell of bodies to their taste. Rabbit's ability to delaminate his own sensory appreciation from the girl's unique personhood is, on the one hand, nothing less than offensive. Yet this is no erotic fantasy. It is a description of bodies that assert their own unalterable existence. Lest we miss that fact, Updike returns to the theme later in the novel as Rabbit engages his wife Janice in a bout of late-night cunnilingus. "I would have taken a bath," Janice says at first,

> but she smells great, deep jungle smell, of precious rotting mulch going down and down beneath the ferns. When he won't stop, crazy to lose his face in this essence, the cool stern fury of it takes hold of her and combatively she comes, thrusting her hips up to grind

her clitoris against his face and then letting him finish inside her beneath him [...] Long after she has fallen into the steady soft rasping of sleep [...] Janice's taste is still on his lips and he thinks maybe it wouldn't be such a good idea for Sealtest. (733–34)

The simple fact that he includes such a moment in the narration, the association of the genitalia with rotting mulch, and then the invocation again of the ice cream flavor, exemplify Updike's need to make the body strange, to force the bizarre mystery of its intractable physicality back upon us. Updike once asked in the title of an art review essay he wrote, "Can Genitals Be Beautiful?" His writing seeks to attend to the physical facts and derive its sense of beauty from those physical facts. "If men and women have sexual parts and a sexual purpose," he asks, "how can an art of representation suppress them?" (*Higher Gossip* 310). If our ideas about beauty don't line up with the facts of creation, perhaps the ideal needs to change.

The body is a genuine source of truth for Updike, and his sex scenes reveal it. At the beginning of one of the Maples stories, the series of short stories tracing the fate of Richard and Joan Maple's ill-fated marriage (and the stories that most closely track the dissolution of Updike's marriage to Mary Pennington), the body is rendered as a powerful army, ready for mutiny. "Twin Beds in Rome" begins by describing how the increasingly estranged Richard and Joan's "lovemaking, like a perversely healthy child whose growth defies every deficiency of nutrition, continued: when their tongues at last fell silent, their bodies collapsed together as two mute armies might gratefully mingle, released from the absurd hostilities decreed by two mad kings" (*Maples Stories* 55). Their bodies long for each other despite the husband's and wife's growing antipathy. In this sentence it is the body that knows better and the mad king of rational argument that insists on violence. Bodies know things—in this case the peace that Richard and Joan lack.

More than free love or the sexual revolution, Updike's sex scenes celebrate the vulnerability, even humility, that being a body comprises. When Alexandra, one of *The Witches of Eastwick* (1984), reflects on the wild pagan revelries of her casually intimate coven, she cannot help being struck by "the human awkwardness of it all"

(117). There is a tender comedy to how bodies in Updike's novels are so jarringly exact. Swerving from his usual style, Updike has one of his characters take on the voice of fantasy's contemptuous generalizations and makes the point explicit. In *Memories of the Ford Administration* (1992), the history professor Alfred Clayton attempts to spurn a less-than-coy student's advances while reflecting, "against the age-old abstract ideal of the *jeune fille* stood the disconcerting particularity of every instance, the unique female individual with a chin too sharp, some baby fat still to lose, a dreadful vulgar near-childish voice, or an unairbrushed pimple beside her slightly bulbous nose" (82). Narcissistic fantasies feed on airbrushed bodies, but gratitude loves this exact, unrepeatable, given body's physical singularity. As Christopher Gabriel surmises of pornography's need to avoid details in Updike's last novel, *The Widows of Eastwick* (2008), "The guys who watch this stuff [. . .] don't want a ton of reality" (241). Sexuality is one of the most powerful forms of expressing human love, and Updike's work jolts us free from the bleak, mass-produced, Pavlovian stimulants that are little more than cheap imitations. Remember that gleaming bit of chicken skin? Updike's descriptions can teach us to love not what might be but what *is* given.

Moreover, Updike's writing about sex deploys a Christian anthropology in which people are first and foremost *lovers* before they are *knowers*. Updike's characters are lovers insofar as they are often involved in affairs, but even more so in St. Augustine's sense that the human creature is what it is because of how it loves. Praise is not merely an effulgent feeling but the expression of love that makes people the most fulfilled, the most like fully *human* beings. The pagan *ars erotica,* or sensual art of love, for which Updike's *Couples* became famous, is at the same time an invocation of Augustine's *ordo amoris,* the "order of the loves" whereby Christians learn to love in the right way. Indeed, one reason why Updike's prose confuses some Christian readers is that the *ordo amoris* in his fiction is not opposed to, but is inextricable from, the *ars erotica*. Updike's belief in the spirituality of pleasure is first evident in his instructive 1963 review of Denis de Rougemont's *Love in the Western World* through—as Prendita Sengupta has argued—his engagement with the Indian concept of *sringara rasa* in *S.* (1988) and all the way to his last novel, *The Widows of*

Eastwick (Sengupta 84). Updike strove to understand the full spirituality of love in the body's full physicality.

Augustine's *Confessions* opens with what may be the most succinct definition of *ordo amoris*: "To praise you is the desire of man, a little piece of your creation. You stir man to take pleasure in praising you, because you have made us for yourself, and our heart is restless until it rests in you" (*Confessions* 3). Updike's work upholds the truth of Augustine's claim—his characters take pleasure in praising, and he takes pleasure in his writing's ability to praise. In his short story "Augustine's Concubine" (1975), Updike directly addresses Augustine's theology of love. Events in Updike's personal life suffuse its background: he wrote it from his single rented room in Back Bay, Boston, just after having separated from his first wife, Mary Pennington, but prior to marrying his second wife, Martha Ruggles Bernhard. Yet the personal struggle with guilt and desire notwithstanding, it is (perhaps all the more so *because* of the guilt) an overtly theological manifesto that addresses itself to Augustine's theory of well-ordered loves.

In Updike's story Augustine is a haughty, nay-saying antagonist to his unnamed concubine's innocent love of life. Using italicized text from different passages of the *Confessions*, "Augustine's Concubine" purports to tell the story of Augustine falling in love with, living with, fathering a son with, and then finally renouncing his relationship with his "concubine"—he to marry and she to enter a convent. It begins with the famous lines from Book III of the *Confessions*, "To Carthage I came, where there sang all around me in my ears a cauldron of unholy loves" (*CES* 828). The question the story poses is, Just what does count as an "unholy love"? In order to answer that question, the story vacillates between quotations from Augustine's original text to snippets narrating Updike's Augustine character's relation to the concubine, beginning with their flirtatious dialogue at a party. Their banter is fraught with echoes of the story's opening quotation. Is theirs an unholy love? "Why do you hate me, Aurelius?" she asks not long after meeting him (828). He demurs and follows it up with "Love your dress" (828). "It's just a dress" she replies, as if to highlight the fact that a dress is not worth loving (828). Isn't she more lovable than a dress? And indeed her allure is no materialistic trapping to Augustine, as it "sharpened within him his hollow of famine, his hunger for God" (829). She elicits another order of yearning.

Yet she lacks his sense of guilt and shame, of self-consciousness. She is "frontal" both in how she stands with him at the party and in her confidence (828). Updike writes that Augustine sensed she was "*new,* new, that is, to life, in a way not true of himself, youth though he was (*aet.* eighteen), or true of the Carthaginians boiling about them" (828). This newness has something to do with her conviction of "having been created for love" (830). Her innocent lack of self-consciousness irks him, as if she has not attained the feeling of alienation he sees as necessary to understand the human relation to God. She refuses, in other words, to think that a self is necessarily opposed to the world of things. Augustine eventually turns on her, hardening his heart against her charms, diagnosing her sins.

> Concupiscentia. Its innocence disturbed him, the simplicity of her invitation to descend with her into her nature, into Nature, and to be immersed. Surely such wallowing within Creation was a deflection of higher purposes. Like bubbles, his empty spaces wanted to rise, break into air, and vanish. Their bodies would become one, but his soul was pulled back taut, like the hair at the back of her skull. (832)

Concupiscence is a hallmark of disordered love. Yet Updike pushes against our preconceived notions of what constitutes disordered bodily loves. It is not lust that she loves. No, her wholehearted embrace of Creation, "wallowing" in it, no longer hollows Augustine's hunger for God but is now condemned as her own false attempt to fill that hunger. What changed? He longs for the "higher purposes" that Creation in itself does not offer, but why does this cause his soul to pull back now when it used to push it forward? Here Updike is both invoking and revising the order of the loves Augustine establishes in the opening pages of the *Confessions*—that loving the right things in the right order brings people to the happiness God intended. Though the Augustine character becomes the villain of the story (Updike's guilt for leaving Mary must play some part in this), Updike is more interested in provoking a rereading of Augustine's psychology in more physical terms. He's offering his own version of the *ordo amoris,* though it turns out much closer to Augustine's than the story's condemnation of the Augustine character might make it seem.

It is not in the *Confessions* but elsewhere, in *The City of God,* that Augustine gives his fullest explanation of the order of the loves. There he clearly establishes that human beauty, of the sort that draws him to the concubine in Updike's story, is itself a "lesser good" that can either bring a person closer to God or take him further from God, depending on whether or not that beauty is treated as an end in itself or a means to knowing God. Augustine wants to affirm the goodness of human beauty while warning against loving it in any other way than as a gift from God. Beauty is not an end in itself; the truly fulfilled person understands this and loves beautiful things accordingly.

> For bodily beauty is most certainly created by God. But it is a temporal, carnal, and lesser good, and it is loved wrongly when it is preferred to God, who is eternal, inward, and everlasting good, just as gold is loved wrongly by misers when they desert justice for its sake, although the fault lies not with the gold but rather with the man. This is true of every created thing. For, although it is good, it can be loved both rightly and wrongly—rightly when the proper order is preserved, wrongly when the proper order is overturned. [. . .] Thus it seems to me that a brief and true definition of virtue is "rightly ordered love." (*City* 173)

If a person loves beauty to the detriment of other goods, such as justice or friendship and especially God himself, then their love is not rightly ordered.

Note, however, that though Updike clearly invokes the concept of the *ordo amoris* in his Augustine character's response to his concubine's immersion in creation, it is not the *ordo amoris* that causes the Augustine character's repulsion toward her. In Updike's version, Augustine condemns his concubine's paganism out of a thinly disguised self-love. He cannot accept that she does not value his individual selfhood as he does, for "she had had a husband and had accepted that husband and her lover as if they were kindred manifestations of the same force, as if he himself were not incomparable, unique, with truth's sole Lord within him. For this she was rightly punished" (*CES* 833). Updike covertly uses the historical Augustine's ideas, and his exploration of the contradictions of psychological interiority, to render judgment against the Augustine character's gift-denying pride. If we judge the Augustine character, we do so because he suffers from the disordered loves that the historical Augustine first explained.

"Augustine's Concubine" ends praising the concubine's piety in the cloister she joins after Augustine leaves her. Instead of Augustine's guilty, self-conscious alienation from the flesh, she has achieved a shameless love of all things natural. *She* has rightly ordered loves, whereas Updike's Augustine seems to have unwittingly propagated the Manichean Gnosticism that the historical Augustine so powerfully argued against.

> Her complacence, which had never doubted the body's prerogatives, seemed here, in these corridors cloistered from the sun, to manifest purity. Her shamelessness became a higher form of self-surrender. Her placid carriage suggested triumph. It was as if her dynamic and egocentric lover, whom she had never failed to satisfy, in his rejection of her had himself failed, and been himself rejected, even as his verbal storms swept the Mediterranean and transformed orthodoxy.
>
> She was a saint, whose name we do not know. For a thousand years, men would endeavor to hate the flesh, because of her. (834)

Augustine's concubine's "shamelessness became a higher form of self-surrender" in a way that the Augustine character's fascination with the self and its contradictions, its shame, missed. In pursuing "higher purposes," he misses her "higher form" of humble love. His selfishness betrays the confession that opens *Confessions*: "To praise you is the desire of man, a little piece of your creation."

While Updike's descriptions of sense experiences set him apart, the strenuous affirmation of the body is something he shares with several contemporaries. Compare, for example, Updike's unexpected descriptions of lovable bodies with Walker Percy's consistent theological emphasis on the meaning of embodied experience for spiritual fulfillment. Both writers published their Kierkegaard-inspired breakout novels almost at the same time (*Rabbit, Run* in 1960 and *The Moviegoer* in 1961), and both portray the importance of bodies for thinking about fiction and what it tells us about human experience. Yet Updike's style seeks to convey affection for those bodies whereas Percy's indirectly gestures toward it.

For example, the physician Thomas More in *Love in the Ruins* (1971) has begun to diagnose cases of two different diseases, what he calls "angelism" and "bestialism": opposed but twin reactions of the psyche to the contradictions of embodiment. More believes that the experience of what he calls "abstracted" lust is excellent evidence that the two states of alienation "are not mutually exclusive": It "is not uncommon nowadays to see patients suffering from angelism-bestialism [a combination of the two diseases]. A man, for example, can feel at one and the same time extremely abstracted and inordinately lustful toward lovely young women who may be perfect strangers" (*Love* 27). When combined, angelic abstraction and bestial bodies turn into despair. Angelism-bestialism suffers from the belief that sexuality is more fulfilling if abstracted from *this* particular body.

Love in the Ruins goes on to explain the theological underpinnings of Percy's denigration of abstracted fantasy. When Thomas More comes back from church sexually aroused, his wife Doris asks, "My God, what is it you do in church?" According to More, "What she didn't understand, she being spiritual and seeing religion as spirit, was that it took religion to save me from the spirit world, from orbiting the earth like Lucifer and the angels, that it took nothing less than [. . .] eating Christ himself to make me mortal man again and let me inhabit my own flesh and love her in the morning" (254). Christianity—and its Eucharistic ritual—frees the body to enjoy itself as *this* body in *this* place in *this* intimate way to *this* person.

Yet take note how Percy's prose lacks the sensuous enactment of such a claim. While Percy shares Updike's theological insistence on the body (though a decidedly more Catholic version), he does not perform that love of variability and peculiarity in his prose with Updike's eager adjectives. Where Updike indulges in cheerful lyrical pirouettes ("Like bubbles, his empty spaces wanted to rise, break into air, and vanish") Percy is sardonic ("what is it you do in church?") and didactic ("it took religion to save me from the spirit world"). Percy's is not a theology of sense so much as a theology of the stumbling block, rendered in prose adequately perturbing. And indeed, as much as Percy saw his times as cursed by the complacencies of a hypocritical Christendom, Updike sought to describe those times with unmistakable love. When only nineteen, Updike wrote home from Harvard that writers like Proust and Joyce, inventors of a whole new style, were not what these times needed. According to this young freshman with a sense of his own literary vocation,

> this age needs rather men like Shakespeare, or Milton, or Pope; men who are filled with the strength of their cultures and do not transcend the limits of their age, but, working within the times, bring what is peculiar to the moment to glory. We need great artists who are willing to accept restrictions, and who love their environments with such vitality that they can produce an epic out of the Protestant ethic [. . .] Whatever the many failings of my work, let it stand as a manifesto of my love for the time in which I was born. (Tanenhaus)

"A manifesto of my love." It is hard not to view the Rabbit novels Updike would later compose as the fruition of this early desire to create a Protestant epic imbued with love.

THE SENSES OF SENSE

His love for the world around him is what drives Updike's theology of sense. His writing does not offer theological allegories; at times Updike's realism verges on an almost a-religious empiricism. Moreover, Updike is suspicious of representing theological truths about the nature of God. Rather than pretend to depict Providence in action, his spiritual truths about the meaning of gratitude and love come from descriptions of the purely human experience of embodiment (Viladesau 26–29). Yet, on the other hand, Updike does think that a *sense* of God reshapes the human experience of beauty and he writes accordingly.

To clarify how, let me distinguish Updike's theology of sense from its broader theoretical contexts and explain why I think it so central to postsecular aesthetics. Updike's sense is *not* what philosophers have called "common sense"—quite the opposite. Descartes thought he could identify the pineal gland as the embodied location of human consciousness's ability to turn sense perception into meaning. He thought it housed a "common sense" held by all people. In the wake of Descartes's turn toward this common sense, Thomas Reid and other members of the Scottish School of Common Sense attempted to provide a more consistent case for the epistemology of empirically grounded rationality. Their work was crucial in establishing the notion of a universal common sense capable of serving as a secular, philosophical authority for the ground of human judgment. Updike's empirical sensibility, however, is perhaps closer to that of Reid's contemporary David Hume, who insisted that routine repetitions do not amount to causal arguments. Sensation does not justify ideas in the minds of Updike's characters. To the contrary, Updike's theology of sense is not at all schematically "common" (in the sense of necessary or the key to a universal subjectivity) but instead is given by God and received by his creatures. Updike's theology of sense emphasizes how gratitude and love participate in perception. This means, however, that sense is unquestionably "common" insofar as this sense of "sense" is absolutely open and available for cultivation. For the Protestant Updike, however, it gains its final and fullest sense in the revealed Word of God.

Updike's Protestant view of natural theology apprehends the natural world and the quasisecular domain of literature as part of the created order. Accordingly, it offers a different way of thinking about literature that is neither secularist nor sacramental. Nor is it, for that matter, "postsecular" if that term means the "partial faith" celebrated in John McClure's *Partial Faiths*, and neither is it the "belief in meaninglessness" of Amy Hungerford's *Postmodern Belief.* McClure's and Hungerford's studies imply that late twentieth-century American literature bore witness to new ways of thinking about religion and culture and that something had changed in the relationship between religion and literature, something which "postsecular" might be flexible enough to name. There are two sides to this shift: First, religion has not gone away in literature but is in fact thriving in new ways. The second thesis their work shares, however, is that the increasingly pluralist sensibility of contemporary American culture was wearing away at the role of confession-specific doctrines (and the religious institutions that supported them) and that new "partial faiths" or "postmodern beliefs" were imagining a variety of ways to be "spiritual but not religious." Defining work by Tracy Fessenden and Danielle Haque, however, has challenged both the truth and the usefulness of such historical explanations because their emphasis on the weakening of confessional content promulgates the very same secularization narrative they attempt to complicate.

Nevertheless, McClure and Hungerford have cleared new ground for understanding the persistence of religion in the apparent secularity of literary culture and academe. So, too, has the extensive work done since to trace the vicissitudes of religion and secularity, as exemplified in the 2014 special journal issues by *American Literature, American Literary History,* and *Religion and Literature,* which were dedicated to addressing the relationship between religion and postsecularity. Now scholars are looking to the postsecular less as a way of understanding late twentieth-century literature and more as a theoretical position that, for a number of historical reasons, has taken up the meaning of secularity for literary studies (Coviello and Hickman 645). Lori Branch's essay in *Religion and Literature* situates the emergence of the postsecular within the history of that discipline. She contends that literary studies (especially in US English departments) have practiced a ritualized "resecularization," or process of disavowal. For decades, literary scholars have used religion to represent an irrational past still clinging to the field, a past that a truly robust academic discipline must disavow and supersede. To study literature well means to secularize it. Branch instead contends that postsecular studies provide a way to confront this ritual practice without reinscribing it once again. In attending to religion and secularity, literary studies can better redress the cultural work literature accomplishes. For Branch, a "postsecular perspective encourages us to investigate religion both in terms of the ways secularism has constituted it, as private belief in various propositions sincerely or halfheartedly held, and as a much broader shifting, transforming range of practices and experiences that has to do with the *real construction* of selves and meaning" (Branch 26). Understanding how scholars theorize that "real construction of selves and meaning" requires thinking about religious sources as well as aesthetic strategies—which is why, I believe, the study of postsecular aesthetics is such a pressing question for literary studies. Does religion actually shape the way literature contributes to the "real construction of selves and meaning"? Updike's writing demonstrates one way it has.

Updike's apparently secular yet fundamentally theological narrative style is a striking example of postsecular literary form because of how it expresses what the Swiss theologian Karl Barth called "secular parables of the truth." Barth was Updike's most consequential theological influence, and Updike's conception of the writer's vocation bears witness to that fact (Plath 31, 187). For Barth, secular parables are secondary forms of witness to God's truth but are not the Word of God itself, nor sacramentally related to it. Barth's secular parables, George Hunsinger explains, are made of "words which conform and agree materially with the Word, not as equals but as servants, and not by any capacity of their own but by grace" (254). Hunsinger's point is that Barth's way of understanding literature as "secular parables" demonstrates the lordship of Christ and Christ's freedom to use works of literature that otherwise appear to have little redemptive relevance. The redeeming power of a secular parable to reveal the incarnate Word is not intrinsic to the words themselves but instead depends on Christ's external saving action. The agency is not in the words, but in the Word, which sharply differentiates secular parables from sacramental theology. As Barth explains, secular literature speaks of "the One whom no single human word will declare, but to whom each may well point, so that He for His part may well declare Himself in such words, making them the instruments, signs, and attestations of His self-revelation and therefore His truth" (*Church Dogmatics* IV.3.1, 123). Literary words are less like sacraments than the tools neatly stowed up on that basement workshop shelf in *A Month of Sundays,* waiting for their Lord's use.

Updike gestures toward the empirical methods of his secular parables in his novelistic homage to *Hamlet,* Shakespeare's most sustained theological reckoning with Protestantism's dawning cultural authority. In *Gertrude and Claudius* (2000) the Gertrude character defends Hamlet's decision to stay in Wittenberg rather than coming home to Denmark. She explains,

> there's a ferment going on in cultivated circles to the south, various bits of ancient knowledge the Crusaders brought back, the Arabs and the Byzantine monks have been transcribing them for centuries but nobody read them, something about a new way of looking at the world scientifically, whatever that is, letting nature tell us about itself in little details, one after another, as if women and children and millers and farmers haven't been doing that all along. Instead of taking everything on faith from the priests and Bible, I mean. Instead of arguing from first principles, you deduce your principles from a host of observed particulars. (80)

Wittenberg's Renaissance-inspired ideals, in Updike's rendering, participate in an emerging science of "letting nature tell us about itself in little details." The Book of Nature has newly attained authority. Gertrude's remark that the new ferment enshrines the millers' and farmers' views of the world neatly echoes the concept of vocation that Max Weber famously associated with the Reformation's celebration of secular labor. In *Sources of the Self* Charles Taylor calls the legacy of this cultural shift the "affirmation of ordinary life," which he argues continues to inform the models of modern subjectivity in contemporary society (211). Everything matters, not just the sacraments or other explicitly sacred rituals. Updike once identified that his goal in writing was to "give the mundane its beautiful due," and Gertrude explicitly identifies that artistic ideal with a trajectory of Reformation-inspired thinking (*Early Stories* xvii).

Yet note how she emphasizes its empirical leanings: "You deduce your principles from a host of observed particulars." The details come first. As Updike writes in his 1962 short story "The Blessed Man of Boston, My Grandmother's Thimble, and Fanning Island," "a piece of turf torn from a meadow becomes a *gloria* when drawn by Dürer. Details" (*CES* 354). Details make the art and thereby become transformed. This empirical approach to particular details seeks to know the thing, if not *in-itself*, then *for-itself*. The computer programmer protagonist in Updike's 2004 novel *Villages* wonders at the "atomic brilliance of reality, its reserved but implacable pop-up quiddity" and feels overwhelmed at the sublimity of details, as "if every atom in the universe were an individual, with its own private story" (302, 133). If not quite down to the atomic level, Updike's realism seems as if it were trying to tell as many of those private stories as it can, to restore the essential wonder of their "pop-up quiddity."

Updike's Protestant approach is considerably different from the dominant studies of sense and the senses in theological aesthetics and continental philosophy. In theology the brilliant, field-defining work of Hans Urs von Balthasar's multivolume study, *The Glory of the Lord,* is focused more on the history of aesthetics and the beauty of Christian forms than on the anthropological implications of specific sensations. In fact, studies on Christianity and the senses are relatively rare in contemporary theological aesthetics despite a strong medieval tradition and a growing interest in the theology of embodiment. Gilles Deleuze's innovative, influential philosophy, on the other hand, makes prominent use of sense and deals directly with questions of how desire informs human conceptions of it. Crucially, Deleuze opened a path forward out of the linguistic boundaries that phenomenological hermeneutics set for sense, which has been followed by a host of new object-oriented, realist attempts to rethink old ontological questions. Yet much of this new philosophical work slights the rich tradition of theological aesthetics and theological anthropology. Of them all, the most apropos to Updike's theology of sense is Jean-Luc Nancy's work, especially *The Sense of the World*, which explicitly brings the notion of sense to bear on the Christian theology of the body. Nancy's prose has an affectionate relish for concrete sense-details evinced in neither his phenomenological precursor Maurice Merleau-Ponty nor his contemporary Jean-Luc Marion. Moreover, Nancy is perhaps closest to Updike's work in his concern for the contradictions that arise in refusing to choose between fidelity to the particulars of sense experience and the necessarily preexisting assumptions about the whole those particulars can assemble.

Nancy's confession that attempts to define the "sense of the world" always ends in an aporia is particularly instructive. While the very concept of sense demands some kind of apprehension of the whole, the assumption that such a whole can be conceived is extremely naive. Nonetheless, it is equally naive to believe that philosophy could entirely do away with the concept of an intuitive sense of the whole. Even though Nancy claims "there is no longer any sense of the world"—because any idea of "world" suggests an artificially constructed unity—he nevertheless insists on the obvious fact that there "is something, there are some things, there is some there is—and that itself makes sense, and moreover nothing else does" (4, 55). The somewhat obtuse illocution aside, affirming in some way that "there is some there is" is easy enough; asserting that "nothing else" makes sense without that "there is" also seems straightforward enough. In Updike's words, "What is is absolute" and thought must reach toward it. But how?

Nancy does not deny that people necessarily experience this "there is," or that those experiences undoubtedly *make sense* regardless of philosophical handwringing. Yet how does one affirm "What is is absolute" without imposing on "what is" an artificial, humanly constructed world of pale ideas? While Nancy is right to identify the crisis in continental thought's concept of sense, and although his work is helpful insofar as it illuminates the pitfalls of too facile definitions of sense, it lacks Updike's basic insight that our emotional and spiritual relationship to "what is" is the fundamental ingredient of our epistemic explorations of it. This is due mostly to the fact that Updike's literary representations of sense experience provide an affective aspect unavailable to philosophy's conceptual determinations. Updike's sense of the world begins with love for its details.

Accordingly, my argument begins from Updike's singular representations of sense and the peculiar theological assumptions they demonstrate. Whether the neat order of tools on a basement shelf or the feel of pubic hair, such examples provide the core of Updike's theology of sense. To use Gertrude's words, this book should qualify as a work of Protestant "ferment" insofar as it insists that "observed particulars" demonstrate to the senses the sense of God's goodness. Updike's love of "observed particulars" is good advice for novelists as well as for literary critics and theologians.

Yet I do not merely want to collect a catalog of such examples, since this book is meant to offer a theoretical argument about the postsecular elements of aesthetic experience. So let me add one more layer of theological context here. If sense for Updike is not the common sense of modern philosophy, neither is God the only means of securing the value of sense. For Updike, God is not a necessary addition in order to affirm the world as good—the world is good and worth loving in itself. That is one reason why his work is better described as *secular parables* rather than *sacramental*. Updike's superficial (and at times apparently godless) sense descriptions demonstrate "the nonnecessity of God" in sense experience insofar as the sense of God is *"more than necessary"* (Jüngel 24). Readers shouldn't fall for the apparent secularity his exacting realism might convey at first blush; the impression of God's irrelevance is in fact a Christian's homage to God's freedom. In *God as the Mystery of the World* Eberhard Jüngel (one of Barth's most thorough expositors) succinctly summarizes what he thinks are the three basic truths discovered by modern theological anthropology:

a. Man and his world are interesting for their own sake.
b. Even more so, God is interesting for His own sake.
c. God makes man, who is interesting for his own sake, interesting in a new way. (34)

God is not the logically necessary explanation for how the world works. Human culture and the world it inhabits can and should be known for their own sake. Secular parables are true sans any divine imprint.

Protestantism's natural theology gives creation—and God—that dignity. In *Roger's Version* (1986), Updike's novel to address natural theology most directly, Roger Lambert exclaims, "my God, anybody's real God, will *not* be deduced!" (88). Updike's God is not logically necessary to establish the goodness of the physical world, and neither is the goodness of the world an ontological proof of God's existence. The superfluity of God's love for the world, however, makes him *more than necessary* to the world. God is not a logical necessity, like the prime mover, but the eternal giver of good gifts, which means that the gift of life is freed to be intrinsically interesting for its own sake.

Furthermore, few literary critics have placed Updike's theological *ressourcement* squarely within the aesthetics of his secular parables. While Updike's use of Karl Barth's theology (Hunt, Webb) and Kierkegaard's existentialism (Boswell, Crowe) have been thoroughly explored, and other studies have pointed toward his dialectic of belief (Bailey), his imagination (Farmer), or his juxtaposition of myth against gospel (McTavish), the theological implications of Updike's surface dwelling aesthetics of embodiment and their relation to a more general theology of the arts has provoked less critical attention. Ralph C. Wood's *The Comedy of Redemption* (1988) included Updike as one its four central novelists, and Andrew Tate's 2008 *Contemporary Fiction and Christianity* contains an excellent chapter on Updike's theological strategies. Yet other surveys of religion and literature, such as Thomas Haddox's *Hard Sayings: The Rhetoric of Christian Orthodoxy in Late Modern Fiction* (2013), only include Updike with a dismissive derision. Both McClure and Hungerford avoid mentioning his work entirely except, in Hungerford's case, as a parenthetical aside in an endnote. I hope to redress this situation by making this study less a methodical "interpretation" of Updike's work than an attempt to isolate the postsecular aesthetics it suggests, and thereby plumb the theoretical depths of its shallow surfaces.

CHAPTER 1

Touching

A FEW PAGES into the first of the Rabbit Angstrom novels, Rabbit is walking down the street to fetch the car he shares with his pregnant wife, Janice. As he strolls, he "now and then touches with his hand the rough bark of a tree or the dry twigs of a hedge, to give himself the small answer of a texture" (*Rabbit Angstrom* 15). If he feels in the rough bark of a tree and dry twigs of a hedge an answer, what was the question? What does he want to know—and how could tactile pressure provide a verbal answer? The possibility of a nonlinguistic answer is later complemented by the novel's portrayal of language as a form of touching. Rabbit feels words spoken by a prostitute as if she were touching him, as his "name in her mouth feels like a physical touch" (72). Touch can respond with an answer; words can feel like a touch.

The answer of a touch and the touch of a word are represented in these descriptions as everyday experiences. They are, in Kathleen Stewart's term, "ordinary affects." "Ordinary affects," she writes, "are public feelings that begin and end in broad circulation, but they're also the stuff that seemingly intimate lives are made of" (2). We experience them personally and publically, but they shape who we are, how we act, and why we act as we do. Rabbit, for example, feels not only the familiarity of his town in those trees and twigs but also a thrilling escape from his marriage in another's sexually suggestive voice. Updike's portrayals of touch are ordinary affects insofar as they convey to Rabbit how he feels about the world he experiences in common with others. As such, Updike's sense of touch operates on an affective plane different from the one Rachel Greenwald Smith finds in the "neoliberal novel" of Updike's era. For Smith, such novels establish "parallels between personal experience and the economic logics that underlie neoliberalism" (8). She cautions against how these neoliberal novels misrepresent personal sense experiences as fundamentally private, individualistic affairs. For Kathleen Stewart, on the other hand, ordinary affects "are more directly compelling than ideologies, as well as more fractious, multiplicitous, and unpredictable than symbolic meanings" (3). Neither an ideology nor a symbol, the ordinary affect of touch compels and unsettles.

Updike was never an ideological writer (Fromer 31). Politically, his work will frustrate both the liberal and the conservative if they come to it expecting confirmation. Yet this is no diplomatic strategy or apolitical quietism. Updike's avoidance of ideological positions is the natural product of his fascination with the world of sense experience which we all share in common. In this chapter I argue that, in contrast to much of contemporary affect theory, Updike firmly places human language alongside touch as twin affects of a common, creaturely experience. *To touch, to feel*: These verbs for tactile experiences also describe the emotional sense of common, human connection that literature often elicits. For Updike, both words and bodies exist to touch and feel the Creator's creation. His work presents examples of how the sense of words and the sense of touch are principally experienced as emotional connections to creation. In Updike's hands, touch is never a purely personal experience but one that orients his characters in a shared world of common, created objects.

Moreover, when Rabbit's hand reaches out for that common world, it discovers that what he touches, touches him back. The touch of a tree or a hedge is meaningful because it provides "a small answer" to Rabbit's unstated question: Who am I? In Updike's novels and stories, in his autobiographical essays, and in his poetry, we learn the meaning of who we are from the people, things, and places that touch us back. He shows us how a caress, even a firm grasp, can be a passive reception and an affirmation. This orienting aspect of touch shares notable parallels with the way that one of Updike's fellow contemporary novelists, Don DeLillo, uses the sense of touch to respond to the disorientation of modern societies. While postsecular critics have emphasized the religious significance of language in DeLillo's novels, I show that touch, too, orients an otherwise disoriented modern subject. Having shown how DeLillo's use of touch corresponds with Updike's, I close the chapter by comparing Updike's writing about style with John Dewey's remarkable *Art as Experience*, in order to demonstrate how Updike's theology of sense offers its own theory of aesthetic experience.

WORDS TOUCH

An Easter sermon delivered in Updike's dystopian novel, *Toward the End of Time* (1997), draws its moral from the conviction that words touch. The aging protagonist, Ben Turnbull, finds himself in a near future where the government has ceased to function but Americans still go to church on Easter Sunday. The priest preaches on the biblical scene where the newly risen Christ tells Mary Magdalene not to touch him. *Noli me tangere*. The story has a wealth of iconographic imagery associated with it, but this priest instead focuses on the relationship between touching and hearing, between male and female, between rushing and waiting. The moral of the sermon is that it is better to be *touched by* Christ than *to touch* him.

Beginning with Mary's mistaking Christ for a gardener, the priest narrates: "The strange man, whom she has mistaken for the gardener in this disorienting place, says her name: 'Mary.' She turns and says, '*Rabboni*,' which is to say, 'Master.' At this point she must have reached out in the joy of recognition for He says, 'Touch me not.' *Noli me tangere*. Jesus spurns her instinctive attempt at contact.

Why?" (*Toward the End* 116). As he listens to the sermon, Ben reflects that this must be because Christ "was in what quantum theory calls superposition—neither here nor there, up nor down. He was Schrodinger's cat" (116). Ben's immediate turn to a scientific explanation for the risen Christ's atomic structure betrays his willingness, even desire, to believe in this risen Lord. Nearing death himself, he is primed for encouragement in such a belief. Instead of a reflection on Christ's resurrected body, however, the priest notes the difference between how Christ speaks to Mary and how Thomas touches Christ.

> "A little later in the same chapter," our inquisitor preached, "Jesus invites His disciple Thomas to touch Him, to ease Thomas's doubts. Thomas has said he will not believe in the risen Jesus unless he sees in His hands the print of the nails, and puts his own hand in the wound of sword-thrust in Jesus's side. Jesus obliges. He lets Himself be intimately touched to ease the other man's doubt. It is a guy thing. For Mary Magdalene, seeing must be believing. Jesus tells her not to touch Him because He is not yet ascended to the Father. He is in a fragile in-between condition. Still, He has some orders for Mary: she should go tell the disciples that He is risen. Mary obeys. Like so many women in the Bible, she accepts her subservient role and obeys. But because she needed to weep, to stay at the tomb and come to terms with her feelings, it was she and not Peter or the other disciple, whom Jesus loved, usually identified as John, son of Zebedee—it was not these but Mary who first sees the risen Christ and who hears her name pronounced by Him: 'Mary.' For the people of Biblical times, spoken language was as good as a touch, each word lived in their ears. They didn't have TV, they didn't have MTV or animated holograms, for them the spoken word was the hottest entertainment around. 'Mary.' '*Rabboni.*' 'Touch me not.'" (116)

The spoken word touches Mary because she was ready to be touched—in "coming to terms with her feelings," Mary feels Christ in a more powerful way than Thomas. Thomas touches Christ, but Mary *is touched by Christ*. Where Thomas skeptically intrudes, she graciously receives.

The novel then sets up a similar juxtaposition between the apostle Paul and Christ's disciples. Paul receives the greater gift in being touched by, rather than being able to touch, his Lord. Thinking back on the sermon about Mary Magdalene, Ben falls into a hallucinatory reverie in which he becomes the apostle Mark assisting on a missionary journey with Paul (Acts 13:5). For Paul, words take on forceful liquidity that pours out of his mouth. As Mark listens, Paul names the cities to which they will travel, and the "names tumbled from Paul's mouth like cheerful imprecations; he loved language as it spilled through his lips" (126). The names tumble and spill; they have mass and gravitational pull. Words are not air; they are to be swilled and savored like a good wine. They take shape and create sensations of feeling—like the feathers Felicia Alden keeps discovering in her mouth in *The Witches of Eastwick*. In that novel one of the witches, Jane Smart, uses the *Book of Common Prayer* to cast a spell on Felicia, and she begins pulling feathers from her mouth when she talks. Like when Mary's own name suddenly touches her ear, the nonmetaphorical physicality of the feathers surprises. The words take form and brush against their speaker's body. This association of words with the light touch of feathers is no merely descriptive flourish. Rather, it is at the heart of one of one of Updike's most celebrated stories—another story about the touch of Christ, "Pigeon Feathers" (*CES*).

After "A&P" (1961), Updike's "Pigeon Feathers" (1961) may be his best-known short story (*CES*). It describes a young boy, David Kern, and his existential crisis of faith. David is unsure about his belief in God but is only disgusted by his pastor's idea that the resurrection of the dead is merely a metaphor for how our deeds might live on in others. When his father claims that "the earth is nothing but chemicals" in his ongoing debate with his wife over organic farming, she insists, "If you'd just walk out on the farm you'd know it's not true. The land has a *soul*" (266). In contrast to the pastor's metaphorical afterlife and his father's chemicals, David's mother thinks that even the blind matter of the land has a soul. In bed one night, fretting about death, David yearns for assurance that the resurrection of the body is a true and certain thing. If it is not true, he will miss what it feels like to walk and to experience how things feel: "*Never walk again, never touch a doorknob again*" (271). The prospect so frightens him, this lack of tactile sensation—what Rabbit might call a *lack of an answer*—that he puts his hands up in the air.

> David prayed to be reassured. Though the experiment frightened him, he lifted his hands high into the darkness above his face and begged Christ to touch them. Not hard or long: the faintest, quickest grip would be final for a lifetime. His hands waited in the air, itself a substance, which seemed to move through his fingers; or was it the pressure of his pulse? He returned his hands to beneath the covers, uncertain if they had been touched or not. For would not Christ's touch *be* infinitely gentle? (271)

His hands in the air, David waits to be touched, waiting to be told who he is: Is he a child of God or, like his father's view of dirt, "nothing but chemicals"?

While David is unsure of Christ's touch (or, rather, left to his faith) at that moment, he becomes sure of His touch once he begins to use those same hands to dig a hole in the ground at the story's close. Once the problem is recast in light of God's role as the Creator and his own creaturely status, everything changes for him. Following his grandmother's request, David has shot some pigeons roosting in the family's barn and must bury them. His encounter with the dead birds bears resemblance to a proof for the immortality of the soul but, in all truth, reads more like an assertion of the triumph of the pleasure principle over the reality principle. The passage makes its point by enacting the sensuousness of the commonplace in lavishing adjectives onto the humdrum pigeons' not-so-gray feathers, completely eschewing any attempt at philosophical or theological argument. The sentences caress the feathers' iridescent whorls with their own unhurried luxury. It is worth reconsidering the passage in the entirety of its unfolding as David handles, drops, and then finally buries the birds:

> He had never seen a bird this close before. The feathers were more wonderful than the dog's hair, for each filament was shaped within the shape of the feather, and the feathers in turn were trimmed to

fit a pattern that flowed without error across the bird's body. He lost himself in the geometrical tides as the feathers now broadened and stiffened to make an edge for the flight, now softened and constricted to cup warmth around the mute flesh. And across the surface of the infinitely adjusted yet somehow effortless mechanics of the feathers played idle designs of color, no two alike, designs executed, it seemed, in a controlled rapture, with a joy that hung level in the air above and behind him. Yet these birds bred in the millions and were exterminated as pests. Into the fragrant open earth he dropped one broadly banded in slate shades of blue, and on top of it another, mottled all over in rhythms of lilac and gray. The next was almost wholly white, but for a salmon glaze at its throat. As he fitted the last two, still pliant, on the top, and stood up, crusty coverings were lifted from him, and with a feminine, slipping sensation along his nerves that seemed to give the air hands, he was robed in this certainty: that the God who had lavished such craft upon these worthless birds would not destroy His whole Creation by refusing to let David live forever. (285–86)

The gross egotism of this conclusion, the circularity of its reasoning, should not distract from but emphasize the aesthetic means by which the conclusion is drawn: the force of sense *against* the form of reason. Updike's lyrical style makes all the difference here. The ostensible logic of the passage is that if God makes common pigeons beautiful, then He will keep me alive to appreciate that beauty. Were we to reduce it to logic, the argument is less than convincing—how do we get from "God makes things worth appreciating" to "God will keep me alive to appreciate them"? Yet the way the prose immerses the reader in a sensuous experience enacts its own theologically sober praise for created life. Like the pigeons, David Kern is a loved creature. Moreover, the "infinitely adjusted yet somehow effortless mechanics" and "controlled rapture" of the pigeons' feathers could just as well refer to the style of the sentence as to the feathers. Updike takes care to ensure that the passage's conclusion overwhelms with its own sense of created purpose. Here a "slipping sensation" "seemed to give the air hands," and David feels touched. The dead pigeons become witnesses, not only to the truth of eternal life but also to the gratuitous beauty of Creation and the human creature's need to know and feel that beauty, to be "robed in this certainty" that a lavish Creator gives and to feel it as a robelike "slipping sensation along his nerves." The passage is finally about how the most modest experiences of God's creation can touch us.

The palpable reality of the Creator is a theological conviction that Updike seems to associate with his mother and the Plowville farm that his family moved to from Shillington when he was thirteen years old. While *The Centaur* (1962) was an overt homage to his father, Wesley Russell Updike, *Of the Farm* (1965) was the same for his mother, Linda Grace Hoyer. In an introduction to the Czech edition of *Of the Farm*, Updike writes that the novel's "thematic transaction, as I conceived it, was the mutual forgiveness of mother and son" (*Picked Up Pieces* 78). The similarities of the mother and son figures in *Of the Farm* to the ones in "Pigeon Feathers" (and the fact that both demonstrate the views Updike attributes to his mother in *Self-Consciousness*) suggest that David Kern likely got the idea of holding his hands out for Christ's touch from his mother. The mother character in *Of the Farm* claims that her belief in God depends on her ability to touch him. In one scene the Updike-stand-in-protagonist, Joey Robinson, listens as his new wife, Peggy; her son Richard from her previous marriage; and his mother banter back and forth. As the conversation takes an intellectual turn, Joey's mother glosses Plato's story from the *Symposium* about the origin of gender difference for the young Richard. Then Peggy adds that the differences between the sexes were psychological as well as biological.

> My mother, who liked to do her own amplifying, said, "I've never believed in those. I'm a very coarse customer. I believe only in what I can see or touch."
> "And God," Richard said.
> My mother's head dipped forward in surprise and, as if to make something useful of the gesture, she took another slice of baloney. "God?"
> "We discussed it before we came. He—me—said you believed in God."
> "And you don't?"

Richard looked at us, at Peggy and me, for help, which came, instead, from my mother. She said, "I see and touch God all the time." The froglike shininess of fascination returned to his yes as he looked at her. She went on, "If I couldn't see and touch Him here on the farm, if I lived in New York City, I don't know if I'd believe or not. You see, that's why it's so important that the farm be kept. People will forget that there could be anything except stones and glass and subways." (*Of the Farm* 70)

How wonderful that added irony: she picks up a piece of baloney and asks, "God?" Is this God-talk just more baloney, or is it, like baloney, a kind of everyday, tangible, Pennsylvania Dutch experience? For Richard's mother, God is either there to be touched like boloney or a bunch of metaphysical boloney. The novel goes on, however, beyond an invisible God to how invisible people can be touched by simply speaking of them. When Peggy complains to Joey's mother that she continuously harps on not seeing the children from Joey's prior marriage, his mother replies, "I talk about them, Peggy, when I do, because I'm a garrulous old freak and because talk is the only way I can touch them now" (105). Here talk is not the touch of a word in the ear, or the word flowing over—or feathering—the lips, but a kind of lesser touch, something to make up for the absence of a shared touch between two immediate bodies.

Is talking about someone a way of touching them? And what about the dead letters on the page that make up Updike's writing? Is claiming that such printed words touch merely a rhetorical flourish? I think what Updike's descriptions reveal is that both words and touching are ordinary affects that help us take hold of the world. Touch is a way of reaching out and feeling, of caressing or appreciating, but also of connecting. In its rigorous and attentive form, touching becomes a form of active reception. In his early autobiographical essay, "The Dogwood Tree: A Boyhood," Updike recalls a nearly tame squirrel that lived close to their house, which he had named and would feed. In the reciprocating touch of that squirrel Updike discovers an otherwise intangible abstraction: life itself. When he recalls "Tilly's tiny brown teeth shivering against my fingertips," he can only conclude, "That was life" (*Assorted Prose* 124).

Rather than parse the concept of "life itself," Updike provides a sense experience—tiny brown teeth shivering against fingertips. This is the point of touching, to receive the gifts life offers by ever so gently— like David Kern—reaching out to feel.

Writing may never touch in the same way that a body touches, but it is a way that a body can come to know *what* it touches in a new way. In Updike's case, writing uses words to touch in a manner similar to the aural touch of the word in Mary Magdalene's ear. Jean-Luc Nancy, the contemporary phenomenologist most invested in touch's religious resonances, contends, "Writing in its essence touches upon the body" (*Corpus* 11). He clarifies: "Writing is not itself a touch, but it is a form of touching" because writing "is the touch of being touched. When touching is an act of being touched. It seeks outwards, and receives" (17). Writing is not a solitary retreat into the writer's psychological interiority but the reception of a gift; it is a way of opening oneself up to the outside world. To use words to explore creation, as Updike does, is to reach out in order to be touched. It is to wait, like Mary Magdalene at the tomb, trying to feel what there is to feel.

This way of thinking about the active passivity of touch is an essential aesthetic insight. *Touching Feeling,* Eve Kosofksy Sedgwick's book on affect, avers, "The sense of touch makes nonsense out of any dualistic understanding of agency and passivity" (14). At its best, affect theory takes the modern subject down from its untouchable height: to know is not only to see and speak but to touch, and *be touched*. According to Lauren Berlant, this kind of attention to embodied sense experience is a better way to rethink how we know, since "the affective turn brings us back to the encounter of what is sensed with what is known" (53). Yet this turn toward the senses has come at the cost of categorizing the body's affective resonances as distinctly separate from what are too often characterized as the strictly linguistic aspects of textual study.

Donovan O. Schaefer's recent work on the place of affect in religious studies is a striking recent example. *Religious Affects: Animality, Evolution, and Power* uses several theorists to think through the prelinguistic modes of feeling involved in religious culture. Schaefer's definition of *postsecularism* as "those moments when religion flows over the boundaries of language or thought" promises to treat the ways in which merely theorizing language is insufficient for postsecular studies (10). Moreover, the argument in Schaefer's chapter "Savages," that prior "to language, moral decision making—in humans and other animals—is produced from embodied regimes of affect," suggests that he has Updike's high regard for the animal aspects of human experience (133). Recall Updike's sense that "we should behave, if not like monkeys, like 'savages'—that our instincts and appetites are better guides, for a healthy life, than the advice of other human beings" (*Self-Consciousness* 257). Yet instead Schaefer claims that the symbolic structure of language "is of no value" for the study of religious affects (10). While work such as Schaefer's is undoubtedly informative and compelling, the reduction of sense to a phenomenon utterly distinct from or even opposed to what he calls the "linguistic fallacy" (20) enables the too-neat binary opposition of emotion/language and thereby fosters the very animal/human binary that his study seeks to upend.

Updike provides a more coherent way to understand affect. According to Christian theology, not only is the created world *spoken* into being but the Gospel of John makes the striking claim that "the Word was made flesh" (John 1:14). Christianity's doctrine of Creation asserts the direct participation of words in the substance of material bodies; the doctrine of the incarnation—that Christ is fully divine and fully human—completes it with the teaching that the body itself communicates. Many of Updike's passages about God, and certainly the ones I've cited thus far, have a hard time separating words from bodies. Take, for instance, his inclusion of God's role in his psoriasis in the "At War with My Skin" chapter of *Self-Consciousness*. Updike would often seek out a sunnier clime during the winter months because the sun would help heal his psoriasis spots. He writes about the spiritual idea of God's forgiveness as "a tactile actuality" that he would experience during these ritual winter trips.

> To be forgiven, by God: this notion, so commonly mouthed in shadowy churches, was for me a tactile actuality as I lay in my loathed hide under that hard pellet, that suspended white explosion, of tropical sun. And the sun's weight on my skin always meant this to me: I was being redeemed, hauled back into mankind, back from defor-

mity and shame. The sun was like God not only in His power but also in the way He allowed Himself to be shut out, to be evaded. Yet if one were receptive, He could find you even at the bottom of a well; one could board a plane in a blizzard, bounce for a few hours in the fuselage's pastel tunnel, slide far down the lines of longitude, and get out, and He would be there, waiting. That sun-softened humid air would hit your face like an angel's kiss at the airplane's exit door, at the top of the stairs. (68)

Forgiveness has a "tactile actuality" because the "sun's weight on my skin" becomes a form of redemption, of being "hauled back into mankind." As Joey Robinson's mother felt she could touch God on the farm, Updike feels the touch of God's forgiveness in the sunshine. The sense experience incorporates Christianity's overarching claim about the Fall and Redemption. In his body he registers the feeling of what it means to be forgiven and redeemed. It is an affective response to a purely physical experience that at the same time becomes sensible through two very distinct and special words in Christian teaching: *forgiveness* and *redemption*.

Christian theology has a long tradition of explaining how speech about God works in the bodies God made. It is a fertile resource that writing on religion and affect theory, such as Schaefer's, rarely plumbs. The published version of Rowan Williams's 2013 Gifford Lectures on natural theology make use of that tradition, however, and they demonstrate the continuity between the body's affective responses and its use of language (*Edge of Words*). One chapter in particular, "Intelligent Bodies: Language as Material Practice," takes up "the study of autistic conditions" to "underline the fact that our conversational practice rests on a closely woven scheme of physical interaction" (97). For Williams, conversation is less about communicating information and more about establishing the meaningful presence of another body. Williams draws on Phoebe Caldwell's work on autism and concludes that her ability to draw severely autistic people into forms of communication through touch helps us see how intimately touch and language are interrelated. Williams insists that "it is a mistake to think of speech originating in the (practical) need to communicate information: it has its roots in simply articulating and testing mutual recognition" insofar as its primary aim is to establish "a world in common" (99). Language is first and foremost a way that bodies try to establish a common world; like touch, it establishes a rapport, a way of being together more than accomplishing a transaction. Williams argues that people are people not because of their ability to use language but because they are "another centre of meaningful experience, another point of view, another intelligible situation" that may or may not be able to communicate with words (115). The body and the word exist in common as ways to share the "meaningful experience" of being human—in all its senses.

Updike strives to express that common, creaturely world with his readers. Whether it is a summer night's tableau or the radiator by the front window or the sun on his skin, touch orients Updike's writing toward the substantiality of shared sense experience. In "The Dogwood Tree" Updike claims that the "difference between a childhood and boyhood must be this: our childhood is what we alone have had; our boyhood is what any boy in our environment would have had" (*Assorted Prose* 132). He calls the common environment he seeks to describe "middleness with all its grits, bumps, anonymities, in its fullness of satisfaction and mystery" (147). Note that it is texture that defines that middleness for him—"grits" and "bumps"—and that the textures bear their own mysteriousness. Updike confesses that something unknown, because unnoticed, lurks behind each blank page he seeks to fill: "Blankness is not emptiness; we may skate upon an intense radiance we do not see because we see nothing else. And in fact there is a color, a quiet but tireless goodness that things at rest, like a brick wall or a small stone, seem to affirm. A wordless reassurance these things are pressing to give" (147). That pressing "wordless reassurance" is what touched Updike. It inspired him to write in such a way that the books he gives to readers do not merely indulge their own creative linguistic patterns but seek to unfold a firmly grasped, given world.

ORIENTING TOUCH

The body's ability to orient a character's sense of reality is a concern that Don DeLillo, a writer Updike rarely enjoyed, shares. As different as their novels' themes and style may be, Updike's and DeLillo's shared interest in the body suggests its importance for late twentieth-century American literature. In 2006, when the *New York Times Book Review* published its polled results of the top five novels of the past twenty-five years, it put DeLillo's *Underworld* (1997) at number two. Updike's complete tetralogy, *Rabbit Angstrom,* came in at number four. Whatever value lies in such rankings, it highlights what the two works have in common. Both novels cover most of the second half of the century and do so in such a way as to capture key shifts in social mores, political ideals, economic realities, and technological changes. DeLillo's work as a whole, however, is more concerned with the global flows of capital, technological developments, and the experience of alienation and fragmentation. Updike's attention to the lyrical details of suburban and small-town life can seem hidebound in comparison. On the other hand, Updike once aptly captured the similarities and differences between DeLillo's and his own style with the barbed complement: "Though always a concept-driven writer, whose characters spout smart, swift essays at one another, he has shown himself—in large parts of *Underworld,* in almost all of *White Noise*—capable of realism's patient surfaces and saturation in personally verified detail" (*Due Considerations* 267). The details of realism's patient surfaces are, of course, Updike's territory, not DeLillo's. Yet such realist points of contact indicate how both novelists focus on embodied experience.

DeLillo's follow-up to *Underworld*, *The Body Artist* (2001), eschews sprawling plots for the slimmer, more concentrated dramatic form that DeLillo's novels have taken since the turn of the millennium. And despite critical attention to DeLillo's almost magical view of language (Hungerford 52), *The Body Artist* inaugurated a more concentrated focus on the body, culminating with *Zero K* (2016). As Laura Barrett has noted, "These recent novels seem to wallow in the inadequacy of language" while simultaneously gesturing that this very inadequacy "can only be communicated by words" (253). DeLillo has become more and more interested in how literature that attends to the sense experiences of embodiment can become a mode of imaginative resistance to the dehumanizing scale and pace of the modern world. This is not to claim that *The Body Artist* retreats into Updike's rural Plowville or small-town Shillington. While it refrains from the global plotlines of his other novels, *The Body Artist* nonetheless remains in the rarefied milieu of performance art.

From a seaside cottage, the novel follows the "body artist" Lauren Hartke's grief over her husband's self-inflicted death, her surprise at discovering a mentally ill man living in the house, and the composition of a new work of performance art called "Body Time." Despite its inclusion of a dying spouse, the novel is far from sentimental. First, Lauren's relationship to her husband, Rey Robles, is presented only in the sparest of deadpan domestic dialogue, evoking little to no emotional connection between the two. Their banter keeps an ironic distance throughout. Second, her grief is experienced more as disorientation than as loss. She dwells less on the person of Rey than on what it feels like for her to be living now without him. The nameless stranger, whose presence mysteriously seems to predate Rey's death, gives human form to the unfamiliarity Lauren feels all around her. Lauren's subsequent disorientation inspires her, and rather than seek to overcome it, she instead makes a goal of it, formalizing the stark austerity of the human body as such in her new performance.

Touching in *The Body Artist* can seem less to connect people to their place, or even others, than to disconnect and disorient them. Lauren touches her own body in order to erase its familiarity, to become closer to the nameless stranger's absent sense of self. Her body becomes a work of art in which the goal is not to paint the canvas but scrape it clean. "It was time to sand her body," DeLillo recounts as if describing a monk's self-disciplined renunciation (78). "She used pumice stone on the bottoms of her feet, working circular swipes, balls, heels, and then resoaped the foot and twisted it up into her hand again" (78). And yet there is something in this contact that reassures her: "She liked to hold a foot in a hand. She patiently razed the lone callus, stretching the task over days, lost in it, her body coiled in a wholeness of intent, the kind of solemn self-absorption that marks a line from childhood" (78). The further she goes down this road the more it sounds like a monastic struggle against the flesh. "She ate dull light dinners, quickly," DeLillo writes, "getting it over with," as if such indulgences were too much (79). She uses "a monkey-hair brush on her elbows and knees" because she "wanted it to hurt" (86).

All this attention to her body is no manicure: The goal is a kind of self-denial, where the self is commensurate with her body's idiosyncrasies. She touches her body to erase its identifying qualities. "This was her work, to disappear from all her former venues of aspect and bearing and to become a blankness, a body slate erased of every past resemblance," for only then would she become "someone who is classically unseen, the person you are trained to look through, bled of familiar effect, a spook in the night static of every public toilet" (86). She is working to prepare her body so that it can express the same lack of identity she sees in the stranger with whom she shares her house. One section of the novel is a review, printed in the text without comment, of "Body Time." The reviewer claims that "Hartke is a body artist who tries to shake off the body—hers anyway" (106). Her work attends to the experience of the body with precise and fixed thoroughness, but it is the body as an abstract, physical form: *the* body, not Lauren Hartke's unique body. It is the body as pure form.

She pushes on the processes of change a body undergoes, interrogating its role in creating a person's sense of identity. At one moment she looks at her face in the mirror, trying "to understand why it looked different from the same face downstairs, in the full-length mirror in the front hall, although it shouldn't be hard to understand at all, she thought, because faces look different all the time and everywhere, based on a hundred daily variables, but then again, she thought, why do I look different" (65). While it might seem that the context of the full-length mirror changed the way she perceives her face, in fact Lauren becomes increasingly convinced that only the passing of time and the kinds of changes it registers can truly tell her who she is. "You are made out of time. This is the force that tells you who you are. Close your eyes and feel it," she reflects (94). Then, in the novel's final line, she confesses that her body orients her in ways that nothing else seems able to achieve. She returns to the house after the stranger has left and immediately opens up a window in order "to feel the sea tang on her face and the flow of time in her body, to tell her who she was" (126). The touch of time—a concept as abstract and difficult to explain as Updike's touch of God—orients her. The touch of time, even more than her body's unique distinguishing marks, tells her who she is.

DeLillo places the body's sense of touch at the forefront of his portrayal of the sense of self. As in Updike, touch tells us who we are. Alongside the sense of touch, too, there is the sense of meaning that it creates: in this case, time flowing. For Updike, this second sense of meaning is just as crucial. For example, Updike's parents planted a dogwood tree in the side yard of their house at 117 Philadelphia Avenue in Shillington the same year he was born. "This tree, I learned quite early," Updike explains, "was exactly my age, was, in a sense, me" (*Assorted Prose* 121). In which sense? Was it because he grew up climbing it so often that the feel of its bark on his hands is part of his identity? Not quite. Despite its place as the essay's central conceit, the tree was far from a vivid presence in his childhood. Updike confesses that he "never observed [the dogwood tree] closely, am not now sure what color its petals were; its presence was no more distinct than that of my shadow" (121). No vivid memory springs forward of its annual fragrance, the feel of its velvet blossoms, its swaying shape in a storm. Yet its shadowlike presence persisted whether the young Updike was noticing it or not.

In its indistinct persistence, the dogwood tree anchors an entire chain of Updike's sense memories, for merely "mentioning it seems to open the possibility of my boyhood home coming again to life" (121). The tree opens an entire scene.

> With a sweet damp rush the grass of our yard seems to breathe again on me. It is just cut. My mother is pushing the mower, to which a canvas catch is attached. My grandmother is raking up the loose grass in thick heaps, small green haystacks impregnated with dew, and my grandfather stands off to one side, smoking a cigar, elegantly holding the elbow of his right arm in the palm of his left hand while the blue smoke twists from under his mustache and dissolves in the heavy evening air—that misted, too-rich Pennsylvania air. (121)

The side yard's dogwood initiates a vivid series of palpable connections: The damp grass rushes upon him, the mower is pushed, the haystacks impregnated, the elbow elegantly held, and the air itself feels heavy. While the prose's overall effect is visual, a scene emerges of people touching and feeling, coated in a misty evening. Indistinct to any sense memory itself, the dogwood tree nevertheless initiates several.

The little phrase Updike uses to introduce the dogwood tree, "in a sense," is central to the case I've been making for how his theology of sense thinks about touch. The tree is not directly registered by any one sense, yet it somehow incorporates all of them. Moreover, in some small way, the dogwood tree truly *is* Updike. If he attempts to define himself in words, he must say something about his experience of the dogwood because it's part of who he is; it is, therefore, in a sense, he himself. That "in a sense" correlation between Updike and the tree, where the two nearly meet to become one, is how Updike's writing touches on the tableau of his boyhood. It isn't quite a metaphor or a simile. Instead, the dogwood tree orients his sense of self within his other senses.

"The Dogwood Tree" further develops that orientation when it leaves the front and side yards to go inside the house. "I remember waiting with [my mother] by a window for my father to return from weeks on the road," he writes, "in the Shillington living room. My hands are on the radiator ridges, I can see my father striding through the hedge toward the grape arbor, I can feel my mother's excitement beside me mingle with mine. But she says this cannot be; he had lost his job before I was born" (124). The touch of his hands on the radiator ridges orients the whole scene—gives it a tactile anchor in spite of the fact that it is a false memory. Updike's writing will often associate looking and touching; touch orients the speaker within a particular vantage point. Touch does not necessarily render any specific object more vivid (such as the dogwood tree) or tell the historical truth (the hands on the radiator cannot speak, only feel); it grounds the body in a place—*this* place and not another. Touch gives to the body the sensations to create a deeper sense of belonging *here* and not just anywhere. It is an orienting experience that reveals Updike's unique history of belonging to the place that is Shillington, to the people of Shillington.

When Updike sets out to map the geography of Shillington in "The Dogwood Tree," his hands are no longer gripping a radiator but his father's hair and ears. Just beyond Shillington's poorhouse "was a woods that extended along the south of the town. Here my parents often took me on walks. Every Sunday afternoon that was fair, we would set out" (126). On these walks, Updike writes, "I would lag farther and farther behind, until my father would retrace his steps and mount me on his shoulders. Upon this giddy, swaying perch—I hesitated to grip his ears and hair as tightly as I needed to—I felt as frightened as exultant, and soon confusedly struggled to be put down" (126). Here again the prehensile contact orients the memory. Updike's hands on his father's head hold the scene together, even as those same woods later bestowed those same hands their first opportunity to "cup my hands over [a girl's] breasts, small and shallow within the stiffness of her coat" (127). The suddenly sexual association of those childhood walks with the woods of his teenage years, the movement of his hands from his father's head to a young girl's breasts, traces the passing time with passing touches.

Updike's autobiographical writing consistently associates his sense of self with such memorable experiences of touching. While Kathleen Verduin is to right to name "self-consciousness" as "eminently Updike's hallmark theme" (329), the autobiographical works characterize self-consciousness as a way of feeling, an embodied orientation in space and time. It is not a disembodied interiority or pure self-awareness. When Updike writes his memoirs, *Self-Consciousness,* the book explores not a deep psychological essence but the surfaces he touched and how they felt. For example, when Updike returns to Shillington in the book's first chapter, it is again to mix the sense of touching with walking, and walking with his deepest sense of identity. Titled "A Soft Spring Night in Shillington," it maps his town based on visceral sense experiences from his childhood. Now he is an adult visiting his mother, but his walking is again rendered in terms of touch: The town is as soft as the spring night, and his walking probes its surfaces, touching its "tenderest parts" and finding in them his own sense of self: "I had propelled my body through the tenderest parts of a town that was also somewhat my body. Yet my pleasure was innocent and my hope was primitive. I had expected to be told who I was, and why, and had not been entirely disappointed" (*Self-Consciousness* 40–41). Shillington must be walked through, touched, like a reflexive patdown one might give oneself when recalling a misplaced set of keys—except this time it's to find out who you are. And it's not yourself but—like the answering pressure of Rabbit's hedges—the town around him. Your identity is in your body, which is also your town. As with the dogwood tree "in a sense" being he himself, now the town "was somewhat my body."

At the beginning of "On Being a Self Forever," the closing chapter of *Self-Consciousness,* Updike turns again to his body and his "odd habit of tracing what I see with a mental finger or pen—outlining a shoe or foot, drawing diagonals across window-panes, tracing a curtain pattern while my real finger slightly twitches. This, too, this idiotic tic, is myself" (212). While Updike connects seeing with touching here, he also associates his twitching finger with who he is. His hands, after all, produce his authorial signature. They contain the common hiccup he runs into while signing his name, a stab of graphite lodged in his index finger from a "freshly sharpened pencil that I accidentally gave myself in junior high school one day, hurrying between classes in the hall" (213), and the "faint bad smell that is always (somehow satisfyingly) there" on his other index finger (214). For Updike, this "embedded data compose my most intimate self" (214). His most intimate self is somehow lodged in those unique hands.

And yet not only in those hands. He goes on to elaborate that his "own deepest sense of self has to do with Shillington and (at a certain slant) the scent or breath of Christmas. I become exhilarated in Shillington, as if my self is begin given a bath in its own essence" (*Self-Consciousness* 220). Note how, as in the beginning of "The Dogwood Tree," he again uses breath—as if the spirit of Shillington is life itself, though in the faintest of touches. Here, however, the breath becomes a bath that flows over him. For Updike, the self is not something you achieve or find; instead it comes as a gift in the body's experience of a specific time and place. Shillington has given the gift of this self—of his body!—to him. Of these small-town origins Updike writes, "I loved Shillington not as one loves Capri or New York, because they are special, but as one loves one's own body and consciousness, because they are synonymous with being" (30). A self becomes such from its body's immersion in its surroundings. It revels in the goodness it finds in the given world of experience because that world defines it, whatever existential uncertainties that self may agonize over.

Indeed, the existential anxieties of self-consciousness are as characteristic of Updike's work as its love of small-town American life. "On Being a Self Forever" rehearses them, but, as in the ending of "Pigeon Feathers," they are stylistically overwhelmed by the prose's sensuous, lyrical warmth. He describes his Shillington boyhood in terms of its "winter light," which "has the eggshell tint, the chilly thrilling taste, of my self" (243). The color of light, unique to this place and time, is an everyday sense detail that composes his sense of self. For Updike, the truth of the self lies nestled in "the snug opaque quotidian" (234). Rather than explaining what he means by associating himself with Shillington's "scent of Christmas" and "eggshell tint" of winter light, he weaves together images that convey the truth of that "snug opaque quotidian" through their diction and consonance. These things touch him: The quotidian is "snug," the winter air "thrilling" (*thrill*, in Middle English, meant "to pierce or penetrate"—just like a sharp breath of winter air), and these adjectives do the kind of grammatical work that propositional statements do for philosophers. They express truth and, in this case, truth about the role of words in the ordinary affects of felt experience. The truth here is not in the correctness of the memory, however, but in the fundamental emotional relationship it expresses between a person and the world that makes him.

ARRANGING HANDS

Where Updike's theology of sense differs from most of affect theory is in its insistence that words, in a sense, touch. Not metaphorically, but *in a sense*. Touch, whether in the word that reaches out or the hand that grasps, is a way of feeling that is also a way of knowing. It provides the ordinary affects that tell us who we are: creatures that belong to the created world in which we find ourselves. This is fundamentally a theological insight delivered via Updike's attention to the sense of touch. We learn the world's truth through feeling it. As I argued in the introduction, Updike's adjectives are more concerned with adoration than accuracy; his habit of piling them up conditions the perceptions they refer to with the predisposition of a creaturely gratitude.

The significance of this gratitude is why Kristiaan Versluys is right to extricate Updike's realism from any *das Ding an sich* and insist instead on its affective artistry. He writes that Updike's "prose is baroque, unsparse, untidy, and full of dangling ends and seemingly unconnected *obiter dicta*. This superabundance of meanings—the refusal of the tale, even a short one of a mere six pages, to lead in a straightforward manner to its predestined end or telos—is a way of demonstrating the fertility of the human mind and of dramatizing meaning-making in action" (41). Stressing the baroque nature of Updike's prose opens the full aesthetic import of his style: His "superabundance of meanings" is a meandering over the artist's sense of things, never the means to tying up a "straightforward" plot. It is, I would add, how he imbues the sense of meaning into the sense experiences that his realist prose describes. As Versluys also points out, it is this Whitmanesque quality of his leisurely accumulated and often luxurious catalogs that moves his prose more than its epiphanies: "Nothing much happens in an Updike story except for the slow unraveling of feeling and circumstance" (30). This unraveling unfolds the mysteries of the material world through layered prose that proves the prescience of Robert Detweiler's phrase for Updike's work: "secular baroque" (Detweiler 131). These baroque occupations place Updike alongside unexpected company. In "The Literature of Exhaustion," Updike's antirealist contemporary John Barth cites Borges's definition of the baroque as "that style which deliberately exhausts (or tries to exhaust) its possibilities and borders upon its own caricature" (Barth 73). The baroque in Updike is not Borges's hermetically sealed performance *sui generis*; rather, it is the attempt to saturate prose in the palpable—or some might say secular—world of the senses. Words can touch, in part, because of how Updike's style arranges them.

That style, including the disposition of gratitude it expresses, suggests its own theory of subjectivity. Only a few pages into "On Being a Self Forever," Updike begins considering his own writing style by referring to "the modernist dissolution" of the self (218), citing Rimbaud's famous line, "*Je est un autre*" (218). In light of the chapter's title, it seems this should be the moment Updike sets up his opponent, perhaps even as a straw man, in order to make his case for the unified persistence of the self in the Christian afterlife. As mentioned in the introduction, he does something close to that with Alain Robbe-Grillet's dissolution of the narrative subject in *A Month of Sundays*. Instead he turns to the work of Robbe-Grillet's French contemporary, Michel Tournier. Updike cites Tournier out of admiration for what Tournier attempts to achieve in his prose, expressing an affinity for Tournier's desire for unmediated experience. "Our brains are no longer conditioned for reverence and awe," Updike laments, but he thinks Tournier's prose attempts just that (216). The passage Updike quotes is from Tournier's novel *Friday* (originally *Vendredi ou les limbes du Pacifique*), not only a rewriting of Daniel Defoe's *Robinson Crusoe* but also a manifesto for what was heralded in the sixties as the "death of the subject." Tournier was a lifelong friend of the vitalist philosopher Gilles Deleuze, and in several respects *Friday* pays tribute to Deleuze's philosophy and is every bit as radical as Robbe-Grillet's work. The novel reverses Defoe's original scenario, where Robinson Crusoe learns to have dominion over both Friday and the island through Robinson's use of instrumental rationality. Instead *Friday* offers an account of how Robinson opens himself up to the island's power over him.

In the passage Updike quotes in *Self-Consciousness*, Tournier's Robinson character provides an account of perception that exemplifies Updike's narrative style according to a posited "primary, direct mode" of knowledge. Robinson writes that a "self unrelated to others" exists "comparatively seldom." But in the "primary, direct mode" of perception,

> the objects are all there, shining in the sun or buried in the shade, rough or smooth, light or heavy; they are known, tested, touched, even cooked, carved, folded, and so on; whereas I who do the knowing, the tasting, touching, and cooking, have no separate existence except when I perform the act of reflection which causes *me* to emerge—a thing which in fact rarely happens. In that primary state

of knowledge my awareness of an object is the object itself, the thing known and perceived without any person knowing and perceiving it. We cannot use the image of the candle shedding its light upon objects. We must substitute another: that of objects shining unaided, with a light of their own. . . . Then suddenly there is a click. The subject breaks away from the object, divesting it of a part of its color and substance. There is a rift in the scheme of things, and a whole range of objects crumbles in becoming *me*. (qtd. in *Self-Consciousness* 218–19)

Robinson has written this in his journal. As an individual alone on an island, he reflects on his relationship to the objects around him; as he has yet to meet Friday, he inhabits, to use the title of Deleuze's appreciative essay on Tournier, "a world without others." Robinson's line of argument is that the consciousness of such an isolated subject is a secondary kind of awareness, something that lacks the immediacy of reality's true force. The primary state of knowledge would be a consciousness that received objects without the intervention of the Enlightenment's symbolic candle of reason—one that did not organize objects according to limitations of the subject's ability to synthesize information but experienced objects as a multiplicity of illuminating surfaces. Such objects are "shining unaided, with a light of their own." But in the secondary mode, there is "a rift in the scheme of things" that causes "a whole range of objects" to dissolve in the subject's reordering of those objects as so many cognitive representations.

Tournier's character is not so much exhibiting an epistemic naïveté here as forcing the issue: *Either* the objects dissolve *or* the subject does. Either you get the objects radiant or the subject coherent, but not both. What Updike takes from Tournier, however, is that this either/or is indebted first and foremost to a reverence for things. When objects shine "with a light of their own," the receiving subject does not construct them through any a priori categories but receives them in innocence and wonder at their sensuous import, in a power of perception that enables a deeper, fuller relationship to one's surroundings. It's not an either/or epistemology but a question of emotional investment. Updike omits a section from this passage in *Friday* that not only makes this clear but also evokes Updike's own aesthetic, what he once called "the clarity of things" (*Always Looking* 3). The need to dominate, order, and control the world of things that Robinson felt now begins to recede in his innocent reverence for the island. In the "primary, direct mode" of knowing he becomes his sense impressions of the island.

> In that innocent, primary—as it were, primeval—stage which is our normal mode of existence there is a happy solitude of the known, a virginity of things comprising all things in themselves like so many functions of their own essence—color, smell, taste, and form. In this sense Robinson is [the island]. He is conscious of himself only in the stir of myrtle leaves with the sun's rays breaking through, he knows himself only in the white crest of a wave running up the yellow sand. (Tournier 93)

Notice that familiar phrase: "in this sense." The dogwood tree was, "in a sense, me," and the town "somewhat" my body, and Robinson is "in this sense" the island. Robinson speculates on the self's relationship to things in the same way that Updike associates his own internal sense of self with the specific sense experience of things in the external world. It is a relationship of innocent sensation, unabashed in its goal "to give the mundane its beautiful due" (*Early Stories* xv). Tournier's character finds himself saturated with an innocent reverence for the island and becomes "conscious of himself only in the stir of myrtle leaves" and the "the white crest of a wave." Updike's refusal to absolutely demarcate the affective valances between a word and a touch is here mirrored in the way that a self becomes indistinguishable from its sensory experiences.

Updike's sensuous style is suffused with similar moments of attentive sensitivity—yet what distinguishes his from others is the overt gratitude it expresses. His recognition that the self is determined not only by the external world that touches it but also in the self's emotional relationship to that world is a key contribution that Updike's work can make to the field of aesthetic theory. John Dewey's *Art as Experience* remains one of the best attempts to clarify the stakes involved in that transformation of a sense of meaning into a sense experience—and vice versa. Dewey makes the case for understanding our experiences with works of art in any medium as the refining and intensifying of everyday experiences. Adapted from the inaugural William James Lectures that Dewey presented at Harvard, *Art as Experience* maintains the continuum between emotional affects and aesthetic effects. Dewey helps clarify what Updike is trying to do with his analysis of Tournier's work because of his emphasis on how aesthetic experience intensifies the ordinary affects of perception.

The most mundane experiences are full of missed perceptions that the literary, musical, or visual arts can teach us to heed. Yet Dewey's peculiar genius is to clarify how the style of a writer like Updike can shape the kinds of perceptions his writing registers, primarily because Dewey argues for the creative spark contained in new perceptions. We tend to think of perception as passive. Dewey writes, however, that perception must muster its forces in order to assimilate with accuracy: "Perception is an act of the going-out of energy in order to receive, not a withholding of energy" (55). For everyday perceptions this is true; but even more so an artist's creativity is an efflorescence of such an "act of the going-out of energy." A writer's recorded observation is a willed participation in the world, not a subtraction from it into some other autonomous, purely imaginary realm. Dewey argues that in exemplifying creative perceptions the artist makes possible a way of perceiving what we would otherwise merely recognize and therefore pass by. His title for the lectures, "Art as Experience," means that art is not opposed to everyday sense experiences, or merely one more sense experience just like all others, but the quintessence of experience as attuned perception.

For Dewey, all forms of experience are informed by this kind of aesthetic experience. So the words and syntax chosen to create David Kern's study of the pigeon feathers can create the possibility of perceiving what might otherwise lack the form of "geometrical tides" or the "mottled" "rhythms of lilac and grey." The following passage works through the paradox of active passivity that Updike's description of the pigeon feathers can help develop for the reader:

> But receptivity is not passivity. It, too, is a process consisting of a series of responsive acts that accumulate toward objective fulfill-

ment. Otherwise, there is not perception but recognition. The difference between the two is immense. Recognition is perception arrested before it has a chance to develop freely. In recognition there is a beginning of an act of perception. But this beginning is not allowed to serve the development of a full perception of the thing recognized. It is arrested at the point where it will serve some other purpose, as we recognize a man on the street in order to greet or to avoid him, not so as to see him for the sake of seeing what is there. (Dewey 54)

Updike's descriptions go beyond arrested recognition in order to see, as Dewey has it, "for the sake of seeing what is there." Updike renders the merely recognizable world—in which perception limits what it perceives to the immediate use values that "serve some other purpose"—in such a way as to point his readers beyond initial appearances to the full dignity of recognition as intense discovery.

Dewey is clear that these more intense perceptions, if they are to achieve the quality of experience beyond habitual recognition, are as much emotional commitments as sense data. What I have called Updike's gratitude is precisely what makes his unique perceptions possible: There is "no such thing in perception as seeing or hearing *plus* emotion. The perceived object or scene is emotionally pervaded throughout" (55). Emotion—and in Updike's case usually the emotion of grateful love—provides the necessary component in order that passive recognition might become active perception. In Updike's artistry, perception always begins with an emotional attachment to what it perceives. This is the reason why even Updike's religious fiction is more in the spirit of Nietzsche's yea-saying to life than work traditionally associated with it, such as Robbe-Grillet's catalog of bloodless empirical data (as the title of the earliest comprehensive piece of literary criticism written on Updike's work, Rachael Burchard's 1971 *John Updike: Yea Sayings,* testifies).

Dewey is explicit that the perceiving self of the aesthetic subject is neither the impermeable self of modernity nor the dissolved self of postmodernity but is composed through the processes of sense experience. It takes the arts, however, to enhance and galvanize those experiences. Literature does not create the sense of a self in the purely linguistic, intellectual experience of reading; literature delivers the self to the renewing powers of the senses in a new way—a new sense, as it were. According to Dewey, the artist must teach the philosopher to put away the bad habit of splitting the world into subjects and objects. Only then can we begin to understand how subjective creativity and the objective environment both co-inhere in the self. Dewey writes, "The uniquely distinguishing feature of esthetic experience is exactly the fact that no such distinction between self and object exists in it, since it is esthetic in the degree in which organism and environment cooperate to institute an experience in which the two are so fully integrated that each disappears" (259). The subject *is* its relation with its environment: Neither subject nor environment achieves a hegemonic shaping force, but the two inextricably constitute each other. To return to Updike's praise for Michel Tournier in *Self-Consciousness*: Crusoe *is* the island. Or to put it in more theological terms: David Kern *is* the Creation.

It is misguided, therefore, to characterize Updike's work by its nostalgia for the passing world of his youth (D. Miller 16). His autobiographical writing is not an attempt to grasp after a fleeting past. Rather, it is an attempt to catch and reinvigorate certain kinds of perceptions. Renewing the present-tense aesthetic experiences of his readers is the end goal of Updike's descriptions. Take, for instance, the obviously autobiographical poem "Shillington." On one level it appears to be a nostalgic eulogy for the town of his past. But paying attention to the sense experiences in the poem opens up a very different orientation—one toward the present. The poem, like so much of Updike's writing, is about leaving and staying, about how memory and the senses intertwine. Yet it is also about how specific sense memories continue to orient the speaker's present. Curiously, the eyes cannot discover the familiar knowledge at hand. "Shillington" contrasts the sights of a rural town's capitulation to suburban sprawl with the redemptive, playful touch of the town's children. Here is the poem in full:

> The vacant lots are occupied, the woods
> Diminish, Slate Hill sinks beneath its crown
> Of solvent homes, and marketable goods
> On all sides crowd the good remembered town.

Returning, we find our snapshots inexact.
Perhaps a condition of being alive
Is that the clothes which, setting out, we packed
With love no longer fit when we arrive.

Yet sights that limited our truth were strange
To older eyes; the town that we have lost
Is being found by hands that still arrange
Horse-chestnut heaps and fingerpaint on frost.

Time shades these alleys; every pavement crack
Is mapped somewhere. A solemn concrete ball,
On the gatepost of a sold house, brings back
A waist leaning against a buckling wall.

The gutter-fires smoke, their burning done
Except for, fanned within, an orange feather;
We have one home, the first, and leave that one.
The having and the leaving go on together. (*Collected Poems* 15)

If "every pavement crack / Is mapped somewhere" in the speaker's memory, it is the touch of a waist on a wall, the solid heft of a concrete ball that unfolds that map. For if, in returning, "we find our snapshots inexact," it is because life is not in the *view* of those snapshots but in the clothes we pick up, pack, handle, and use to clothe ourselves. The deeper sense of place is not in those visual memories but instead "found by hands." The poem does not so much try to visualize Shillington as much as reach out and touch it. To hold on to those horse-chestnut heaps and touch a finger to the frost. Not to retrieve the past, or to become one of those children today, but to use both remembered and imagined sense experiences to orient the present: "The having and the leaving go on together." Like the hands on the radiator, these hands find that what they once touched continues to touch Updike in profound ways.

To claim that these literary representations of sense are a kind of tactile orientation is a claim that goes to the heart of Updike's contribution to postsecular aesthetics. His writing does not seek to stop or halt time, a Romantic conceit that held little interest for him. Rather, like the world it seeks to praise, his writing is a gift to the reader that opens up the possibility of new sense experiences. New hands are finding his Shillington in the poem, but the reader's hands are also rethinking how and what they touch.

The next chapter will address the ontological implications of Updike's version of affect theory and how his writing makes it possible for "sights that limited our truth" to become "strange" through his verbal descriptions of visual phenomena.

CHAPTER 2

Seeing

IN THE EARLY SCENES of the 2013 film *Words and Pictures* a beleaguered English teacher, played by Clive Owen, asks his nonplussed students why they should care about John Updike. He interrupts their stupefied silence with belligerent disbelief: "You should care because Updike wrote"; then, pausing, he dramatically closes his eyes and softly recites from memory—"The lesson over he went to the garden patch and joined his mother. He punched her stomach and I watched them pretend to box. Above them, on the single strand of wire strung to bring our house electricity, grackles and starlings neatly punctuated an invisible sentence." After a cut to a dreamy crush spreading across one student's face, and letting the appropriate downbeat pass, Owen increases his volume: "You ever heard that before? Updike has handed you an image that was never described before. What do you think of his gift?" The moment in the film, and its quotation from *Of the Farm*, epitomize a popular perception of Updike's writing: It is a consummate purveyor of pictures made with words. Updike's legacy, it seems, has less to do with graphic sex these days and more to do with his visual style, how he paints on the page's canvas images "never described before," images that poetically render the visible world anew.

Critics, too, contend that Updike wrote in such a visually sensitive way that, as Donald Greiner puts it, the "details paint the portrait. The reader *sees*" ("John Updike" 182). But what do we "see" when we read Updike? I wager not all that much. Perhaps we might imagine some general scene, most likely distinct in a few foreground spots but fringed with haze. As for that neatly punctuated sentence on the electrical wire: I know both grackles and starlings sometimes display an iridescent shimmer, and in different ways, but which is purple and which more jade, and was it on the back of the neck or down where the wing begins? Is the sun above, in front of, or behind those indistinct grackles? Even words as illustrative as Updike's would never lead two readers to imagine the exact image in their minds. Yet this is no weakness or shortcoming because Updike's realism does not in fact lie in his evocative images. It is one of the hallmarks of Updike's prose that it decidedly does *not* capitulate to the "reality effect" that Roland Barthes famously identified with Flaubert's realism. According to Barthes's analysis, the stylistic trick of a "reality effect" emerges in Flaubert's scene-enriching descriptions. Such descriptions have no intrinsic significance to the narrative other than establishing its aesthetic validity as a fully imagined world (143). To the contrary, Updike's descriptions have less to do with fixing a precise but ultimately reflexive image in the reader's mind and more to do with cultivating the reader's emotional attachment to the world *as such*. His sentences create a virtual experience of wonder and reverence for the plenitude of the visible world, lending his verisimilitude a genuinely affective end. Instead of a reality *effect*, it would be more appropriate to say that his writing cultivates a reality *affect*.

Updike's acclaimed realism does not merely make readers see certain things with words; it encourages them to feel certain ways toward what can be seen. In doing so, it offers its own vivid sense of what it means to be a fully human being: one whose curiosity about the world begins with loving it. The previous chapter explored Updike's sense of self and the role of touch in establishing a sense of belonging. Here I show how Updike's photographic style describes a world of visual experience, no matter how familiar or apparently dull, that is both precious and terrifying, but ultimately lovable. His words' characteristic sensitivity to line, shape, and color expresses what I call an *affective ontology*—a philosophical conviction that we know and understand creation insofar as we learn to love it.

To convey creation's inherent goodness afresh is, for Updike, the end of his precise verbal images. This chapter explores how the affective ontology at the heart of Updike's theology of sense illustrates Augustine's dictum that love alone is capable of seeing (qtd. in Balthasar, *Love Alone* 392). Human vision in Updike's writing is not a bare field of perception but begins with a predisposition to feel at home in the world. Accordingly, the truth content of Updike's lyrical descriptions should be located in their reverence, not their lifelike plausibility. When Updike writes in the short story "The Sea's Green Sameness," "All I hope for is that once into my carefully spun web of words the thing itself, *das Ding an sich,* will break: make an entry and an account of itself," he is referring not to visual verisimilitude but to the possibility that prose can render the reader open to seeing the thing itself (*CES* 304–5). Representation is not an end in itself. This affective ontology permeates Updike's art criticism as well as his novel about American cinema, *In the Beauty of the Lilies,* and betrays a clear correspondence between Updike and one of the most astute critics of visual culture in late twentieth-century American letters—Susan Sontag. Rather than attend to Updike's many pronouncements on the visual orientation of his craft, in this chapter I will catch Updike in the act of looking—first, in how he writes about visual art and, second, in how he portrays his characters' responses to realism's apogee, the cinema. For Updike the critic and Updike the novelist, the visual (and visually oriented) arts succeed in teaching us *how* to see the world only insofar as they convince us *why* to love it.

LITTLE PLENITUDES

Updike's attention to visual detail is part of why he enjoyed writing about painting as much as he did. Though it is worth reading on its own merits, Updike thought of his art criticism nonetheless as a kind of calisthenics, a tuning exercise to keep his fingertips in sync with his eyes. His essays on art tell us a good deal not only about how and why Updike notices things but also about what he wants his readers to notice and why. For instance, he voices his enthusiasm for Fairfield Porter's creative use of color, exhorting us join in his wonder, for "where else but in *The Harbor—Great Spruce Head* (1974) have we seen painted those leaden lavender cores at the heart of radiant cumulus?" (*Just Looking* 122). That phrase, "leaden lavender," attempts to honor the singularity of this specific cloud color with an equally attentive expression. Yet the lyrical luster used to name this dull, metallic shade emanating from a "radiant cumulus" is in itself a lesson in Updike's way of noticing: Naming is a form of response. Writing is not the work of a solipsistic, inward gaze but the task of forming an adequate response to what has been given to see.

A painter's knack for pulling colors out of white surfaces again catches Updike's adulation in Winslow Homer's iconic image of innocent boyhood repose, *Boys in a Pasture* (1874). He muses that "there is something of Greek drapery in the color-gouged fold of the sunlit white sleeve" on one of the boys (43). The fold does slip into a shadow, but that shadow hides a whole spectrum of visibility in its subtle reclusion. Such observations demonstrate a willful desire to appreciate the sly inventiveness of the artist's creative relationship with sense data. In Updike's appreciative eyes, Homer's sometimes too sentimentalized view of rural American boyhood weaves that other Homer's wine-dark sea into homespun regalia. Updike confesses that appreciation is indeed the preeminent goal of his art criticism, writing that the "effort of an art critic must be, in an era beset by a barrage of visual stimulants, mainly one of appreciation, of letting the works sink in as a painting hung on the wall of one's home sinks in, never quite done with unfolding all that is in it to see" (*Still Looking* xv). To unfold the image by spreading it out into words. To secure oneself from the "barrage of visual stimulants" not by closing one's eyes but by opening them to receive the panorama of a single image's myriad rewards.

This approach to writing about what has been seen and what might be seeable expresses a basic philosophical assumption. The fact that Updike kept looking, or rather kept writing about looking, demonstrates an ontological conviction about the nature of things and the meaning of human being. He gives this conviction a name when he recalls his first encounter with Paul Cezanne's *Pines and Rocks* (1896–99) in the Museum of Modern Art, musing, "What did it mean, this oddly airy severity, this tremor in the face of the mundane? It meant that the world, even in such drab constituents as pines and rocks, was infinitely rewarding of observation, and that simplicity was composed of many little plenitudes, or small, firm arrivals" (11). A common rock deserves its belabored homage even as distant cumulus clouds disclose new hues to the attentive eye.

Plenitude is not necessarily dependent on some notion of beauty as stunning brilliance. As often as adjectives like *splendor* or *radiance* appear in Updike's oeuvre, an intensity of light and color is not what rewards the viewer of *Pines and Rocks*. The apt synonym for *plenitude* here is not *pulchritude* but *amplitude*. Cezanne's little arrivals are firm and dense, bursting with a specific *thisness* that is nonetheless a fathomless *muchness*. There is so much in those pines and rocks; so much to see, to know, to love. Plenitude, a concept born in Platonism but baptized and adopted by medieval Christian philosophers and theologians via Plotinus, originally expressed how the conceptual possibilities of the human mind related to the nature and structure of the created order. To every conceivable idea, Plato thought, there must be some matching reality. The world of human experience is equally expansive as the world of conceivable possibilities. "What is, is" was Updike's succinct but awestruck appraisal of this ontological mystery at the heart of materiality (*Just Looking* 35).

Remnants of this ancient notion infuse Updike's prolixity. Yet the fact that this medieval metaphysics of plenitude should persist in Updike's late twentieth-century writing is far from unprecedented. Arthur O. Lovejoy's classic study, *The Great Chain of Being*, puts plenitude at its center, arguing for its persistence throughout most of Western cultural history. According to Lovejoy, this philosophical ideal of ontological multiplicity persists from classical times right into the modern era. He defines its inexhaustibility as a function of the creativity that brings all things into being—whether trees or telephone poles, fine art or fine weather. Lovejoy explains the concept of plenitude as the world's inexhaustible forms, the *plenum formarum* in which creation multiplies itself. Plenitude is "the assumption that no genuine potentiality of being can remain unfulfilled, that the extent and the abundance of the creation must be as great as the possibility of existence and commensurate with the productive capacity of a perfect and inexhaustible 'Source,' and that the world is the better, the more things it contains" (52). When Updike thrills to discover in Cezanne's *Pines and Rocks* the rewards of observation, he assumes the basic sense of this enduring concept of plenitude—that the world's full range of forms are fundamental to its goodness. His writing, too, participates in this abundance of creation. In order for the artist to pay homage to an "insatiably creative" God, in Lovejoy's words, he must "add something of his own to the creation" (296). The writer adds to those possibilities with words; writing is not opposed to life but is its facilitator. Accordingly, the aesthetic ideal of plenitude is more than a mere occasional insight prompted by Cezanne's "airy severity" for Updike. It infuses his understanding of the ideal in any aesthetic experience.

Prose written with an eye for plenitude assumes that the world in all its multiplicity is a gift worth commending. It is a philosophical conviction that is also a moral value. To keep giving that gift is one reason why Updike writes the way he does. Something is always waiting to reveal itself to the patient admirer. There is a moment in *The Centaur* when Peter Caldwell's father has just picked up a hitchhiker on the way into town. "It's a dirty town" is the hitchhiker's judgment on Alton as it comes into view (90). Yet Peter's only response is "To me it looked so beautiful" (90). How can a realist's sensibility allow for such diverging impressions? Yet the divergent opinions are no mere matter of perspective. The hitchhiker is wrong; he has not seen correctly. Peter sees truly in part because Peter sees a plenitudinous gift in Alton.

This moral relation to being is routinely ignored in the realist turn in contemporary theory, from Bill Brown's "thing theory" to Graham Harman's "speculative realism" to Markus Gabriel's "new realism." Ever since proclaiming that "continental philosophy needs a total overhaul in the name of realism and essentialism," Harman has led a reconsideration of how philosophy approaches metaphysics (109). Yet many of these approaches, whether Brown's attempt to think through the agency of objects and "the mutual constitution and mutual animation of subject and object" or Gabriel's insistence that "thoughts about facts exist with the same right as the facts at which our thoughts are directed," lack the moral dimension of Updike's affective plenitude (Brown 19; Gabriel 6). While these new ontologies have discovered important ways around idealism's subject/object divide, they do not provide a moral account for why the world is worth carefully perceiving in the first place. Yet such is largely the lesson Updike imparts in his 2008 Jefferson Lecture in the Humanities, "The Clarity of Things" (*Always Looking*). When Updike opened that speech with the question "What is American about American art?" he sought to define more precisely what he elsewhere calls the American "morality of representation," or the way an image conveys its own values (*Still Looking* xiv). He can help us understand the moral responsibility we owe to objects. While Updike's Jefferson Lecture meanders chronologically through the series of paintings included in the NEH program *Picturing America*, it confidently asserts a single aesthetic ideal as the backbone of this morality of representation— "the clarity of things." This clarity in things is inseparable from their status as gifts, an insight Updike's theology of sense can bring to contemporary realist ontologies and their relation to aesthetics.

John Singleton Copley, whose paintings Updike has often admired in print and from whom Updike first derives the critical ideal of clarity, may have been apprehensive to hear that painting should artlessly defer to the things it represents. Copley wished his painting more refined, not simple. He wanted to be more like his English contemporaries. He yearned to, in his own words, "acquire that bold free and graceful stile [sic] of Painting that will, if ever, come much slower from the mere dictates of Nature, which has hither too [sic] been my only instructor" (qtd. in *Always Looking* 6). Updike turns this lament into Copley's strength and legacy, the impervious heritage he bequeaths to his American successors. The way Updike conveys Copley's penchant for the clarity of things over the embellishments of illusion is most instructive, though, about Updike's own aesthetic intentions. Much of what he claims about Copley in the lecture hints at his own aims.

Though Copley's response to the "mere dictates of nature" was no shortcoming in Updike's eyes, it did prompt Copley's peers to decry a too-fastidious austerity in his painting. Updike quotes Copley's friend reporting back to him that the Royal Academy's famous Joshua Reynolds, while admitting that Copley's work certainly showed promise, found in his *Boy with a Flying Squirrel* (1765) "a little Hardness in the Drawing, Coldness in the Shades, An over minuteness" (6). The Pennsylvania-born painter Benjamin West sent a similar judgment to Copley, claiming that some of the English painters found it "too liney, which was judged to have arose from there being so much neetness [*sic*] in the lines" (6). What Reynolds saw as a slightly harsh, "over minuteness," West calls "liney." Updike asks, "What did Benjamin West mean by this word? A line is a child's first instrument of depiction, the boundary where one thing ends and another begins. The primitive artist is more concerned with what things are than what they look like to the eye's camera. Lines serve the facts" (9). For Updike, the primitive artist is duly focused on "what things are" more than the stylistic techniques of illusion, such as shading or spatial composition. Yet note how Updike distinguishes the definition of a thing from its apparent qualities when he separates "what things are" from the "eye's camera" of visual perception. Lines, in Copley, serve the facts, not ocular illusions. They are the artist's expression of reverence for the created world.

Eighteenth-century American painters in this style are usually called *limners*. The limners' lack of fleshy depth or suggestive atmosphere is sometimes considered a mark of their art's immaturity, but it distinguishes their conceptual fidelity for Updike. If one compares something like the Beardsley Limner's *Boy in a Windsor Chair* with Copley's *Boy with a Flying Squirrel,* Copley's silky contours seem like baroque ornamentation. Yet comparing Copley's portrait to Joshua Reynold's *Portrait of Master Bunbury* evinces Copley's distinct affinity for the limner's harsher, demarcating style. If Reynold's use of shaded borders emphasizes the boy's imaginative interior life, Copley's lines give his portrait the dignity of defined space; "over minuteness" respects the empirical facts if not the realistic illusion of them. Updike thinks this limner style entirely justified, for it exemplifies "a resolute attempt at likeness and an honest notation" that is justifiably suspicious of artistic illusion.

> The conventions of illusionistic painting, providing through tint and brushwork the sense of recession in space and of enclosing atmosphere, are not demanded by every culture. In the art-sparse, mercantile world of the American colonies, Copley's lavish literalism must have seemed fair dealing, a heaping measure of value paid in shimmering textures and scrupulously fine detail. "Over minuteness" could scarcely exist, as it did not exist for Holbein or Jan van Eyck. (9)

This quotation is a typical specimen of Updike's critical prose. The mixture of precise, apt diction paired with an amiable demotic— "tint" and "brushwork" alongside "fair dealing." "Art-sparse" is itself a bare expression for the cultural wilderness of the colonial United States. Yet Updike's alliterative "lavish literalism" seems an unnecessary embellishment: Is not literalism reserved, if not austere? To adhere to the bareness of a thing would certainly seem less than lavish. Literalism can be an expression of inherent worth, however, and a way of lavishing what is with its overlooked value. Literalism is its own aesthetic "heaping measure of value." Moreover, to lavish the literal with such phrases is the linguistic correlate to the limner's lini255. Copley provides "a heaping measure of value paid in shimmering textures and scrupulously fine detail" not to make up in exhaustive details what his images lack in the refinements of illusion, but because the world of things is so adamantly specific.

SENSATIONAL RHETORIC

Updike attributes this aesthetic notion of "fair dealing" to what the art historian and critic Barbara Novak calls a "conceptual bias" in Copley's aesthetics. It is a preferential attitude toward the evidential object shared by Copley's contemporary, Jonathan Edwards. According to Updike, "Edwards wrote of 'the clarity of 'things,' of things as the mediators between words and ideas, between empirical and conceptual experience" (10). Here Updike is recycling an influential argument of Novak's; note the doubled quotation marks around "things." He gives the impression that the phrase he uses for the title of the lecture and the subsequent essay—"The Clarity of Things"—was Edwards's phrase. But is it neither Edwards's nor Novak's. While Updike directly quotes Novak's study of Copley when he refers to Copley's "conceptual bias" in the lecture, there is no mention of "the clarity of things" to be found in Novak's argument, which opens her influential study *American Painting in the Nineteenth Century.*

The phrase is, in fact, that of another art critic, Carrie Rebora, paraphrasing Novak's characterization of Edwards's preaching. In "Copley and Art History," included in the Metropolitan Museum of Art's 1995 exhibition catalog, *John Singleton Copley in America,* Rebora writes that Novak

> identified "Copley's realism as a unique union of object and idea" comparing him to the theologian Jonathan Edwards, who relied on the clarity of "things" in his preaching as Copley did in his painting. This clarity of things, Novak proposed, was, and still is, at the core of the American experience, and she attributed Copley's greatness to his invention of means for conveying weight, volume, texture—the "thereness" or "being" of people and objects—and his reconciliation of conceptual and empirical experience. (18)

Even though Updike likely got the title from Rebora and the exhibition catalog, the quotation he goes on to cite from Edwards to back up his assertion comes from neither Rebora's, Novak's, nor even Novak's source for her reading of Edwards—Perry Miller's famous study *Errand into the Wilderness,* which Updike had likely read. Instead, it is from one of Edwards's *Miscellanies* volumes—not exactly everyday reading for a theologian, let alone a novelist.

I belabor these intertexual layers, however, not from some idle scholarly curiosity, or even to provide evidence of Updike's intellectual heavy lifting. The truth is that the phrase "clarity of things" reveals a good deal of Updike's affinity for Edwards's thinking. The quotation Updike uses from Edwards to explain this object-oriented lucidity and to support his claim that Copley shared a theologically inspired idea with Edwards conveys Edwards's own reverence for the triumphant substantiality of things: "The manifestations God makes of Himself in His works are the principal manifestations of His perfections, and the declaration and teachings of His word are to lead to these" (qtd. in *Always Looking* 10). Note how words and the created works both point toward God: The works of creation do not receive their sense from words but are sensed as the "principal manifestations of His perfection." Furthermore, the created world inspires wonder and love for those perfections. For Updike and Edwards alike, visual experience is inseparable from emotional responses. Yet the emotional response is at the same time an ontological conviction that the world is fundamentally worthy of our love. Copley's lush silks and satins and liney portraits emanate from an original affection.

Perry Miller characterizes Edwards's understanding of the affections through the relationship of words and things in a way that highlights Updike's sympathy with Edwards. "Edwards's great discovery, his dramatic refashioning of the theory of sensational rhetoric," Miller contends, "was his assertion that an idea in the mind is not only a form of perception but is also a determination of love and hate" (179). For Edwards, ideas are intimately linked not only to perception but to emotional judgments. The rational mind does not operate in isolation from the affections; judgments and inclinations work in conjunction to become affections. We think, in part, through our emotions. In *The Religious Affections* Edwards clarifies how these inclinations relate to our judgments.

> God has endued the soul with two faculties: one is that by which it is capable of perception and speculation, or by which it discerns, and views, and judges things; which is called the understanding. The other faculty is that by which the soul does not merely perceive and view things, but is some way inclined with respect to the things it views or considers; either is inclined *to* them, or is disinclined and averse *from* them; or is the faculty by which the soul does not

behold things as an indifferent unaffected spectator, but either as a liking or disliking, pleased or displeased, approving or rejecting. This faculty is called by various names; it is sometimes called the *inclination*: and, as it has respect to the actions that are determined and governed by it, is called the *will*: and the mind, with regard to the exercises of this faculty, is often called the *heart*." (24)

Edwards's "theory of sensational rhetoric" (Miller's phrase) is rooted in this Christian vision of human judgment as necessarily entailing emotional attitudes. Indeed, for Edwards, true religion was first and foremost a tenderness of heart, of orienting the affections toward what is good and true. "It is an evidence that true religion, or holiness of heart, lies very much in the affection of the heart," he expounds in *The Religious Affections*; "that the Scriptures place the sin of the heart very much in hardness of heart" (45). "Hardness of heart" is a kind of insensitive disaffection, a refusal to love—one of the "external circumstances" Pascal names and Updike uses for the epigraph to *Rabbit, Run*. The purpose of "sensational rhetoric" is to warm the "affection of the heart" and open it up to God's grace.

This idea of "sensational rhetoric" is at the heart of Updike's "lavish literalism." To assert the empirical clarity of things—that things mediate between words and ideas, and not words between things and ideas—is to assert the high place of objects in shaping human culture. Updike's sensational rhetoric, like Copley's "lininess," seeks to give those objects their ontological weight. Yet Updike also shares with Edwards the awareness that a representation in the mind entails an emotional attitude toward the thing represented—not merely to the representation and its beauty or lack thereof but also to the thing in all its material substantiality. To see things clearly, to visually appreciate the full clarity of the given world, demands an emotional predisposition—what Edwards would call an "inclination of the heart"—to be grateful for what one sees.

Updike's comparison of the style of Copley's "lininess" to Winslow Homer's "painterly" flourishes exemplifies how Updike himself seeks to elicit such inclinations through his prose style. He does not only show us things; he wants us to value them, to feel joy at them. Of Homer's *Undertow* (1886) he writes, we cannot but be conscious of the paint itself, of thick white dabbled and stabbed, swerved and smeared into place in imitation of the water's tumultuous action; we simultaneously witness both the ocean in action and the painter at work. These arduous passages of tumbling foam and exploding spray are at once representations of natural phenomena and examples of painterly artifice; thing and idea are merged in the synthesis of artistic representation. (*Always Looking* 16)

According to Updike, Homer's use of curvature and thickness are not merely reflexive embellishments but create sensational impressions in service of the facts. In this case, unlike in Copley's portraits, the thing itself is not static but in motion. Stylistically, Homer's painterly strokes are far from Copley's lininess; their shared conceptual priority of the idea of the thing, however, is apparent in Homer's desire to capture the ocean waters not merely in action but as a painterly form of action. As Updike writes, "Thing and idea merge." Yet note how Updike's own sentence wants to embellish in such a way as to follow Homer's style and simultaneously gesture toward the thing it describes: "Dabbled and stabbed, swerved and smeared" evoke the motion of water as much as a painter's brush, and "tumbling foam and exploding spray" work to match in verbs what Homer achieved in line and texture, pushing us back to Homer's image and continuing through to the thrill of water's weighted spontaneity.

Observations such as this one in Updike's art criticism show how the concept of plenitude entails "inclining the heart" toward appreciation and gratitude—the ontological conviction occasions the affective state, and vice versa. Not only thing and idea merge, but the thing, the idea, and a perceptual attitude toward them. This is, in Updike's writing on American painting, a vital part of what he calls the national tradition's "morality of representation." The moral here is that clear vision depends not on dispassionate judgment but on open astonishment at the given world, a reverential awe at its inherent beauty. The emotional attachment enables realistic exactitude. The moral failing of Hollywood films, for this famously prurient novelist, has less to do with their sex and violence than their failure to respect the morality of representation that he discerns in American painting.

THE BEAUTIFUL, THE GOOD, AND THE GIVEN

Updike's attention to visual detail may intimate his love for all forms of visual experience and the insights of visual culture, but critics are divided on how he valued the motion pictures. It seems obvious that film's photographic realism would inspire an immediate affinity between Updike's descriptive writing and the medium's images. Moreover, Updike's writing about film and film stars would suggest his uncritical fandom. "From curtain-raising to end credits," asserts Jack De Bellis, "Updike has loved the movies" ("It Captivates" 169). Donald Greiner, while recently noting Updike's "command of cinema lore," also reminds us of Updike's suspicion that good novels rarely made good films, singling out Updike's displeasure at the unsuccessful adaptation of *Rabbit, Run* ("Film Version" 176). Peter Bailey sees a profound ambivalence in Updike's view of the movies, however, admitting that though Updike "felt real affection for the movies and movie houses of his youth" he increasingly saw Hollywood as nothing more than "a bright island of make-believe"—the phrase used to describe movies by the Doris Day–inspired character in *In the Beauty of the Lilies* ("'The Bright Island of Make-Believe'" 69, 70). Yet Judie Newman perhaps best grasps the heart of Updike's thinking about film when she writes that "it is the social impact of visual domination that most concerns him," noting the "general ambivalence" toward visual spectacles in Updike's "opposition of cinema and church" in that same novel (124). What Updike fears in "the social impact of visual domination" is an inversion of what he praises in the "morality of representation" in painting: The immediacy of a purely visual culture dulls the senses and lacks the affective nuance that could incline the heart toward more substantial loves.

James Schiff, however, is no doubt right to assume it is "likely, given the hundreds of movies [Updike] watched during his youth, that his sense of scene, narrative, and character has in some significant way been shaped by film" ("Updike, Film, and American Popular Culture" 136). Is not much of Updike's vivid descriptiveness due to the particular forms of visuality the movies have given us? And are not the movies the very height of Western art's quest for mimetic realism, that kind of photographic realism for which Updike is known? Yet the obvious artificiality of paint seems to have held truer to the medieval doctrine of plenitude than the cinema's realistic illusions for Updike. Moreover, Bailey does not go far enough in claiming Updike's ambivalence to the movies. While Liliana Naydan is right to emphasize how *In the Beauty of the Lilies* affirms a "temperate" faith, the movies provide a way "to approach understanding an unknowable, Barthian divinity" only indirectly, through their corrupt privation of plenitude (97). If we read *In the Beauty of the Lilies* in light of the affective ontology that emerges in Updike's art criticism, we can see a condemnation of the disregard Hollywood movies too often inspire toward the world's little plenitudes.

Contra the life-denying tendencies of Hollywood's "bright island of make-believe," let me suggest that the relation between words and images in Updike's writing is delineated against the background assumption that there is always something more to see and appreciate for those who love the given world as such. In the movies portrayed in *In the Beauty of the Lilies,* something fantastically abstract, however "realistic" the moving image appears, siphons the viewer's attention from the given world's little plenitudes. Too smitten with the realistic illusions of the camera, the movies in *In the Beauty of the Lilies* end up teaching the eye to notice, and even to desire, an inferior, banal fantasy. Film's affective ontology is wrong insofar as it celebrates the intrinsic goodness of desire rather than a desire for the goodness of what is. Recall that the clarity Updike celebrates in American painting is not the achievement of lifelike illusion, as if the way to celebrate reality were to create a more believable version of it. No. "The Clarity of Things" unmistakably articulates a tradition of American realism that celebrates the distinctly *good* material reality of things in relation to human sensation. The movies that dominated so much of the American visual culture of Updike's youth, however entrancing they might have been, lack this morality of representation. They lack the same affective relation that raises human desire into a gratified sense of belonging to the essential goodness of creation.

This is why *In the Beauty of the Lilies* should not be read as another example of the standard secularization narrative of American culture where movies come to dominate the culture in proportion to the decline of its religious identity. The cinematic lucidity with which Clarence Wilmot, a Presbyterian minister, loses his faith in the novel's opening pages—following a short, prologue-like cameo of Mary Pickford on set and filming for D. W. Griffith—could imply such a simplistic one-to one-ratio. The first of the novel's four parts follows Wilmot's resignation from the pulpit and his failed attempt to make an adequate living for his family as an encyclopedia salesman during the Depression years. The printed word he peddles lacks the compelling force of the movies he watches (the character is based on Updike's paternal grandfather's loss of faith). Yet the succeeding three parts of the novel go on to follow Wilmot's son, granddaughter, and great-grandson, and their respective relationships with God and Hollywood. In toto, all four sections of the novel comprise a cinematic panorama of the American century as one where the image ascends to its preeminent place in contemporary cultural experience. While the novel begins with the actress Mary Pickford in the news, it ends with the sensationalized TV news coverage of federal authorities raiding a cult compound—much as the Bureau of Alcohol, Tobacco, and Firearms did during the 1993 Waco siege. In Updike's tale, when the century begins, the movies are news and religious passion is dying out; at its close, the news entertains like a movie and religious passion is on the rise. Movies do not replace God any more than God replaces movies.

Moreover, even though the novel associates the loss of God with the rise of an image-driven culture, its consistent emphasis is neither the loss of individual belief nor the religious affinities of moviegoing; instead it emphasizes American culture's fascination with the spiritual power of images and how that fascination mediates the experience of specific characters. Updike's novel explores sensual and emotional experiences through thick descriptions of, to use Georg Lukács's word, "typical" Americans. These characters are "typical" because, while no individual character is ever wholly representative of the American experience, they do represent *one way* of relating to that whole (6–7). Such typical characters help keep the whole—and here that holistic representation is a culture that worships images—in view. The novel explores what it could feel like to be a minister losing his faith, what it could feel like to be a small-town postman, or a movie star, or a member of a cult; and each character bears a typical relation to the seismic cultural changes taking place across the century. Yet in the novel both the characters and their society are mediated through images. *In the Beauty of the Lilies* is less about a decline of belief in God or the rise of television than about how images can affect the cultural values that shape everyday experience.

In the beginning of the novel, movies provide ways of escaping and cherishing the given world of everyday life. Clarence Wilmot escapes from the midsummer grind of his hapless door-to-door encyclopedia sales, and his inability to provide for his family, in the cool relief of Paterson's movie houses. There "he felt released from accusation" as "women of a luminous and ideal pallor licked at his fevered brain soothingly" (*Beauty* 104). It seems the movies provide the kind of comfort his God used to, back when he believed. Yet this interpretation wrongly assumes that God was only a form of escape for Clarence, when in truth what God offered him was a reason for staying. God bestowed meaning and purpose to the everyday, not an escape from it. The passage where Updike describes Clarence's release from accusation in the movie houses paints a situation in which the loss of God is irremediable. The movies present an escape from that loss but cannot restore it.

> Ever since his revelation three years ago of God's nonexistence, he had carried around with him a crusty, stunned feeling—a clinging sense of lostness, as if within a series of ill-furnished, run-down classrooms he found himself in the wrong one, with an urgent appointment elsewhere, for which he was growing every minute a minute more tardy, incurring the growing wrath of some faceless, dimensionless disciplinarian. The sight of his poor family—Stella visibly aged and thinned by their fall, Jared and Ester coming and going with the secretive cockiness of children thrust too early upon their own resources, Teddy at ten growing a shell of deep reserve and plodding stoicism amid the debris of his father's infidelity—was

as painful to him as the sight of a sunstruck row of houses on whose doors he was condemned to knock in vain. Within the movie theatre, amid the other scarcely seen slumped bodies, he felt released from accusation. The moving picture's flutter of agitation and gesticulated emotion from women of a luminous and ideal pallor licked at his fevered brain soothingly. Images of other shadows in peril and torment lifted his soul out of him on curious wings, wings of self-forgetfulness that had not functioned in former days when he and Stella in sober evening finery would attend a Metropolitan production at the Lyceum Theatre, or a Verdi straight from Milan at the Opera House, or a musical play at the Orpheum. (104–5)

The loss of God is wrapped up in Clarence's loss of purpose and identity—the movies he attends complete that sense of loss by immersing him in "self-forgetfulness," which the other theatrical arts had not provided him. When Updike describes the movie theater only a few sentences later as "a church with its mysteries looming brilliantly, undeniably above the expectant rows," he is providing as much as an affirmation of film's transformative power as a critique of the kind of pandering, cultic religion of simple answers portrayed in the novel's last part (105). What would such an escapist transformation truly be worth?

Updike is not insensitive, however, to the ways movies do in fact help us look at the world more carefully. "Eyes had never before seen in this manner," he writes of Clarence's wonder at what he saw in the movies; "impossibilities of connection and disjunction formed a magic, glittering sequence that left real time and its three rigid dimensions behind" (106). We do see new relationships through the camera and the surprising juxtapositions film makes available. Yet it is precisely this need to leave "real time and its three rigid dimensions behind" that Updike mistrusts. The insistence on the conceptual superiority of things over words or images is lost. Whatever new visions the movies provide, there is something unreal about them that betrays the morality of representation Updike discerns in American painting. Clarence seems to know this, and while he relishes the escape from accusation that movies provide, they only exacerbate his sense of the godless world's shabbiness. They don't deliver "little plenitudes" so much as terrifying vacancies.

Clarence's son Teddy feels the threat of that vacuity acutely in the presence of the movies' overwhelmingly idealized sensations. He writhes under the very same effects that his father Clarence found so soothing. "He was not quite the betranced moviegoer his father had been," Updike writes, because Teddy experiences the movies more as a threat than an escape (146). They were "a bit menacing, an alarming and garish profusion" (146). They do not comfort Teddy and offer no substantial diversion. Instead, the energy of their spectacles speaks too loudly of what they are attempting to cover up—the void felt so keenly in the movie house's enclosing darkness both before and after its bright display. The movies did not illuminate so much as terrify.

> Terror would attack Teddy even in the middle of hilarious and romantic sequences, as he realized that these bright projections were trying to distract him from the leaden reality beneath his seat, underneath the theatre floor. Death and oblivion were down there, waiting for the movie to be over. Not so, these movies tried to say. Life was not serious; it was an illusion, a story, distracting and disturbing but at bottom painless and merciful [. . .] these stars led up there a life that was always renewed, movie to movie, without permanent harm, whereas Teddy knew that harm was permanent. The reel of your real life unwound only once. (148)

Teddy refuses to fall for it. Like Richard Maple, who in the short story "Grandparenting" recalls how "sometimes in the movie theater a vast pit of reality and eventual death opened up underneath him, showing the flickering adventure on the screen to be a mere idle distraction from his life, a waste of minutes while his final minute was rapidly approaching," Teddy is all too aware of the movies' distracting qualities (*Maples* 247). Teddy rejects the movies' gaudy inveigling not only because they ignore the "leaden reality beneath his seat" but also because there was something disrespectful uncoiling from within these reels that did not understand the obstinate palpability of the real in the reel. His reaction to the movies is like his reaction to his siblings' brassy approach to life: "There was something a bit off, a bit glib, a bit harsh, that misstated the delicate nature of reality as he needed to grasp it for himself" (*Beauty* 196).

The character Teddy is reminiscent of the portrait in *Self-Consciousness* of the young Updike on his porch or under the kitchen table, hoping to bask away in the innocence of simply seeing and appreciating the world (32–35). The young Teddy does not want to compete; he does not want to jostle or struggle against others (*Beauty* 137). To his mother's and sister's complaints that he get up and get going in the game of life, he replies with exasperation, "Isn't it enough, sometimes, if you just don't make things any worse?" (143). In time he becomes a postman, carrying the citizens' mail down the sidewalk with sincere wonder at his marvelous town. The description of the sidewalks he walks reveals Updike's empathy with Teddy's love for his world of experience. Unlike the films' escapist allure, Updike's description of the sidewalk traces a return to the ordinary, yet with the same sense of amazement that those cinematic illusions first inspired in Clarence.

> And so it was that that unseasonably warm September, as the locusts and poplars and willows and lindens along the streets of Basingstoke turned yellow and slowly dropped their variously shaped leaves onto the buckling sidewalks—blue slate slabs in the oldest section of the town, three-foot concrete widths most elsewhere, and in the less developed districts dirt paths trod in a wavery line beside the roadway—he resumed the walks that he had taken through the town in his earliest days there, only now he leaned against the weight of a leather carrier's pouch and wore a gray-blue uniform and shoes black and thick-soled like a policeman's. (204)

Even as he tells the story of Teddy returning to walk the sidewalks of his childhood rambles, Updike sets up the passage so as to describe the everyday sidewalks—even the soles of Teddy's shoes—in an attempt to return the reader's attention to the experience of walking small-town sidewalks. The description is no screenshot from Hollywood insofar as these sidewalks buckle unevenly. The cause of that buckling, the trees lining them, are named—locusts and poplars; the materials that made them, too, are named and classified in turn. The "waverly line" of the dirt paths does not escape mention either. The passage is imbued with a sense of namable familiarity that evokes not simply the unnoticed but also a sense of the town's small but firm, dense arrivals. Small-town sidewalks have their little plenitudes, too.

Yet it is precisely this smallness that Teddy's daughter Essie longs to leave. How else to escape this dreary everydayness but through the movies? This time, however, that escape is not Clarence's momentary respite. Essie becomes the movie star who abandons her small-town origins for the glamour of New York City and Hollywood. If Updike wrote something of his own aesthetic sensibility into Teddy, he gave to Essie (a character based on his favorite movie star, Doris Day) his ambitions and imperturbable confidence. Unlike her father and grandfather, Essie Wilmot neither cowers before nor seeks consolation in the flicker of film's images. To Essie, the projected image carries a more clearly defined reality. She does not see it as a form of escape so much as a form of possibility, a means of entering a higher, more substantial world. Coming back from her first visit to the movie house without either Teddy or her mother, Essie does not see her home as Teddy saw the sidewalks but as something *less* than the movies' ideal world. Here Updike narrates her sense of loss, even as his own love of describing undercuts it.

> The set-back gray house, with her father in the yard and her grandmother in the kitchen, and Mr. Bear upstairs waiting on her bed, where the day's light was leaking away above the spines of the radiator with their secret pattern of twisting ivy, struck Essie suddenly as sad, and insubstantial, a ghost house, seen by the light of the silvery movie world whose beautiful smooth people rattled all those words at each other and moved through their enormous ceilingless rooms with such swiftness and electric purpose. (252)

It is not that *what* she sees is any less thrilling than a sidewalk. Yet *how* she sees has been altered by the movies; she's looking for something different. She is not, as Teddy was, enjoying the props of her life for their simple *thereness*. No. She sees that very thereness as their curse—that her father and the yard and the house and her little stuffed bear are all in Basingstoke and not in the movies.

A basic value system emerges in the novel's own peculiar morality of representation. In the world of Updike's prose (both critical and fictional), our cognitive judgments on the nature and quality of our visual experiences include, in Edwards's word, an "inclination" to love or hate. Vision is not merely a sensual receptivity or even willful attentiveness to a particular visual field; vision has modes that depend on certain attitudes and emotions, and those attitudes and emotions carry certain value judgments about what is good. These values are informed by an aesthetic ontology derived from a belief in plenitude. Essie's way of seeing is schooled by the movies; her desires are shaped by them as well. Her aesthetic ontology does not value the clarity of things. Things do not mediate between words and ideas for her, as for Edwards; abstracted, idealized images saturate her imagination.

In their ideality, however, Hollywood's images have a very real power. The screen, for both Alma DeMott (Essie's stage name once she arrives in Hollywood) and her audience, offers a way of "lifting them up from fumbling reality into a reality keener and more efficient but not less true" (335). As she walks the streets of her hometown, to which she has now returned as a famous movie star, she cannot help feeling that even "naked of her make-up and costumes, she had more definition, more visible edge, than these shapeless shuffling others who had frightened her that day she went to the movie alone and then, when she came out, looked like a herd of bumbling blind cows" (338). The camera has bestowed on her a new aura of celebrity, but one that works only insofar as it can lift her out of the ordinary and its small-town trappings. The "visible edge" that Essie attains is, in these terms, quite like Copley's "lininess" in its aesthetic function, but not at all in its effects. For the movies' visible edge does not express the ideal concept of the thing, as Copley's does. Nor does it express the ideality that images bring to things, as Updike's descriptions so lyrically intimate. Rather, the movies' visible edge, their ontological hierarchy, celebrate cinematic images as an ideal form of the real. Essie feels more real as Alma DeMott, in comparison to this small town, because of the refinements she has achieved in this image of herself. For Updike, however, though the reality of such images is "not less true" than things, they are less ontologically substantial. While images remain the inescapable mode of human imagining, some images are better than others. Essie has less purchase on her world than Teddy on his; her world has purchased its image.

Essie's son, Clark, grows up assuming the hierarchy of this skewed ontology, and his own life seems most real, most valuable, when it feels like a movie. He acts out several roles, gaining his deepest sense of self precisely as the one who gets credit for *acting* out these roles. When Clark joins a religious group holed up in a compound in the Colorado mountains, he is renamed Esau by the monomaniacal leader, Jesse. At first Clark recoils from his new name because "it did not feel like him yet; he was still Clark to himself, in the credits in his head" (397). His name identifies his role in the script, not he himself. Not only are the credits running in Clark's head, though. His memories of family, too, are construed in terms of "the movies his head would sometimes run" (396). While Clark thinks he has escaped living his life as if it were a movie by joining Jesse's cult, and although he even derides another member's sly allegiance to movie culture (471), his life ends while he holds a gun and delivers noir-inspired lines. "Slick," he spews in repugnance at his latest name and Jesse's command to shoot the women and children before federal agents overtake their compound, "you fucker, I'll give you Slick" (484). True to Hollywood script, he shoots Jesse and helps the women and children out before reciting one of Humphrey Bogart's most famous lines, "Go ahead and shoot. You'll be doing me a favor," as one of Jesse's other male followers shoots and kills him (486).

However subservient Clark is to Hollywood's scripted scenes, he recognizes how deeply the film industry has twisted his experiences. When Clark comes home after an afternoon of busted hopes and an evening of partying to find his mother courting a much older man, he goes into his bedroom, pulls out a half-smoked joint and puts on a half-watched porn flick. The scene is worth dwelling on for the vividness with which it shows Updike's habit of adorning disturbing situations with an easy lyric vitality. It is a key passage for grasping how the novel distinguishes its own descriptions from the falseness of the movies' all too generic clichés. Updike describes Clark watching a brunette maid who looks like "his mother when young, before he was born" and who reveals in her sexual acts "a down-home girl from somewhere's simple wish to please" (433). Oedipal overtones aside, it is clear from other passages in the novel that Clark is frustrated with his mother and at the same time wishes they were closer. As the film continues, Clark finds something erotic in his hatred and self-loathing.

> He had slipped his pants and underpants down on the bed and with his left hand matched the brunette's mouth stroke for stroke, as she kept glancing hopefully upward to the male face, which was off the screen—his mother's look of bright expectancy at its purest, a look he seldom saw anymore, as she expected less and less of him. He'd show her, the bitch. His own eyes rolled back into his skull and his airplane lifted off with a shiver of propulsion and a set of diminishing throbs. When he looked again the butler was jerking off on the maid's face, white gobs like Elmer's glue which she was licking off her fingertips, still girlishly, shrewdly eager to please, and Clark had come all over himself, his hand and pubic hair and the band of his underpants. God, people are disgusting. (434)

As crude as the scene may be, it is more comic than pornographic. It evokes bemused disgust more than any semblance of erotic desire. Yet why must Updike indulge his zeal for vivid diction with "a shiver of propulsion" and "diminishing throbs," or that juvenile reference to "his airplane lifted off"? Why does Updike maintain his characteristically graceful prose while describing such a demeaning disgrace and its sloppy mess of semen?

Reading scenes like this one in Updike's fiction can be a morally disorienting experience. Undoubtedly, there is a moral ambiguity here entirely absent from the porno flick. Updike sounds as though he's enjoying himself in describing all this, but then he ends with "people are disgusting" (which doubles in free indirect style as Clark's and the narrator's conclusion). Would it not be more tasteful to express the interior conflict within Clark more thoroughly instead of patiently picturing for us where his semen lands? There is more at work here, however, than mere descriptive fidelity—"shiver of propulsion" is not an affectless, contentless, reportage of the realistic facts. If Updike is too eagerly cosseting crudeness, the perverse pleasure of his prose is utterly intentional, for the scene is everywhere a perversion of something good: The joy a son can feel in pleasing his mother and her joy in his pride are here turned into the masturbatory fantasy of an incestuous blow job. The mystery of human intimacy becomes humiliation and lonely dissipation. That "shiver of propulsion" enacts precisely this perverted beauty, bearing witness to a latent, crestfallen goodness.

Two of the most astute critics of Updike's Christian influences, George Hunt and Stephen Webb, have argued that an Augustinian theory of evil, where evil is nothing but a privation of the created good, is intentionally evident in such moments of moral disorientation in Updike's writing (Hunt 32–38; Webb 591). Recalling this metaphysical assumption is indispensable when considering the context of Updike's sense of seeing because it feels strange to give "lavish literalism" to semen. This, too, radiates with the clarity of things? Yes, yes, it does. Hunt's elegant analysis of how Updike employs his own unique version of Karl Barth's distinction between "creaturely imperfections" and the "Nothingness" that is evil's privation from goodness is helpful to recall here. "Nature might *seem* evil to us but it *is* not in itself," Hunt writes, "for nature always embodies God's gift of creative grace. Nothingness is the negation of grace, the antithesis to the Creator and creation" (37). The imperfections of creation—those limitations that provide the fodder for so much of literature's memorable scenes of comic relief—are not intrinsically bad. The possibility of transcendent experience that human sexuality offers is not "bad" in its creaturely comedy of bodily fluids. Yet it is bad, becomes destructive, in its negation of that creaturely goodness. Or to put it positively: Beauty still persists in moments of humiliating bathos.

The scene where Clark masturbates offers us a stark look at the clarity of things while simultaneously showing us their rejection in the fantasy world that pornography evokes. The prose delights in rendering service to the clarity of things through its affective ontology of the verbal image it creates. While Clark's fantasy betrays the bleak reality that is the negation of something good, Updike portrays this empty fantasy alongside his own fantastic description of beloved things. The Elmer's glue is no whimsical addendum. The name and its associations with grade-school art projects and American consumerism create a darkly comic disjunction within the scene. Yet Updike's "lavish literalism" heaps loving attention on the white, pure substantiality and quotidian innocence of both the semen *and* that glue. Updike's own "conceptual bias" (Novak's phrase for Copley) is apparent here once again in its attempt to keep pace with the luster of the visible world's forms and surfaces.

The Christian theology of creation's goodness that Hunt identifies in Updike's fiction is unquestionably the source of Updike's unique vision of plenitude. Yet even as that theology has bid people to return to the goodness of the world, it has also helped them escape from its pressing responsibilities. Christianity in Updike's work, too, can provide people with a way of escaping the world—like movies. *In the Beauty of the Lilies* may open with Clarence losing his faith and, desperate in its awful void, becoming a devotee of the movies, but the novel closes with Clark being converted from desperate devotion to the movies only to escape into a narrowly defined religious zeal. Yet this is not a historical argument about how the cinema replaced the church as a form of moral escapism. Rather, Updike warns us that the religion of images has replaced the Puritans' old religion of the word as the galvanizing authority of American culture. The late twentieth-century's celebration of the image, however morally liberated, seems just as life-denying as any stereotype of Puritanical asceticism. What both the Puritans and Hollywood misunderstand is that the task of human beings in this world, as a protagonist that Updike modeled on Nathaniel Hawthorne's famous Puritan minister Arthur Dimmesdale once put it, "is not to love what might be" but rather to love the plenitude of what already "*is* given."

Updike's affective ontology of the image, where the image (whether verbal or visual) not only bears witness to the goodness of the created world but seeks to inspire love for it, is not only an example of the prolonged vitality of Jonathan Edwards's theology in American culture; it is also a prominent example of what Susan Sontag—a critic with sensibilities markedly less religious than Updike's—called for: "an erotics of art" (*Against Interpretation* 14). While Sontag did not share Updike's commitment to Protestant Christianity, her work from the sixties through to the first decade of the twenty-first century provides an excellent example of how Updike's superficial, surface-oriented aesthetics of the body found similar forms of expression in his contemporaries' work. The first two essays of Sontag's incisive early collection of essays *Against Interpretation* (1966) trace an aesthetics of embodiment that clearly corresponds with the affective ontology I've been unfolding in this chapter. Even her late essays demonstrate a surprisingly similar moral critique of the ways visual images can betray the given world through their glossy reduction of reality.

It is not such glossiness, however, but conceptual narrowness that is the target of her early essay "Against Interpretation." Half a century later, it remains a resonant essay on the meaning and ends of criticism and a clear precursor to contemporary affect theory. In it Sontag denounces the critic's need to "interpret" a work of art—in whatever medium—by stifling its several affective valences in favor of determining and then explicating its content. Rather than being against criticism, the essay is a condemnation of the assumption that criticism exists to plumb the depth of a given work of art's ideas. For Sontag, to think of criticism as an "erotics of art" would instead seek "to recover our senses. We must learn to *see* more, to *hear* more, to *feel* more" (*Against Interpretation* 14). Criticism need not close out the sensory world that so much art seeks to open up. Like Updike's art criticism (or his writing on the self discussed in the preceding chapter), Sontag's erotics of art would seek to unleash a work's potential to create fuller, more intense forms of experience.

The goal of recovering our senses in Sontag's polemic against interpretation, however, is that interpretation tends "to impoverish, to deplete the world—in order to set up a shadow world of 'meanings.' It is to turn *the* world, into *this* world. ('This world'! As if there were any other.)" (7). She decries the way that this kind of criticism demeans the fullness—the plenitude!—of reality, of "*the* world," into a simpler, abstracted, and even commodified version of it. Note that here she is not making an argument for Roland Barthes's famous "third meaning"; this is a case not for the inexhaustibility of the work of art but for the inexhaustibility of the true if mysterious world that art participates in and augments. *The* world.

Just as the movies could disrespect the given world in ways that painting tended to avoid, according to Updike, so criticism for Sontag could dull rather than enhance our ability to understand and fully pay attention to the multiplicity of the world. She sounds as if she is defending Updike's "morality of representation" when she laments that ours "is a culture based on excess, on overproduction; the result is a steady loss of sharpness in our sensory experience. All the conditions of modern life—its material plenitude, its sheer crowdedness—conjoin to dull our sensory faculties" (13). According to Sontag, the writer (and especially the critic) must oppose these forms of material plenitude with the plenitude of life (*Same Time*). In her acceptance speech for the Jerusalem Prize, "The Conscience of Words," Sontag enjoins the writer to see that regarding plenitude, "Whenever writers are functioning as writers, they always see . . . more"; she then quickly adds, "Whatever there is, there is always more" (*Same Time* 153). Throughout her writing life, she wrote in order to see more.

Yet this "more" was more than a matter of numbers for Sontag. Prominent for her writing on film and photography, she understood how visual culture shapes visual perceptions. The affinity of their ontological assumptions notwithstanding, Sontag's approach to visual mediums is markedly different from Updike's. Updike has no complaint to lodge against the screen as a medium per se, but he was wary of what it did to American viewers' respect for the everyday world of experience. Sontag shares his skepticism, but her work on French film and her patient, incisive writing on photography find in those mediums the same hope Updike finds in painting. Thus, Sontag could write in a late essay defending the aesthetic notion of beauty that "the standards of beauty in nature are largely set by photography" (13). A category like nature is difficult to extricate from the visual culture that represents it. Yet the fact that nature and culture are in fact quite distinct is of no small matter. For she then insists that nature is the appropriate subject for photography because of how it can deepen our awareness of the world: "What is beautiful reminds us of nature as such—of what lies beyond the human and the made—and thereby stimulates and deepens our sense of the sheer spread and fullness of reality, inanimate as well as pulsing, that surrounds us all" (13). Beauty, in any image, ultimately brings us back to nature.

Sontag shares Updike's reverence for the plenitude of the "sheer spread and fullness of reality" while also maintaining that this belief demands an aesthetic commitment to surfaces and the forms of desire a work of art can stimulate, teach, or even unleash. However, as I argued in the previous chapter, Updike's erotics of art is no simplistically hedonistic aesthetic. His *ars erotica* is at the same time a Christian *ordo amoris.* In the next chapter I show how his sense of taste—and his conviction that the physical experience of tasting should inform theories of aesthetic taste—decidedly includes the bitter, sour flavors that rarely receive a lyrical tribute. Moreover, his conception of aesthetic taste is interested not only in aesthetic effects but in the corresponding pedagogy of desire that the *ordo amoris* entails.

CHAPTER 3

Tasting

ONE OF UPDIKE'S characteristically playful poems, titled "Taste," confesses, "I want to be, like Nature, tasteless / abundant, reckless, cheerful" (*Collected Poems* 59). It is true that his writing belittles tasteful reserve in favor of a cheerful, reckless, abundant creativity. In Nature's plenty he finds an artistic ideal—profligacy has its own profundity. The astounding array of phenomena demands, for Updike, an adequate artistic response, one that the strictures of tasteful decorum would likely fail. The mere quantity of Updike's novels, stories, and poems could be taken to exemplify just such an abundance. Yet even if the poem claims to be "tasteless," Updike certainly is curious about the act of tasting, or what one of his characters calls "the taste of the world" (*Collected Early Stories* 759). In his short fiction, the commonplace act of tasting has more to teach us about beauty than the judgments of well-trained taste. While the aesthetic problem of taste is not the same as the sense experience of flavors, the two are often ambiguously entwined for Updike. Whereas the previous two chapters addressed the affective and ontological aspects of Updike's postsecular aesthetics, this chapter makes a case for how Updike's attention to tasting takes us beyond judgment and into a fuller participation in the created world. In his writing, aesthetic taste takes on a decisively different meaning—a sense more in tune with the senses.

Despite his poem's dismissive tone, Updike does not entirely demean aesthetic taste. He thinks it can become an aptitude for appreciation. What he disdains is the idea that good taste is a way of judging via abstracted, universally applied standards. In Updike's work, taste rightly construed is the skill of experiencing the gift of creation's infinite particularity. Viewing taste as an embodied, experiential quality, Updike emphasizes its development through repetition and variety more than refinement or critique. It is concerned with the theological implications of different qualities of perception, not the forms of judgment Immanuel Kant and Edmund Burke bequeathed to aesthetic theory. Updike's version of taste turns away from modern, secular aesthetics' too narrow concern with ensuring judgments. Instead, it questions how to cultivate an appreciation of the infinite goodness of creation. In Updike's theological construal, aesthetic taste is the creature's way of learning to receive the Creator's gifts.

It is precisely this insight that makes Updike's work unique—who else among Updike's literary contemporaries combined theological concepts with an "abundant, reckless, cheerful" exploration of human sense experience? Not necessarily because of his frank sexual content (though that is part of it since "Taste" unabashedly continues, "Go screw, taste— / itself a tasteless suggestion") but because the meaning of being a creature was not an aesthetic concern for many late twentieth-century writers (*Collected Poems* 59). Updike's use of taste, however, offers an insight into the influence of Christian theology on the milieu of late twentieth-century American literature, in which Updike played a prominent—if not perpetual—role. Using three of Updike's short stories, in this chapter I focus on what readers can extract from the sensual prominence of tasting in Updike's theology of sense. While Updike's fiction has numerous instances of distinctly registered flavors—some tastelessly crude indeed—the aesthetic principles we can draw from them fall under three general propositions.

> 1. Though taste may be learned, it is also surprised by unexpected gifts.

2. Eating, like beauty, reconciles humans with the world of things.
3. Drinking, with or without thirst, is a ceremonial and symbolic gesture.

These propositions are more like anthropological observations than prescribed standards of aesthetic judgment. They show how the sense of taste requires its own "sense" of meaning in Updike's work. Tasting senses insofar as it participates in a human—which is to say, cultural—relationship with the world. While sense perceptions arrive in flavors, chewing, and bodily movements, these three propositions posit that those physical actions are conditioned by the feeling of gratitude, the hope of reconciliation, and liturgically learned rites. Critics have faulted Updike's fiction for its lackluster theological reasoning, but his writing offers a unique theological anthropology of taste precisely because it so thoroughly savors the *experiences* that express the gratitude of an embodied creature (R. Wood 178; J. Wood 208–9). In Updike, aesthetic perception is the key to an accurate anthropology; humans flourish as uniquely human beings insofar as they rightly perceive the giftedness of creation. It is a persistent concept in his work and is vital to understanding his unique contribution to aesthetics.

Nevertheless, religion-curious critics tend to malign Updike's keen sensual attunement. Thomas Haddox has argued that even Updike's theologically infused passages are little more than a "deliberate self-justification, a rhetorical ploy that admits to the compensatory nature of narcissism" (88). In other words, Updike invokes his Christianity to justify putting his self-obsessions into print. Narcissism is no theological category, of course, and Haddox's claim becomes not only more generous but more probable when inverted: that Updike's noted sensual style is in fact the "deliberate self-justification" of his theology of sense. By engaging the field of theological aesthetics, I show how Updike's theological anthropology of taste delivers its own dynamic account of the beautiful.

Updike's use-value for the study of religion and literature has wavered if not declined in recent years, in part because of the neglect that critiques like Haddox's evince toward Updike's theological aesthetics and their corollary theological anthropology. Yet Updike's descriptive attention to the concrete particulars of embodied, human experience exemplifies the field of religion and literature's emphasis on the peculiarities unique to individual literary works. Updike's work demonstrates the fallacy of assuming either religion or literature as internally discrete, self-sufficient domains of culture. In this way, it provides an excellent means for theorizing a genuinely postsecular aesthetics.

While I will limit my comments here to three of Updike's short stories ("The Gun Shop," "The Music School," and "The Full Glass"), Updike's unique understanding of taste is evident throughout his writing across various genres. His other works do not place the act of eating and drinking at their center quite as memorably as *Rabbit at Rest* and its Rabelaisian scenes of unhealthy excess, where Rabbit muses, "God is in the universe the way salt is in the ocean, giving it taste" (*Rabbit Angstrom* 1041). Yet the theological conviction that attention to particular sense experiences expresses the gratitude of human creatureliness surfaces throughout his work: in his poetry from the early "Telephone Poles" and "Seven Stanzas at Easter" to the late long poem *Endpoint* (2009), from the explicit sexual preoccupations of *The Scarlet Letter* trilogy to the raucous paganism of the *Witches* novels, from the details of small-town nostalgia of Olinger and Tarbox to the awkward trysts of *Couples* and *Villages,* and including the intergenerational skirmishes of *The Centaur, Of the Farm,* and *In the Beauty of the Lilies. Self-Consciousness,* too, before finding happiness in the taste of orange juice, concludes that God alone "gives reality its true flavor" (233–34). The theological insight in these works offers one of the unprecedented lessons of Updike's prose: taste, Christianly understood, is how human finitude comes to know itself as good. Embodied finitude is not something to transcend nor is it a result of the Fall but is beautiful in itself. Beauty begins with the finitude of created bodies. This creaturely way of understanding the experience of beauty offers not a privileged vision of God, as it has for so many Christian theologians, but instead a delectable taste of what it means to be human. Updike's creatureliness celebrates the beauty of limitations.

CREATURELY AESTHETICS

Let me begin with the claim that though taste is learned, it is also surprised by unexpected gifts. Usually, tastes are acquired. The same scotch might sting a novice but delight the connoisseur; a steaming bowl of collard greens may provide a nostalgic treat to the exiled Southerner or an inexplicably bitter way to get one's vegetables to the carpet-bagging Yankee. Yet sometimes we are surprised—we find that the greens taste better than they smell, or we find that though we used to love them, they now taste irredeemably drenched in repulsive animal fat. For Updike, such surprises enlighten; they teach us that our taste for the world is *never* fully formed, that we have yet to appreciate the full bounty of the natural world. Moreover, Updike's writing can develop just such a taste in his readers—a taste for the surprising fullness of experience. Updike once characterized his early Olinger stories as all having the same basic point: "We are rewarded unexpectedly. The muddled and inconsequent surface of things now and then parts to yield us a *gift*" (*Olinger Stories* 13).

Often such gifts arrive not because of, but in spite of, our best efforts to reap a reward. Such is the case in Updike's 1972 short story, "The Gun Shop" (*CES*), which explores the mixed blessings of human creaturehood. It stipulates that the "duty of a father" is "to impart the taste of the world" to his son. Adults often enjoy the flavors they scorned as children. The desire for such acquired tastes takes some cultivation—we must learn to like them. In this story "the world" is just such an acquired taste; it is an anticipated compensation that the father must train the child to savor. "The Gun Shop," however, turns that expected taste into the unexpected gift of reconciliation, a gift that comes in the midst of a father's selfish, even violent, impulses. Thus the "taste of the world" is only partially learned; its true flavor comes as a surprise.

"The Gun Shop" opens with Ben Trupp's irked account of his son Murray's turning on him with a kitchen knife. At Murray's birthday party Ben thought the now-fourteen-year-old was acting out of hand. In characteristic Updikean free indirect discourse, "Ben had tapped the child on the back of the head" is later rendered in both his son's and his wife's perspectives as "hit" (*CES* 754). Murray responds to this questionable love tap by pointing the cake knife directly at his father, "Hit me again and I'll kill you." The narrative soon turns from Ben's son in pursuit of his father, also named Murray, which opens the story up to a triptych of tense father-son relationships in which the taste of the world is explicitly associated with the ominous atmosphere of a gun shop. "The Gun Shop" offers a picture of what it might mean to educate a child's taste—not as a matter of refining it, but realigning it, opening it up to the pleasure of unanticipated flavors.

Ben is a lawyer in Boston who has traveled with his wife, two daughters, and son down to his parents' farmhouse in southeastern Pennsylvania for the Thanksgiving holiday. From the birthday cake to the Thanksgiving turkey, the story unfolds between ceremonial meals. Yet the culinary delights that might mute the familial dysfunction known to surface at such gatherings are not the focus of the story. Instead, a Remington .22, given to Ben when he was 13 but now the highlight of Murray's trips to his grandparents, becomes the source of aggravated tensions between three generations of Trupp men when it refuses to fire. This multigenerational, overtly Oedipal drama reaches a surprisingly upbeat resolution in the story's closing paragraph when Ben and the young Murray are shooting at cans with the newly repaired .22. Ben can't hit a single target, but his son, full of "murderous concentration," triumphantly does. It ends with Ben, who used to be in a "murderous mood" himself (756), laughing in relief and joy while saying to his son, "You're killing me!" (765).

All this implied violence, however, is part of a certain flavor that Ben thinks his son should learn to savor as he matures into an adult. When Ben takes his son and father to the basement gun shop of a rural, southeastern Pennsylvania home, a friend of the older Murray expertly fixes the rifle that the young Murray wants to shoot. In the shop Ben's thoughts roam between his father and his own paternal style:

> There was that about being his father's son: one had adventures, one blundered into places, one went places, met strangers, suffered

rebuffs, experienced breakdowns, exposed oneself in a way that Ben, as soon as he was able, foreclosed, hedging his life with such order and propriety that no misstep could occur. He had become a lawyer, taking profit from the losses of others, reducing disorderly lives to legal folders. [. . .] Seeing his son's habitual tautness relax under the spell of this potent, acrid cellar, Ben realized that he had been much less a father than his own had been, a father's duty being to impart the taste of the world. Golf lessons in Brookline, sailing in Maine, skiing in New Hampshire—what was this but bought amusement compared with the improvised shifts and hazards of poverty? (759)

Ben worries that his excessive order and the money gained from his professional success have insulated his son Murray. He has failed at imparting "the taste of the world" to his son in the way that his father was able to for him. The security of success has resulted in an adumbrated palate, one unaware of the world's panoply of bitter flavors.

And smells. The "potent, acrid cellar" that the three Trupps visit is described as a "cave" where "the metallic smell of murder lurked" (759). Ben feels as though the "whole place smelled of death" (765). The smells remind Ben that he is out of his element in the rural gun shop, and the insecurity irks him. When Ben forgets and trips a backdoor alarm, he jumps back with a fear the others find amusing. Though his schoolteacher father hated all forms of what he called "cruel humor," he too laughs at the stupefied Ben. All of these aggressions participate in the young Murray's education into the milieu of death. The older Murray, something of a suffering saint in the story (reminiscent of Updike's portrait of his father in *The Centaur*), obliges in this education with the morbid maxims he dolls out: "Death is a part of life" and "Kill or be killed, that's my motto" (763, 765).

Some of Updike's personal experiences are no doubt apropos, and this deadly story is very much about life. Updike's son David corroborated some of these personal connections while amending others during a question-and-answer period at the 3rd Biennial Conference of the John Updike Society. Adam Begley's biography, too, has chronicled others (347–50). Yet we need not attribute the story's psychological acuity to those circumstances. The story is also an indirect meditation on writing fiction. For it is equally true that the very act of writing, which Updike considered a peaceful and innocent activity, can so easily put friendships and other personal relationships in jeopardy (see, for instance, the teenage David Updike's angry indictment of this aspect of his father's writing in David Cheshire's 1983 documentary, *What Makes Rabbit Run? A Profile of John Updike*).

Writing often destroys in order to create. Perhaps more than anyone else, the theorist Maurice Blanchot has explored writing's destructive forms of negation. For Blanchot, literary language is necessarily violent—it destroys the living thing to replace it with something quite different, words on a page. In his writing Blanchot uses strong verbs like *kill, murder,* and *annihilate* to describe the destructive side of literary creation. As he puts it in *The Work of Fire,* "For me to be able to say, "This woman," I must somehow take her flesh-and-blood reality away from her, cause her to be absent, annihilate her" (322). The words do not represent but replace the person; they "annihilate" the actual living, breathing person with bulletlike letters. Blanchot's Gallic penchant for philosophical overstatement aside, he at the very least serves to warn that writers who profess a realist aesthetic (and often take their characters from actual friends and acquaintances) have waded into ethically troubled waters.

This ethically questionable aspect of realism rumbles beneath the story's violent overtones, but it receives its symbolic portent in Ben's legal profession. Recall how Updike describes Ben's work as "taking profit from the losses of others, reducing disorderly lives to legal folders" (*CES* 759). A novelist who uses real-life experiences to give his fictional worlds a lifelike sheen does much of the same thing, unknotting the twisted complications of personalities and their contexts to weave together a story's meaningful pattern. "The Gun Shop" goes even further, however, to suggest an unnerving affinity between the gunsmith and the writer. Ben is mesmerized while watching Dutch, the owner of the gun shop, work on such recalcitrant material. Updike writes, "Ben had once worked wood, in high-school shop, but this man could shape metal: he could descend into the hard heart of things and exert his will" (763). As a lawyer, Ben knows how to "exert his will" on the truth, and Updike, too, knew how to exert his will on things by recreating them in words. Later the older Murray will remark to the younger Murray about Dutch, "He's what you'd have to call a genius and a gentleman. Did you see the way your dad looked at him? Pure adoration, man to man" (764). This adoration is bound up in a respect for the manly art of destruction.

All this gunmetal adds up to a bitter flavor for a writer looking to bear witness to the beauty of unexpected gifts. How can a father, or a writer, "impart the taste of the world" when his work seems to delight in its own viciousness? Is it a father's duty to embitter his son? There is a stark contrast between the gift-giving connotations of imparting a taste of the world and exerting one's will over the hard heart of things. And yet, in Updike's Christian logic, the violence of this creative act is a *felix culpa,* for it is in the midst of such violence that writing begins its work of reconciliation. Updike tries to shape the quality of sense experience through the specific sense of the world it portrays. Moreover, for Updike it is the writer's duty as much as it is a father's to impart the taste of the world in this way—to lift the sensorium of human experience into conscious appreciation, even praise. Preceding the moment of father-son bonding portrayed in the final scene, Ben receives just such a gift of reconciliation from what he had assumed was the estranged world of his childhood home. When Ben and Murray walk across his parents' land, something catches Ben's attention. He notices

> in the dead grass the rusty serrate shapes of strawberry leaves, precise as fossils. When they had moved here, the land had been farmed out—"mined," in the local phrase—and the one undiscouraged crop consisted of the wild strawberries running from ditch to ridge on all the sunny slopes. At his son's age, Ben had no fondness for the strawberry leaves and the rural isolation they ornamented; it surprised him, gazing down, that their silhouettes fit so exactly a shape in his mind. The leaves were still here, and his parents were still in the square sandstone farmhouse. (756)

The image of the wild strawberries, he realizes with surprise, is an image he knows well. That surprise is imperative to the story. Ben is surprised that the shape of the leaves fit so exactly a shape in his mind. The "rusty serrate" edges of the leaves, "precise as fossils," provide him with a new sense of security that had hitherto been absent. Their familiarity strikes him just as the familial feeling of pride will overcome him at the story's end. His son and father, too, share that same peaceful proximity to him, though his competitive drives have distracted him from realizing it. That such forms of quiet familiarity exist in spite of our failures to realize them—indeed, in spite of our tendency to aggressively degrade them—is the unexpected gift this story seeks to savor. While the smell of death lurking in the gun shop may be pungently powerful, the true taste of the world is hidden in the sweetness of those wild strawberries. Seeking to inculcate Murray with a taste for the struggling world of competition, Ben will instead be given a sudden and new appreciation for the peaceful comfort of that very same world.

Even as "The Gun Shop" acknowledges the destructive side of literary representation, it bears witness to the paradoxical possibility of words to reconcile. This redemptive violence is alluded to in the story's last line, when Ben finally lets go of his aggression: "In his pride and relief Ben had to laugh, 'You're killing me.'" The story's last scene describes Ben missing the target that his son seems to hit effortlessly. The anger and frustration that had been building during the visit instantaneously become "pride and relief." The undiminished violent undertones running throughout the story serve to illuminate this unearned, unsentimental form of paternal solicitude. Moreover, cheap reconciliation is blatantly ridiculed in the moment when, while driving to the gun shop, Ben sees "a Pentecostal church built of cinder blocks, with a neon Jesus Lives. Jesus Saves must have become too much of a joke" (758). While such signs, and Ben's cynical musing, point toward the many ways Christian thought has been used to promulgate a foolish sentimentality, Updike himself believed that the Christian's foremost task was to tell the truth. In accepting the Campion Medal in 1997 from the Catholic Book Club, Updike asserted that Christianity "tells us that truth is holy, and truth-telling a noble and useful profession; that the reality around us is created and worth celebrating; that men and women are radically imperfect and radically valuable" ("Remarks" 4). In fact, he asked of his audience "to be absolved from any duty to provide orthodox morals and consolations in my fiction" because doing so would betray the truth-telling realism with which he sought to portray human imperfection and value (5).

Accordingly, reconciliation is not earned by any of the characters in "The Gun Shop." There is no moral to instruct the reader. Reconciliation comes in the form of a revelation, and Ben's grateful laughter is the only adequate response to such a gift of life-changing knowledge. The importance of such gifts of reconciliation was thoroughly developed in Karl Barth's theology, and specifically in Barth's exposition of the doctrine of reconciliation. Updike often praises Barth's work in both his fiction and nonfiction, and critics have shown how prominent the themes of Barth's theology are in Updike's work (Boswell, *Updike's Rabbit Tetralogy* 15–25; Hunt 30–38; Webb 145–61). The importance of gratitude, along with Christ's work of reconciliation, is one of Updike and Barth's shared concerns, though it has not received the same critical attention as some of their other thematic parallels.

The importance of gratitude emerges most centrally during Barth's discussion of the doctrine of Creation in *Church Dogmatics*, chapter 10, "The Creature." "Gratitude," Barth writes, "is the precise creaturely counterpart to the grace of God" (III.2: 166). In Barth's theological anthropology, to be a human being is to be a creature created by God, which, in its fullest form, is "a being in gratitude" (166). To be fully human is to express creaturely gratitude for the gifts of God. "To be grateful is to recognize a benefit," and, according to Barth, true benefits are God-given. He continues by explaining that to "be grateful as opposed to ungrateful is not merely to receive, accept, and enjoy a benefit, but to understand it as such, as a good which one could not take for oneself but has in fact received, as an action which one could not perform for oneself but which has nevertheless happened to one" (167). Receiving gifts like this is the "being in gratitude" that distinguishes creatureliness.

The closing line of "The Gun Shop," "You're killing me," captures the helpless joy Ben feels at the benefit of, in Barth's words, "an action which one could not perform oneself but which has nevertheless happened to one." He has not been able to give his son the gift of confident manhood—not even the gift of simple paternal approbation. Yet in his furious attempts to outshoot the young Murray, his own selfishness has mysteriously died and he is free to give up the fight (if only for a moment!). It is a theologically rich scene, one that grapples with the meaning of reconciliation, the free gift of grace, and the persistent perversity of selfish desires. Ben thought he wanted to be a better parent, but he is surprised to find he had wanted the wrong thing: His taste for parenting failed him. What he most truly desired was not being a better shot, not even teaching his son a lesson, but enjoying the gift of his son.

If Updike mistrusts the language of taste, it is because he mistrusts any account of the beautiful that does not establish it first and foremost as a gift and the ability to receive it as training in gratitude. The phrase, "You're killing me," according to the aesthetic expectations the story sets for itself, glows with a moving beauty. Its relinquished frustration and incumbent gratitude is quintessentially human, especially insofar as the experience of beauty, like the sudden recognition of those strawberry leaves, can reconcile in the midst of violence. Beauty is the unexpected gift Updike's characters so often receive. In spite of Updike's enthusiasm for Karl Barth's theology and David Bentley Hart's occasional antipathy to it, Updike would certainly agree with Hart's insistence that there "is an overwhelming givenness in the beautiful, and it is discovered in astonishment, in an awareness of something fortuitous, adventitious, essentially indescribable; it is known only in the moment of response, from the position of one already addressed and able now only to reply" (17). Like Hart, Updike emphasizes grateful response as the fundamentally human mode of being, and beauty as its most powerful conduit. Such an understanding of beauty goes beyond the epiphany of a mere moment. It transcends the momentary to become an attitude, a way of being, insofar as beauty so conceived necessitates an awareness of the persistent palpability of goodness. To develop a taste for the world is to develop a sensibility for creaturely gratitude.

GASTRONOMY AND RECONCILIATION

Updike's 1964 story, "The Music School," is haunted with the threat of violence and the promise of reconciliation in ways similar to "The

Gun Shop." While it is guns in the latter, it is an acquaintance in the former. In both stories the protagonist finds himself musing in a place where one of his children is suddenly taking new steps toward adulthood—getting a taste for the world's less saccharine flavors. In "The Music School," the narrator ruminates, "The world is the host; it must be chewed" (*CES* 527). The reference here is to the wafer used in Holy Communion or, as the older Episcopalian Updike's *Book of Common Prayer* would have called it, "The Great Thanksgiving." Appropriately enough, like "The Gun Shop," "The Music School" takes place around the Thanksgiving holiday, when gratitude is more often dogged by guilt and strife than the forgiveness celebrated in the Eucharist. Yet the story demonstrates how eating, like beauty, reconciles humans with the world of things.

If Updike's sense of taste in "The Gun Shop" hopes to educate in us a taste for receiving the gift of reconciliation, in "The Music School" he challenges us to consider that reconciliation through a close corollary of tasting—chewing. That the world "must be chewed" raises two preliminary points about Updike's understanding of aesthetic taste. First, whatever aesthetic theorists have said about the necessity of distance for truly tasteful judgments, *tasting* requires contact. And second, that contact does not merely brush or glance but breaks—and often lingers. There is such a thing as aftertaste. Some foods will leave a residual flavor behind them, sometimes for hours or even through to the next day. Among the other senses there is no complementary word for an aftersight, or aftertouch, or aftersound, or aftersmell. Taste stays with you *and* fades, which is to say that only the taste of a bite of food can create near-immediate nostalgia, a state of limbo between the fullness of the past bite and its fading but still lingering presence. If a familiar smell can suddenly retrieve the past, an aftertaste keeps its continuity. When approached as the taste acquired in chewing, aesthetic experience rejects the principle of distance and requires contact.

Chewing incorporates—in the full etymological sense of that verb—taste. It offers a different way of thinking about beauty than the sense of sight does, which, ever since Justin Martyr, dominates Christian teaching about the educational in-*sight* of beauty. Sight, as illustrated in the act of focusing a lens, demands some level of distance between the one who sees and what is seen. We step back or lean forward to better scrutinize a painting. Yet tasting does not erect a spatial distance between the object experienced and the person experiencing the object. Moreover, chewing the world is not mere mastication but implies digestion, too. Chewing is the first step to food becoming a part of us; differentiation is broken down into nutrition. To impart the taste of the world, then, is not merely an initiation into the world's variety but also participation in it. The Latin root from which we derive our English word for taste, *tangere,* means "to touch." Tasting is as intimate a form of touch as there is (Aristotle taught that there were only four senses, attributing taste to just such a special form of touching). Curiously, the modern homonym of the Latin's "I taste" aptly evokes the flirtatious proximity of its sensual dalliance: *tango.*

The story's opening sentence lacks the tango's characteristic flair, however, when it begins with the lumbering, Germanic confession, "My name is Alfred Schweigen and I exist in time" (522). The intention is to register the Heideggerian predicament the reader and Alfred share—thrown into life, he is stuck existing in time, stuck choosing and acting based on his embodied limitations and partial knowledge. Once Alfred has identified his temporal limitations, and thus established in that first sentence the existential problem of the story, he begins to tell a short anecdote about a young Roman Catholic priest he had met at dinner party the previous night. The priest was explaining a recent change in Church thinking about the communion wafer. Though nuns once instructed their faithful young charges to simply let the wafer melt in their mouth, so as to avoid damaging the host with the vulgarity of chewing, the Church was now demanding that the host be made thicker, "so substantial it must be chewed to be swallowed" (522). In philosophy, and in Reformation debates over transubstantiation, the word *substance* had significant ontological bite. Yet for Protestants and Catholics alike, Updike seems to be implying, the substantial thickness of the host matters if it is to be a sign (or even a fully meaningful symbol) of the Incarnation. Indeed, the sacrament's dense materiality is unwittingly slighted in the Augustinian formula "visible signs of invisible grace."

Updike is suggesting that perhaps "tangible signs of intangible grace" might be the more appropriate formula.

Without developing the implications of the young priest's news, Alfred's thoughts quickly shift to the morning newspaper, where he read of a passing acquaintance's murder (the fictional event is based on Updike's reading of the MIT computer designer Ben Gurley's death, whom he had only recently just met). The victim was a computer scientist who, as Alfred imagines such professionals, with "their sufficient incomes, large families, Volkswagen buses, hi-fi phonographs, half-remodeled Victorian homes, and harassed, ironical wives, [. . .] seem to have solved, or dismissed, the paradox of being a thinking animal and, devoid of guilt, apparently participate not in this century but in the next" (523). This guiltless "man of the future" now lies dead, however, murdered by a single bullet that entered his head from a nearby window as he ate dinner—"a week after Thanksgiving"—with his family; Alfred acknowledges that he does "not understand the connection between last night and this morning, though there seems to be one" (524, 522, 523). He fumbles to name it as he sits outside his daughter's piano lesson in the basement of a church, discerning in the "two incidents a common element of nourishment, of eating transfigured by a strange irruption" (523). Common to both as well is "a flight immaculately direct and elegant, from an immaterial phenomenon (an exegetical nicety, a maniac hatred) to a material one (a bulky wafer, a bullet in the temple)" (523). In linking the immaterial to the material, these events seem to promise some answer to the "paradox of being a thinking animal." The paradox of a soul housed within bodily appetites is one Alfred feels acutely due to his guilt over an adulterous affair.

His daughter and the students in the music school, in contrast, are shyly learning to take pleasure in the immaterial realm of music. The music school, full of nervous, ethereally beautiful young people, is like "another world, a world where angels fumble, pause, and begin again" (524). Something spiritual seems to nourish his daughter insofar as she "does not beg for a reward of candy or a Coke" afterwards, "as if the lesson itself has been a meal" (524). Alfred enjoys seeing this side of his daughter, enjoys the ritual of the lessons: "I love taking her, I love waiting for her, I love driving her home through the mystery of darkness toward the certainty of supper" (524–25). The certain familiarity of chewing up that very material meal helps to make the lesson such a thrillingly immaterial one. Here is another "flight immaculately direct and elegant" between the material and immaterial that gives the meal of her lesson its own "transfigured," "strange interruption" into emerging adulthood.

Yet even as she learns piano, Alfred is struggling with divorce, another form of breakdown. Alfred has yet to fully reconcile his immaterial and material pleasures in immaculate flight. In trying to draw the connections between the wafer, the murdered computer expert, and the music school, he remembers a novel he had once planned to write about a computer programmer. The protagonist was too pure for his adulterous desire and would end up dying from the building anguish he felt from the mere possibility of consummating his adulterous love. This hypothetical novel was going to associate sexual purity with the stars and mathematics, worlds of immaterial beauty like the music school, where "angels fumble" at their instruments. Impure Alfred, however, can only confess his wrongs to the reader—thereby assuaging his guilt by humiliating himself and his inability to control his own animal instincts.

This feeling of guilt reminds him of the liturgy of confession and communion from the rural congregation where he grew up. His church was not angelic like the music students; its music was that of maladroit human bodies. When the congregation confessed, there "was a kind of accompanying music in the noise of the awkward fat Germanic bodies fitting themselves, scraping and grunting, into the backwards-kneeling position. We read aloud, *But if we thus examine ourselves, we shall find nothing in us but sin and death, from which we can in no wise set ourselves free*" (526). Alfred recalls that this congregation's confession of sin was as inelegantly embodied as some of the sins being confessed. "We were a weathered, homely congregation," he confides, "sheepish in our Sunday clothes, and the faces I saw while the wafer was held in my mouth were strained; above their closed lips their eyes held a watery look of pleading to be rescued from the depths of this mystery" (526). Their "awkward fat Germanic bodies," "weathered," "strained," but pastorally "sheepish," preoccupy his memory. The mere memory of chewing the wafer inspires a bodily response in Alfred, for it is a "memory so vivid it makes my saliva flow," from which he concludes "that it was necessary, if not to chew, at least to touch, to embrace and tentatively shape, the wafer with the teeth" (526). That the sacrament is a visible sign of invisible grace is, of course, yet another "direct and elegant" flight between the material and immaterial. Yet Alfred is not so interested in that symbolic resonance. He does not resolve to go back to church and the religious mysteries that launch such flights. No. Rather he concludes that the world—*not* the body of Christ—is the host to chew. The world of sensuous pleasures is to be approached not with guilt or timidity but with spiritual gusto.

The churchgoers' awkwardly substantial bodies are reconciled with the story's ethereal forms of mathematical beauty in the act of not merely tasting the world but also chewing it. Chewing affirms the goodness of the body's materiality and its capacity to be beautiful and to experience beauty. Through Alfred's musings Updike suggests that the moment we begin to think our best aspirations are somehow at odds with the physicality of our bodies, we become alienated from the joys of the given world and humanity's creaturely place in it. Thus the story suggests that the implicit way to solve the paradox of being a thinking animal is to give thanks *as a creature.* To chew the world, rather than gaze at it or eavesdrop on the music of its spheres, is to affirm that loveliness comes to bodies because—not in spite of the fact that—they touch other bodies. Updike's beauty is not an abstract idealization, an imagined possibility; it is not the classical imagination's pleasing proportionality. To see beauty in its purest form demands attention to the particular, which means that beauty finds its beginning and end in the experience of singular bodies.

This predilection for the particular expresses the formal strength of "The Music School" much better than its theological aphorism about the Eucharist. Updike allows the priest, the murder, the music school, and his musings on divorce to dangle as distinct fragments. The differences separating them are honored throughout, as if each moment in the story was itself a host worthy of being chewed on its own, rather than slowly dissolving into the whole. What seem like abrupt transitions in a story about finding connections are in fact the story's formal unity. The liturgy of Alfred's old church and its kneeling, sheepishly dressed parishioners, his daughter's excited entry into adult responsibilities, the futuristic computer programmer of the sixties—each of these facts lingers as a distinct presence after the story ends—and even more so the *things* named in the story, such as the young students of the music school "carrying fawn-colored flute cases and pallid folders of music" whose "awkwardness is lovely" (524). This is the happy truth hidden within these chewable hosts—the Creator's encompassing love for the vivid delights of creaturely experience. Beauty is not the escape from embodied limitations but a reconciliation with their endlessly differentiated splendors: to cherish the awkwardness of adolescent bodies and the muted brown of their instrument cases. Chewing, in this story, becomes Updike's way of exploring taste's formal singularities.

One of the twentieth century's most comprehensive and influential texts in theological aesthetics contends that this reverence for the particular instantiation of form is the vital aesthetic truth of the doctrine of the Incarnation. The first volume of Hans Urs von Balthasar's *The Glory of the Lord* shows that Christ's peculiarity, what he calls the "primal form" of "God and man in an unimaginable intimacy," is the ground from which any true theory of form must grow (25). "Like all other words that are applied to Christ and his revelation, the word 'form' too must be used with care," Balthasar cautions, "which means that its abstract and general conceptual content must be held *in suspenso* in view of the uniqueness of this particular application. What is crucial here is not the word, but the thing itself" (422). A form is not a generic mold. For a writer of Updike's extreme realist ilk, this is true of all linguistic forms—their "general conceptual content" trembles before the bald particularity of an incarnate God's creation.

The fictional form Updike uses in this story, with its stubbornly substantial, juxtaposed anecdotes, reveals a formal appropriation of Balthasar's theology of the Incarnation. The story's meandering form insists on the substantiality of bodies over the conceptual content of its existential themes. In turning to the body's need for food and how the act of eating might impact perceptions of beauty, Updike reinvigorates this central Christian truth by means of his own unique literary form. Alfred may no longer be a believer, but his reveries echo Christianity's central truth, one put well in David Bentley Hart's more recent theology of beauty: "In the end, that within Christianity which draws persons to itself is a concrete and particular beauty, because a concrete and particular beauty *is* its deepest truth" (28).

Flannery O'Connor grappled with this crucial Christian truth throughout her writing career, and she may be the most critically celebrated "incarnational" writer, the doctrine to which Hart is alluding (Lake, *Incarnational Art* 5). While O'Connor's malcontented, misanthropic characters rarely indulge in describing concrete particular beauties, they occasionally glimpse them in a story's final scene. One of her earliest stories (submitted for her master's thesis at Iowa in 1947, but posthumously published) uses food motifs in order to juxtapose the world of concrete particulars with the same all-too-human tendency to despise them that Updike identifies in "The Music School." "The Crop" (1971) is a story about a writer, Miss Willerton, with less than charitable feelings toward the particularities of her own propensity to, like Updike's writer Alfred Schweigen, exist in a specific time and place. (Notably, these stories stand out in both Updike and O'Connor as a rare instance of using a writer-protagonist.) Miss Willerton, who must "crumb" the breakfast table before she commences to write for the day, has increasingly fewer crumbs to share from it (*Collected Works* 732).

Miss Willerton does not think well of her housemates; in her eyes, Lucia is a busybody who watches over Garner in order to see him "put the Agar-Agar on his Cream-of-Wheat" (732). Garner is such a simpleton, though, she wonders if he'd "be capable of doing anything else," "having done it for fifty years." Yet Miss Willerton, or Willie, receives Lucia's attentions, too, whenever she puts pineapple crush on her Cream-of-Wheat. "You know your acid, Willie," Lucia would habitually say, and "Miss Willerton would taste the pineapple crush she had already swallowed." In the story's opening scene, eating is directly related to the three characters' experience of community; both are spoiled by rising acidity.

The bilious relationship between food and fellow-feeling continues once Miss Willerton sits down at her writing desk. Trying to find a subject for her story with an adequately progressive moral, she thinks, "Bakers. No, bakers wouldn't do. Hardly colorful enough. No social tension connected with bakers" (733). She settles instead on the "arty" subject of sharecroppers and begins composing the story of Lot Motun. O'Connor would recycle this character's last name, and its biblical allusion to the parable of the mote and the beam, a few years later in *Wise Blood*'s Hazel Motes. That parable's warning—look to yourself before correcting another's sins—clearly structures "The Crop." For Miss Willerton becomes smitten with her story of Lot, and her own sense of literary taste, to the point of congratulating herself and then including herself in the story and giving that character all the virtues she knows she lacks. Blinded by indulging her longing for another life, her writing is interrupted when Lucia less than politely asks her to go to the grocery store.

The trip to the grocery store culminates in Miss Willerton's total disgust at the banality it contains: "Silly that a grocery store should depress one—nothing in it but trifling domestic doings—women buying beans—riding children in those grocery go-carts—higgling about an eighth of a pound more or less of squash—what did they get out of it? Miss Willerton wondered. Where was there any chance for self-expression, for creation, for art?" (739). She is repulsed by it all and opposes her own higher calling to such squalid lives. Then she sees a couple walking down the sidewalk who could have been the real-life counterparts to her story's characters, and, overwhelmed by the particulars she sees—a woman with "yellow hair and fat ankles and muddy-colored eyes" and "mottled" skin and an "inane grin" next to a "stooped" man with "yellow knots along the side of his large, red neck" and a "rash over his forehead"—her disgust is complete (740). Once home she realizes she must change her subjects—sharecroppers will no longer do because they just became all too real. For Miss Willerton, good writing avoids the ordinary for the "arty" (740).

If Miss Williston wants to become a writer of O'Connor's quality, however, she is going to have to start thinking differently about meals. O'Connor gives her no final moment of revelation, but the broad strokes of this early work make it clear enough to the reader: Groceries matter for a good meal and, by formal implication, a good story. The actual—not necessarily the quotidian, but the world's lack of dramatic pretense, unsavory acid and all—announces itself in "The Crop" as the antithesis of Miss Willerton's aesthetic. While the story does not, like O'Connor's "A Temple of the Holy Ghost," directly allude to the Eucharist in the way that Updike's "The Music School" does, it too explores the physical act of eating as one that can reconcile a writer too prone to idealize with the world of substantial stuff. It asserts, albeit indirectly as O'Connor so often does, that the limitations of life need not be transcended through art. That the very materiality of human creatureliness provides all the material a writer needs. O'Connor's story creates a formal inversion of its own commitment to exploring the awful truth through Miss Willerton's disdain for the people around her. Updike's, however, formally enacts a way of reconciling dissimilarities in a fictional unity without diluting or romanticizing them. However disparate the two writers' styles, both use shame and guilt to produce the pleasures of careful truth-telling.

CEREMONIES

Finally, let me turn to how Updike shows that drinking, with or without thirst, is always a ceremonial—and thus aesthetic—gesture. Updike used the ruminative, concrete, unraveled form of the "The Music School" in two other stories during the middle of his career: "The Blessed Man of Boston, My Grandmother's Thimble, and Fanning Island" and "Packed Dirt, Churchgoing, a Dying Cat, a Traded Car." As their titles suggest, both stories string together several seemingly disconnected ideas in search of a connecting thread, ending with a succinctly stated maxim. This kind of essayistic yet fictive form held special esteem in Updike's opinion of his own work. Making connections and illuminating preexisting patterns were crucial to Updike's literary ideals, and these stories put that task in the formal foreground. When submitting "Packed Dirt" to an anthology titled *This Is My Best,* Updike explained his selection to the editor, writing that if "the story is dense, it is because there was a pressure of memory and worry upon it; as these far-flung images collected at my typewriter, a bigger, better kind of music felt to be arising out of compression" (*CES* 934). He goes on to admit his authorial exultation in the story insofar as "I seemed at last to understand Proust's remark about the essence of the writer's task being the perception of connections between unlike things." The compressed form (his writer's salute to a more "dense" wafer) provided for associations while allowing characters and objects their resplendent idiosyncrasies. Yet Updike's care for the "substantiality" of his stories' various images is equally sensitive to their flow and the liquidity of their associations. His theology of taste becomes fully anthropological in its consideration of the rites that connect the human creature's taste to the world.

Updike's last published short story, "The Full Glass," happily returns to the tributary streams of this associative form. The story conspicuously reiterates the opening theme of "Packed Dirt, Churchgoing, a Dying Cat, a Traded Car," which begins with a nostalgic musing on the packed-dirt paths he recalls from his childhood. "Such unconsciously humanized intervals of clay," the earlier story begins, "too humble and common even to have a name, remind me of my childhood, when one communes with dirt down among the legs, as it were, of presiding presences. The earth is our playmate then, and the call to supper has a piercing eschatological ring" (*CES* 355). These "unconsciously humanized" forms of connection appear in "The Full Glass" when Updike again writes of "my fascination, as a boy, with pathways" (*CLS* 910). The mundane conduits of connection this story is most attentive to, however, are the city's water pipes and the act of drinking water.

"The Full Glass" makes a consciously humanized ceremony out of washing down a daily dose of pills. In doing so it inflects the 23rd Psalm's praise that God's provisions are wonderfully sufficient—"my cup runneth over"—into the experience of an aging twenty-first-century American's habitual pill-popping. In doing so, it includes an argument for the ceremonial, liturgylike aspect of literature. Indeed, it can be read as an updated meditation on the conclusion of "Packed Dirt," when the narrator suddenly addresses a sailor he described picking up as a hitchhiker and attempts to draw the connecting thread between his several images with the concluding line: "We in America need ceremonies, is I suppose, sailor, the point of what I have written" (*CES* 377).

"We in America need ceremonies" may sound like a rather sweeping dictum, but "The Full Glass" recounts a humble example of just such a ceremony. The narrator has developed a nightly ritual in his late, retired years: filling a glass of water to the top, placing it on the sink-top of his bathroom counter, and then using it to get his medications down. The act assumes a ceremonial and symbolic significance in the nightly repetition; in the "full glass feeling" it excites, the simple gesture becomes something of a tribute to life's unanticipated pleasures (*CLS* 905). The intentional habit is

> more than a matter of convenience. There is a small but distinct pleasure, in a life with the gaudier pleasures leveled out of it, in having the full glass there on the white marble sink-top waiting for me, before I sluice down the anti-cholesterol pill, the anti-inflammatory, the sleeping, the calcium supplement (my wife's idea, now that I get foot cramps in bed, somehow from the pressure of the top sheet), along with the Xalatan drops to stave off glaucoma and the Systane drops to ease dry eye. (903)

The fastidious observance of the ritual seems unevenly yoked to its quotidian austerity. Yet that apparent divergence is what such a ceremony hopes to bridge. The simple ceremony of drinking that glass of water is a way of giving thanks for and cherishing the exquisite ordinariness of its "full glass feeling." Remembering his early experiences with this delighted gratitude at a glass of cold water, he recalls how its fullness translated into an enthusiasm to discover what life had in store: "That icy water held an ingredient that made me, a boy of nine or ten, eager for the next moment of life, one brimming moment after another" (905). Even though the "gaudier pleasures" are no longer there for the elderly narrator, something of that "full glass feeling" of "one brimming moment" is achieved in the smallness of his nightly ritual.

This glass of water is not quite a gift of the natural world, like the strawberry leaves of "The Gun Shop"; nor is it from the spiritual world so explicitly summoned by "The Music School." Its mysteries lie squarely in the realm of human culture. The narrator traces that full glass feeling back to his childhood and the subterranean depths fathomed by the accomplishments of modern plumbing: "Filling a tumbler with water at the old faucet connected you with the wider world. Think of it: pipes running through the earth below the frost line and up unseen from the basement right through the walls to bring you this transparent flow, which you swallowed down in rhythmic gulps—down what my grandfather called, with that twinkle he had, behind his bifocals, 'the little red lane'" (903). That glass of water manifests the hidden plumbing lurking in the most everyday and most sacred experiences of beauty. Such human connections were part of what fascinated the narrator of "Packed Dirt," and those old dirt pathways are still a key part of the joy smiling through this old man's reveries.

Another evening rite of invisible connections that gives him that grateful "full glass feeling" is turning off the outdoor Christmas lights. He could have merely flicked the switch in passing but instead always paused, gazing out the window to watch their luminescence disappear into the darkness of the night in perfect timing with the switch. "My hoping to see the current snake through the extension cords possibly harks back to my fascination, as a boy, with pathways," he confides. "I loved the idea of something irresistibly travelling along a set path—marbles rolling down wooden or plastic troughs, subway trains hurtling beneath city streets, water propelled by gravity through underground pipes, rivers implacably tumbling and oozing their way their way to the sea. Such phenomena have given me considerable joy to contemplate, and, with the lessening intensity that applies in my old age to all sensations, they still do" (910–11). The glass was no mere intimation of possible connection; that water traveled before it reached your hand, and, when shutting off its pressure at the faucet, you were in that moment touching all those unseen mysterious places. Its cascading coolness hid the translucent force of its connections, but it chilled with the tactile pressure of other worlds. For Updike, drinking from a tap is never only an act to satisfy thirst; it participates in the miracle of human community and the mysteries of modern society.

The story's nameless narrator did not always take pleasure in the ceremonial aspects of such rites. He remembers visiting his uncle out in the country and how his uncle relished taking him to his spring for a drink, dipping the tin ladle and pulling it up with regal significance: "I disliked these country visits, so full, I thought, of unnecessary ceremony" (905). "Another full moment," however, is remembered from just such a rural setting at a barn dance with a local beauty. It is the formal movements of the dance, their relaxed but titillating points of contact that make the memory vivid. "Women like all that, it occurs to me this late in life—connections and combinations, contact" (911). And so does he—the inconspicuous ceremonial human touch titillates with that full glass feeling where its awkward overstatement only irks.

The keen delights of these guileless ceremonies guide the wandering, inquisitive probing of the narrative. Why does he find these "curious habits" so gratifying? What thrills in brimming water or the hidden pipes that bring it? As in the dance, it is wonder at the surprising "connections and combinations." Yet it is not the intimate feeling of his connection with another as much as simple wonder at the fullness of meaning. The metallic hint and surprisingly sweet tinge of plain tap water suggest that his ritualized swig is an adequate gesture, one capable of recognizing an unsung dignity. To eulogize too profusely, to embellish to the point of "unnecessary ceremony," would corrupt the resigned awe he feels. It would insert selfish neediness, a thirst for pleasure in place of gratified acquiescence.

Though "The Full Glass" revels in its simple pleasures, it is also a poignant story about letting go. Several of Updike's characters harp on their fear of dying and their desperate need to witness the life of the world in action. This narrator, however, is peacefully pleased at the prospect of oblivion. Of sleeping in an extra hour, he can only shrug that the "world is being tended to, I can let go of it, it doesn't need me" (914). It is an unusual sentiment for an Updike character, but an admission entirely in keeping with the author's repeated conviction: The world in itself, with or without his witness, is gloriously delicious. In fact, his resignation has made life's pleasures even sweeter. "My life-prolonging pills cupped in my left-hand, I lift the glass, its water sweetened by its brief wait on the marble sink-top. If I can read this strange old guy's mind aright, he's drinking a toast to the visible world, his impending disappearance from it be damned" (914). The passing time makes the water sweeter, and it tastes better because of the ritualized performance. The flavor actually changes, in Updike's rendering, when experienced in a certain way—in a ceremony of slow gratitude. Moreover, the story's resigned, elegiac tone is all the more poignant, no doubt, since Updike himself disappeared from this world only months after "The Full Glass" was first published.

The story is its own form of a toast to the world it applauds. If the writer's duty is to impart the taste of the world, to exhort the practice of chewing it, then it is also to raise a toast to it. In this gesture of the raised glass, we come to what I take to be the most profound aspect of Updike's treatment of taste: In it we see how taste is neither fully "disinterested" (to use Kant's term) nor the pawn of appetite. To return to my first point, good taste can be taught. Though Updike's poem "Taste" decries the snobbery and class loyalty associated with the idea of taste—and rightly so—Updike understands the cultural foundations of our desires. He grasps that desires are not purely biological drives but learned. What philosophers and sociologists have called "second order desires," the desire *to* desire what one reasonably believes is good but not immediately desirable, is a subtle motif appearing throughout Updike's fiction (C. Smith 9). The toast is a tribute that in its accolade becomes an affirmation to the reader of what is desirable and why. Yes, the world must be chewed—but it deserves an elegantly stated toast, too. We are surprised with gifts, but those gifts should teach us to love and long for what has been given. In the gesture of the toast Updike affirms the value of cultivating a second order desire for the given world—even without its "gaudier pleasures." Raising the glass is a way of affirming a life lived desiring good things. The ceremony of the act confirms it not only as meaningful, but the simple pleasure of drinking as fundamentally good. Good taste thrives on the ceremonies that teach us to enjoy creation's goodness.

"Cultural liturgies" is what the philosopher James K. A. Smith calls "the formative pedagogies of desire that are trying to make us a certain kind of person" (24). It is a helpful term for thinking about how Updike's aesthetics are always also a form of anthropology. Smith is referring to the kinds of actions, often routine but not necessarily, that shape our desires. This could mean the kinds of experiences we have in a shopping mall, or the songs we listen to, or the commercials we watch, or the books we read. A cultural liturgy is something secular, something from the world, that, when chewed, shapes who we are, what we want, and our attunement to the world we inhabit. Cultural liturgies are "identity-forming practices" that "aim our love to different ends precisely by training our hearts through our bodies" (35, 25). One of Updike's earliest critics, Michael Novak, noticed how his prose offered a liturgylike performance of Christian faith. In a 1963 essay for *The Commonweal* titled "Updike's Quest for Liturgy," Novak wrote that Updike was "beginning to make faith intelligible in America, to fashion symbols whereby it can be understood" (191). I would add in clarification that the intelligibility Updike offers is, like true liturgy, not merely cognitive but fully sensual in its symbols. Raising that glass on a nightly basis is a way for the narrator to train his heart through his body. Even this watery necessity is wonderful and worthy not only of repetition but of full-hearted celebration.

Smith's "cultural liturgies" offer a theological explanation for a host of recent theory that has drawn on ancient philosophy as much as contemporary sociological theory, from Michel Foucault's "care of the self" to Pierre Hadot's "spiritual exercises" to Pierre Bourdieu's "habitus." These concepts all point toward the effect our bodies have on what we desire and to the fact that those effects are not merely biological but can be trained. As such, they tie theories of perception to theories of human culture. Yet Smith pushes these cultural theories to confront a cultural theology based in Christianity's teaching that humans long for God and that that longing is a definitive component of the human creaturely experience. The full glass and its full glass feeling are a kind of cultural liturgy—both as a nightly gesture and as a story that seeks to praise life's inconspicuous joys. By turning the act of drinking into a gesture explored through a short story's controlling idea, Updike allows his readers to experience a taste of what is truly desirable.

The toast of that full glass is raised in the spirit of a transformative cultural practice. If taste is first and foremost acknowledged as receptivity to the gift of God's beautiful creation, then that kind of joyful openness can be cultivated through the simple ceremony of a raised glass *or* an intricately told story of that raised glass. Stories can educate one's taste for the world; stories can witness the world's particular beauties in their uniquely achieved formal beauty. Their aesthetic tensions can express the unsentimental fact of human finitude as the infinite good of being the Creator's creature.

Updike's theology of sense is achieved in refined perceptions. Yet its aesthetic education is the hallmark of a Christian culture whose liturgy promotes the work of gratitude as humanity's highest flourishing. Gratitude is not natural for spirits too easily wearied by their bodies' failure to become a fantasy. For instance, when Marty Tothero, Rabbit Angstrom's high school basketball coach, confides his experience of disappointed middle-age life to his former star, Tothero's mistaken diagnosis is that there is a problem in the world's food supply: "You eat and eat and it's never the right food" (*Rabbit Angstrom* 43). Updike repeats the diagnosis two more times in the Rabbit series, in case we missed the first (734, 1054). Yet the ceremonial rite of Updike's full glass feeling and its theology of sense stand solid against such a conclusion. They quickly diagnose Tothero's problem as a deficiency in desire and a misunderstanding of the importance of gratitude for any meaningful conception of human experience. Raise your glass, Tothero, and wait a moment: toast before you drink and it tastes *better.* The reason people need ceremonies is to teach their bodies to sense the world in all the finitude of its created goodness, to know and savor the goodness of a God that, as Updike puts it in his memoirs, "gives reality its true flavor" (*Self-Consciousness* 233–34).

The next chapter turns to Rabbit's instinctual desire for reality's true flavor, his *lack* of truly Christian ceremonies, and his misguided attempts to listen to what Coach Tothero once told him was our only guide: the heart.

CHAPTER 4

Hearing

THE VERY FIRST sentences of *Rabbit, Run* associate sounds with bodies in motion: "Legs, shouts. The scrape and snap of Keds on loose alley pebbles seems to catapult their voices high into the moist March air blue above the wires" (*Rabbit Angstrom* 5). From the ground-level scrapes and snaps, those voices arc up through the air, and the basketball soon follows from Rabbit's hands, "whipping the net with a ladylike whisper" (6). Harry "Rabbit" Angstrom is unusually attentive to his sensations; whether he is playing basketball or walking down the street, he is "abnormally sensitive on the surface, as if his skin is thinking" (35). The things Rabbit hears, however, register far down below the surface. The net's "ladylike whisper" touches something in Rabbit: not only the feeling of accomplishment that might come with athletic prowess but a sense of the way things could—and should—be. When Rabbit tells the Reverend Eccles later in the novel, "I don't really have a plan. I'm sort of playing it by ear," he's not only admitting to his lack of calculation and tendency to follow wherever his heart might lead (90). He's also confessing his ear's intimate access to his heart; Rabbit's most spiritual sense is hearing.

Sounds lure him to long for something more, the more complete fulfillment he associates with grace. If, as I argued in the previous chapter, descriptions of tasting provide Updike with opportunities to demonstrate the goodness of the body's limitations, then his descriptions of hearing affirm the goodness of that body's deeper longings. To be graceful in his movements and to feel the grace of God are, for the most part, one and the same for him. The "motions of Grace" named in the book's epigraph from Pascal—"The motions of Grace, the hardness of the heart; external circumstances"—are as much spiritual grace as the fully human good of athletic grace. Later in life Rabbit will go so far as to connect his idea of sin with the lack of that athletic grace, reflecting to himself that he "doesn't blame people for many sins but does hate uncoördination, the root of all evil as he feels it, for without coördination there can be no order, no connecting" (664). Feats of coordination carry an aural grace, too. In one of *Rabbit, Run*'s especially poignant scenes Rabbit hits a perfect drive in a game of golf he plays with the Reverend Eccles, telling him that the drive's perfect arc was precisely what was missing in his relationship with Janice. "The sound" of the shot, however, "has a hollowness, a singleness he hasn't heard before" (115). The sound announces its flawlessness even before he can follow it with his eyes. That hollow singleness touches something inside Rabbit.

This association of graceful athletic motion with sound continues some pages after the opening scene when Rabbit, driving south after having left his wife and child, turns on the radio. The opening basketball game and this moment of driving are two of the novel's best-known scenes. Both scenes, however, render Rabbit's search for grace through the association of motion with his instinctive abilities, of "playing it by ear." Once a popular standard starts playing, then Rabbit begins to calm down from previously feeling cramped and anxious about his life. He sits back and "glides on down the twilight pike lefthanded," as if running the floor for a left-handed layup (22). As Michael Szalay argues, "Rabbit searches for a new body on the road" (138). For Szalay, that body is coded in racial stereotypes. During the drive South, Rabbit hears an essential purity in the radio's music—a "beautiful Negress" singing "Without a Song"—and falls prey to the hipster's fetishization of black bodies and the belief that black bodies are more authentic and more graceful than white ones (*Rabbit* 22). I will address the racial issues Szalay raises later in the chapter, but I point out here that Rabbit's need for what Szalay calls "authenticity" is also Updike's portrayal of the character's desire for a fuller, more happily embodied life (Szalay 139). That's what spirituality is in all the Rabbit novels: the fullness of embodied living. When Rabbit's old basketball coach Tothero urges him to do "what the heart commands" since the "heart is our only guide," Rabbit follows his heart in very, very physical ways (47). He leaves his wife to move in with a prostitute in search of the fulfillment that eludes him. In doing so, Rabbit follows his instincts. Sex and spirituality have equal representation in those instincts. Rabbit's "feeling that there is an unseen world is instinctive," and the fact that "more of his actions than anyone suspects constitute transactions with it" points both toward the grace of his golf drive and his sexual promiscuity (201). Yet Rabbit seems unable to pursue the invisible with anything like success, whether spiritually or physically. Instead, "every time in his life he's made a move toward it somebody has gotten killed" (767). Is Rabbit's spirituality downright evil?

While the previous chapters have addressed issues of affect, ontology, and habit alongside the sense experiences of touching, seeing, and tasting, this chapter unpacks the apparent contradiction between Rabbit's spiritual longings and his selfish actions through the ethical implications of Rabbit's tendency to "play it by ear." I argue that Updike's portrayal of what Rabbit hears provides a unique vantage for reconsidering the ethical value of empathy for postsecular aesthetics. Undoubtedly, Rabbit makes unethical choices throughout the series with Nietzschean abandonment. The most problematic charge against the novels, however, is not that Rabbit himself is selfish, racist, or misogynistic but that the novels' style and structure are unable to cultivate genuine experiences of difference. As Dorothy Hale has persuasively demonstrated, critical appreciation for the social value of the novel in general has long depended on its ability to provide readers with experiences of alterity (899). There are a variety of ways a novel does that, and getting inside Rabbit's head would be a shocking way to experience a different perspective for many readers. Yet Susan Keen has shown how critics often take Hale's point a step further, placing value in the novel's ability to provide virtual experiences of empathy (viii–ix). The four novels that make up *Rabbit Angstrom: The Four Novels* (the title of Knopf's Everyman's Library edition of all four novels in one volume) provide only a few such opportunities. Nevertheless, I want to read *Rabbit Angstrom* as challenging the ethics of empathy with its own narrative version of (what I will call) the ethics of peace.

In particular, I want to argue that Updike's postsecular aesthetics complicate the way we think about ethics. Finding something beautiful, as I argued in the second chapter, always includes a value judgment. Yet too often literary ethics are overly simplified to purely secular, rationalist forms of deliberation. That kind of simplification cannot understand Rabbit's strange mix of egoism and sensitive spirituality. One of the more useful points that Charles Taylor makes in *A Secular Age,* however, is that our notions of ethical behavior are wrapped up in a "three-cornered picture" (637). In contemporary society, a confusing mix of three different but internally coherent value systems motivates ethical prescriptions. There are

> secular humanists, there are neo-Nietzscheans, and there are those who acknowledge some good beyond life. Any pair can gang up against the third on some important issue. Neo-Nietzscheans and secular humanists together condemn religion and reject any good beyond life. But neo-Nietzscheans and acknowledgers of transcendence are together in their absence of surprise at the continued disappointments of secular humanism, together also in the sense that its vision of life lacks a dimension. In a third line-up, secular humanists and believers come together in defending an idea of the human good, against the anti-humanism of Nietzsche's heirs. (636–37)

Thinking about empathy in the midst of this three-cornered picture places the standards by which we judge literary ethics against the broader goals of these different philosophies. Taylor's point repeats one made earlier by the moral philosopher Alasdair MacIntyre's *Whose Justice? Which Rationality?* and *Three Rival Versions of Moral Inquiry.* Taylor's and MacIntyre's divisions into a "three-cornered picture" or "three rival versions" help clarify how ethical prescriptions for the work of the novel will necessarily be different according to their assumptions about the end goals of human action. Empathy, for example, is rarely as good as creative expression in the Neo-Nietzschean perspective, but it may be better in the secular humanist or religious perspective. This three-cornered picture offers an efficient way to identify the various ethical assumptions behind Rabbit's helter-skelter desires.

The contemporary importance of empathy and narcissism as ethical categories for the novel makes this three-corned picture even more relevant today. In recent books such as Leslie Jamison's *The Empathy Exams* (2014) and Kristen Dombech's *The Selfishness of Others* (2016), David Foster Wallace's critical dig against Updike has become a preoccupation. No doubt the presidency of Donald Trump has contributed to the cultural preoccupation with the perils of narcissism. While the ethical experience of empathy has its religious sources (e.g., the Good Samaritan), these conversations tend to assume its entirely secular application. Indeed, both Dombech and Jamison shirk religious convictions in their accounts of literary empathy. Functionally, this means that the "ethics" under discussion for the most part refer to only one corner of Taylor's three-cornered picture—the secular humanist's adaptation of Immanuel Kant's ethics. Like Kant's categorical imperative, Jamison and Dombech assume we should be empathetic because it's the right thing to do for anyone, anywhere, anytime. Whether this kind of ethical prescription is truly secular in the a-religious sense or not, it often ignores crucial aspects of the religious and Nietzschean sides of the three-cornered picture.

Furthermore, the either/or of the empathy-narcissism test for a novel's ethics is misleading. While welcoming the stranger and exhortations to neighborly care are key components of Christian teaching on love, the motivation for these actions comes from its Christology and ecclesiastical traditions. Empathy would be only one of a series of concerns, not the single driving factor. According to ethicist Stanley Hauerwas, Karl Barth played a decisive role in teaching contemporary Protestant ethicists to reason from within their own theological tradition. In opposition to Kant's idealization of (secular) rational deliberation, Barth "sought to do nothing less than displace human self-consciousness as the legitimating notion for the creation of ethics independent of God's revelation in Christ. By doing so he has returned theology to the presumption that there can be no 'ethics' separate from theology, particularly when theology is understood as an activity of the church" (Hauerwas 49). A truly postsecular approach to ethical criticism should open up a space for Hauerwas's insight that Christian ethics are most persuasive when they speak from their own theological tradition.

Nevertheless, theological ethics so construed has not had much of voice in postsecular criticism, despite the fact that narrative theology—Hauerwas's biggest contribution to the discipline—rose to prominence at the end of the twentieth century. In 2001 Hauerwas was famously dubbed "America's best theologian" by *Time* magazine, largely for his provocative insistence on the fairly pedestrian claim that theology takes the Christian story as its preeminent subject. While Updike never directly wrote about narrative theology, Barth's influence on his work has made it as much illustrations of narrative theology as Keirkegaardian existentialism (Boswell, *John Updike's Rabbit Tetralogy* 7). In fact, I will argue that Updike's insistence on a Christian conception of the "good" over the "right"—a key component of narrative theology's response to Kantian ethics—makes Rabbit Angstrom a crucial voice for thinking about postsecular literary ethics (see Hauerwas 71). In order to better understand how the Rabbit novels do that, this chapter turns to Patricia Highsmith's series of novels about Tom Ripley and their portrayal of a Nietzschean vision of the good alongside Rabbit Angstrom's explicitly religious account. Highsmith's best-known character is a celebrated example that demonstrates a number of affinities with Updike's skepticism toward the ethics of empathy and highlights the importance of understanding the different ethical traditions their work engages.

The five novels Highsmith wrote about Tom Ripley from 1955 to 1991, which critics aptly call the *Ripliad* (for the novels' *Iliad*-like celebration of violence), neatly run alongside the four novels Updike wrote about Rabbit Angstrom, from 1960 to 1990. Both series share similar Kierkegaardian-inspired themes, and both series have an epochal reach to them, covering the span of four decades. Both protagonists, too, have become Highsmith's and Updike's best-known characters, though Highsmith went so far as to occasionally sign her letters "Tom," a level of direct identification that Updike would have recoiled from with Rabbit. If Rabbit was Updike's "way in—a ticket to the America all around me" (*Rabbit Angstrom* vii), Ripley was the expatriate Highsmith's ticket *out*. Yet both characters appealed to middlebrow readers (Perrin 15). Perhaps the most important difference between them is that Ripley is a permanent outsider who creates his own inside, and Rabbit is a permanent insider who has felt outside ever since his high school basketball career ended. Ripley would have hated Rabbit, should the two have ever met—he left America to avoid such tasteless suburbanites. Rabbit, on the other hand, would have likely thought such a morose, queer fellow should either love America or leave it. Yet the two characters are equally notorious for their immorality. While Ripley murders, Rabbit is not entirely guilt-free of his daughter's death, not to mention the fact that he sleeps with his daughter-in-law. As much as Ripley is celebrated by the likes of Slavoj Žižek for his near-sociopathic tendencies, others denigrate Rabbit for his narcissism. Both are infamous examples of flagrantly immoral characters that the novelists, and their readers, nevertheless somehow enjoyed returning to novel after novel.

Another common trait between the two series is that music offers defining experiences to both Rabbit and Ripley—indeed, their idea of how they most want to live is wrapped up with what they listen to. The novels represent examples of a good life in the characters' attitudes toward music and other sounds. Those lives, however, are drastically different. For Rabbit, the theology of grace looms ever in the background; for Ripley, a Nietzschean vitalism. As exemplars of what Taylor thinks of as the religious and neo-Nietzschean corners, these two characters complete his three-cornered picture of contemporary moral discourse. Moreover, both displace the dominant role of reader-identification in the ethics of novel reading, and the role of empathy in defenses of the novel's social value. They offer instead a view of literary ethics that puts secular assumptions about human rationality and the cultural work of the novel in tension with alternative, postsecular ways of thinking about the novels and ethics—ones that rely less on visual metaphors of perspective and more on the aural experience of dissonance and harmony.

HARMONY

Not long after the basketball scene that opens *Rabbit, Run,* Rabbit decides to get in the car and leave town. His trip is unsuccessful, however, and he soon turns around to drive back to his hometown with the "soothing" "music on the radio" "mak[ing] a beam he infallibly flies in on [. . .] The last quarter of a basketball game used to carry him into this world; you ran not as the crowd thought for the sake of the score but for yourself, in a kind of idleness" (34). This "world" is an athlete's idyll: where the body's movements are effortlessly integrated into the game's shifting rhythms. The music he hears on the radio and the memory of basketball games go together as moments of feeling effortlessly in sync, moments of perfect coordination when Rabbit acts according to his instinct.

Updike uses Rabbit's sense of hearing throughout the *Rabbit Angstrom* tetralogy to indicate such moments of fulfillment. They signal Rabbit's intrinsic desire for a fuller experience of happiness, that state of flourishing the ancients called *eudemonia*. Yet while Aristotle thought such happiness came only to the disciplined and wise, Rabbit associates it with his body. In Updike's characteristic free indirect style he writes, "The body lacks voice to sing its own song" (73–74)—as if singing a song were the pure expression of what Rabbit's body sought in those basketball games, a melody for the joy the body experiences in graceful motion. That promise dogs Rabbit throughout the novels; four decades and four novels later he will die in search of it, once again on a basketball court.

The very next day after Rabbit feels like his body has found its song, however, he eats in a restaurant where "he can just make out a hint, coming it seems from the kitchen, of the jangling melody that lifted his spirits last night in the car" (54). The experience, and its barely audible hint, reminds him not only of the previous night but of that free and easy feeling of graceful perfection that he was searching for and still knows is out there. Again in *Rabbit Is Rich*, though the popular style has changed, the "radio is what he enjoys, gliding through Brewer with the windows up and locked and the power-boosted ventilation flowing through and the four corners of the car dinging out disco music as from the four corners of the mind's ballroom" (647). Listening inside his portable studio, the music envelops him, "fills him too full of pointless excitement. Some music does that" (651). Such pointless excitement is admittedly different from the fourth quarter feeling he felt from the radio in *Rabbit, Run*. Yet later it nonetheless sets "that hopeful center inside his ribs jingling" (869). It is music capable of "making the soul jingle" (870).

In *Rabbit at Rest* Rabbit's trip from Brewer, Pennsylvania, to the South is repeated, this time as an aging retiree's escape to his condo in Florida. "On the road again" is the narrator's arch allusion to the escape of his younger years, "with the radio again" (1451). And, "again," the radio has spiritual associations. When the announcer he happens to be listening to begins a barely coherent stream-of-consciousness riff Rabbit thinks, "This guy must think nobody is listening, gagging it up like this. Lonely in those radio studios, surrounded by paper coffee cups and perforated acoustic tiles. Hard to know the effect you're making. Hard to believe God is always listening, never gets bored" (1450). The moment provokes a question: Is God listening? If he is, what does he hear? Nothing too interesting, apparently. Rabbit begins to wonder how this music has kept even him interested. It occurs to Rabbit, as he drives on listening to the "music of your life, some of the announcers like to call it" (1467), that the "songs of his life were as moronic as the rock the brainless kids now feed on" (1468). It must not be the content that he loved—what was it? What was it about the music that pulled at his heart so strongly? It is the promise of perfect coordination.

The music on the car radio is not the only sound that Rabbit registers with such spiritual longing; the novels develop a variety of other sounds that bring him similar experiences. For instance, the different times he lies in bed listening to the rain hit the leaves of a copper-beech tree just outside the Springers' house. After Janice falls asleep "he lies awake listening to the rain, not willing to let it go, this sound of life" (734). And again, in *Rabbit at Rest*, when Nelson informs him that he had to have the old copper-beech cut down, "Harry couldn't argue, and couldn't tell the boy that the sound of the rain in that great beech had been the most religious experience of his life. That, and hitting a pure golf shot" (1277). The sound of the rain, like the basketball and the music of a car radio, provide Rabbit with religious experiences. The "pure golf shot" the much older Rabbit refers to is the moment from *Rabbit, Run* that I referred to earlier, when, after Eccles insists on knowing what "this thing that wasn't there" in his relationship with Janice actually is, Rabbit hits a perfect shot and shouts "That's *it*!" (114, 116). The thing that was missing is precisely that graceful, instinctual joy that listening to the rain or the radio, or playing basketball, gave him. The "sound of life."

The sense experience of hearing evokes the spiritual context in which Rabbit acts. Updike reveals something of his approach to these sounds in the Rabbit novels in an introduction he wrote for a collection of Karl Barth's essays on Mozart. Knowledge of Barth's daily ritual of listening to Mozart for an hour in the morning is now a commonplace in theological circles, so often has it been invoked to soften some wrongheaded caricature or another of Barth's reputation for being suspicious of human cultural achievements. Yet Updike's introduction reveals a less remarked aspect of Updike's work—its own theological approach to aural beauty. Updike asserts, "Mozart's music, for Barth, has the exact texture of God's world, of divine comedy" ("Foreword" 11). Rabbit's experience of the sounds of basketball and the radio, like Barth's Mozart, have the exact aural resonances of God's world, of divine comedy.

There are two specific reasons why this narrative arc of a divine comedy matters. First, Updike's affirmation of the body and the centrality of love in his conception of religious experience is perhaps best exemplified by Dante's *Divine Comedy*. That context matters again here insofar as Updike's belief in God's world as a divine comedy means that God is in the act of reconciling, restoring, and recreating the creatures who rebelled against him. Belief in this larger narrative context for the whole of creation means that all that is natural in God's world is not a part of that creaturely rebellion but fundamentally good. The first way that music in *Rabbit Angstrom* sounds like a divine comedy, then, is that it makes Rabbit aware of something else, something better, a grace-filled world where instinct and ethics work toward the same end.

Second, it means that music encourages Rabbit to look for that grace in the here and now of living. Updike closes his introduction to Barth's work on Mozart with the assertion that "Mozart's music, like the teeming drama of the Bible and like good crisis theology, gives us permission to live" while simultaneously affirming the difficult freedom in that world-affirming permission, since those "who have not felt the difficulty of living have no need of Barthian theology; but then perhaps they also have no ear for music" ("Foreword" 12). Rabbit has just such an ear. Isn't this precisely what he means when he claims to be "playing it by ear"? His ear for music has little to do with so-called music appreciation or understanding what precisely it is about Mozart's compositions that led Barth to his conclusion. Rather, Rabbit has an ear for music because he receives the knowledge it provides: that grace can be a fully physical experience. He feels in it permission to live.

Avis Hewitt has noted that in *Self-Consciousness* it's not only permission but an "obligation to live" (48). This "obligation to live" shouldn't be understood as moral permissiveness or unethical irresponsibility, which is always a possible misinterpretation of the Rabbit novels. I'll turn to such ethical concerns soon, but first: This obligation is also an aesthetic point about the relationship between theology and the arts. Beauty bears witness to the goodness of creation, to the glories of being alive. As such, it is inherently lovable. The scholar of theological aesthetics Hans Urs von Balthasar famously wrote, "Lovers are the ones who know most about God; the theologian must listen to them" (*Love Alone* 12). Expressing how to love the truly good is something the creative artist—the lover of beauty—can do in ways a theologian cannot. Aesthetic beauty has its spiritual lesson, and Updike's approach to Barth's writing on Mozart betrays his high view of what theology can learn from the creative artist's representations of beauty. The sounds of life are worth listening to.

Rabbit's unflappable cheerfulness throughout *Rabbit Angstrom* is Updike's own leitmotif for asserting the "divine comedy" at the heart of human experience. Rabbit memorably exclaims, in a fit of patriotic joy, "All in all this is the happiest fucking country the world has ever seen" (1387). The exclamation equally applies to Rabbit himself. When Lucy Eccles tells Rabbit she can't understand why her husband likes him so much, Rabbit merely responds, "I'm just lovable" (18). The short novella "Rabbit Remembered" (2000) corroborates his claim when it returns to the other characters of *Rabbit Angstrom* after Rabbit has died. What is it about Rabbit that the other characters remember? Mostly that he was happy and lovable. In a mixed review, his son Nelson remembers that his father "was narcissistically impaired. [. . .] He never grew up. [. . .] He was careless and self-centered, but he had his points. People liked being around him. He was upbeat. Since he never grew up himself, he could be good with children, even with me when I was little. The smaller they were, the better he related" (*Licks of Love* 248). This echoes Nelson's frustration with his father in *Rabbit Is Rich*, "That's what gets me, his happiness. He is so fucking *happy*!" (*Rabbit Angstrom* 741). The novella casts Rabbit's self-centered search for happiness in terms of the Dali Llama's spirituality, invoking Rabbit's abiding fascination with the figure. While the Rabbit novels are dotted throughout with references to him, *Rabbit Is Rich* treats the spirituality of Rabbit's happiness most thoroughly. With an allusion to "Long-Legged Fly," one of W. B. Yeats's most powerful poems on artistic creativity, Rabbit wonders "what it would be like to be the Dalai Lama. A ball on the top of its arc, a leaf on the skin of a pond. A water strider in a way is what the mind is like, those dimples at the end of their legs where they don't break the skin of the water quite" (830). So much hangs on that "quite." This facility between mind and matter, a unity of grace, motion, and infinite sensitivity, is the aesthetic relation that Updike posits as happiness. "Rabbit Remembered" ends with Nelson wryly quoting a line from the Dali Llama's book that haunts in its shallow vacuity: "The very motion of our life is towards happiness" (*Licks* 357). Rabbit's narcissism *may* be a child's innocent pleasure, and the Dali Llama's happiness *may* be pop psychology: It seems that happiness will not rise to the level of philosophy in Updike. And yet the Christian Updike *does* believe that the motion of the whole universe is towards happiness. A divine comedy.

That is precisely what Updike appreciates about Barth's writing on music. The Rabbit novels mirror that holistic, Christian narrative framework of divine comedy. They provide the narrative context for a Christian theology of the "permission to live." Take, for example, this footnote of Barth's from *Dogmatics* on how a musician can teach a theologian. Replace "Mozart" with "Updike," and the theological context of Rabbit's soul-jingling response to music becomes clear. Indeed, it more or less sums up the entirety of my argument about the theology of sense in Updike.

> Why is it possible to hold that Mozart has a place in theology, especially in the doctrine of creation [. . .]? It is possible to give him this position because he knew something about creation in its total goodness that neither the real fathers of the Church nor our Reformers, neither the orthodox nor Liberals, neither the exponents of natural theology nor those heavily armed with the Word of God, and certainly not the Existentialists, nor indeed any other great musicians before and after him, either know or can express and maintain as he did [. . .] He had heard, and causes those who have ears to hear, even to-day, what we shall not see until the end of time—the whole context of providence. As though in the light of this end, he heard the harmony of creation to which the shadow also belongs but in which the shadow is not darkness, deficiency is not defeat, sadness cannot become despair, trouble cannot degenerate into tragedy and infinite melancholy is not ultimately forced to claim undisputed sway. (III.3: 298)

The "harmony of creation to which the shadow also belongs but in which the shadow is not darkness." It is an excellent description of the daylight suffusing *Rabbit Angstrom*. The jaunty young father who abandons his family, and the aging father who sleeps with his daughter-in-law, cast dark shadows over the "harmony of creation."

This is no small part of Rabbit Angstrom's moral context, nor is it a marginal tangent in Barth's *Dogmatics*. Barth puts Mozart's insight into his theological anthropology in his notion of "gladly," a definition of the human that betrays Barth's distance from the ethics of secular humanism and completes the Christian narrative context of Rabbit's permission to live. Barth writes, "In his essence, his innermost being, his heart, [man] is only what he is gladly. If we do not speak primarily of what he is gladly, we do not speak of his essence, of himself" (III.2: 267). The human creature is not in essence a linguistic creature or a rational creature. The human creature is essentially a creature who is glad in his love and praise. Updike portrays in Rabbit, a character who "has no reflective content; it's all instinct," precisely that glad essence (465). Rabbit's cheerful happiness, like Mozart's music, offers an image of what the theological anthropology of "gladly" looks like. When Rabbit says he plays it by ear, he means that he hears music in the very heart of it all—in the rhythmic "*thorrumph thorrympth*" of his own heart (1478). He can hear that fundamental movement of the universe: a divine comedy moving toward happiness.

What hearing in the Rabbit novels illustrates about Updike's theology of sense is that Rabbit's experience of beauty in music is an experience of the created order. Grace is not opposed to the created order but is its fulfillment. When he feels happiness enter his ears like the happiness he feels during a basketball game, that feeling expresses the gladness at the heart of human existence. Once that is clear, his "narcissism" begins to have a theological context in which deviating from that essential gladness is more than mere selfishness: It is not only acting on selfish instincts but is what Christians call *sin*, a rebellion against grace and its place in the created order as such. Rabbit is not merely unethical; Rabbit is a sinner.

DISSONANCE

The harmony of creation promised in the radio's popular standards is not all that Rabbit hears in the novels. He hears the echoes of his sin, too. My account thus far of the way music draws Rabbit toward the promise of this "gladly" is undoubtedly too narrow for the scattered tableau of human desire in *Rabbit Angstrom*. He is alert to dissonant sounds as well; as he grumbles in *Rabbit at Rest*, "Life is noise" (1349). Noise is a part of what Rabbit hears, and I will show how that noise relates to the harmonious context as sin—what Barth calls the *shadow* in Mozart's glad music.

Right after that opening scene of the basketball game, Rabbit runs home to find the door locked: "In fitting the little key into the lock his hand trembles, pulsing with unusual exertion, and the metal scratches" (*Rabbit Angstrom* 8). The domestic scene, unlike the basketball court, requires "exertion" and registers a dissonant scratching sound instead of the basketball net's "ladylike whisper." His wife Janice is inside watching TV and drinking an old-fashioned, and it bothers him that the door was locked or, more probably, that she didn't open it for him. After coming in, he "presses the door shut and it clicks but then swings open again an inch or two. Locked doors. It rankles: his hand trembling in the lock like some old wreck and her sitting in here listening to the scratching" (9). The sound of the metal scratching on metal bothers Rabbit; the idea of someone listening to him gracelessly falter bothers him even more. The sound makes him feel ungainly, "like some old wreck," and that is precisely what he then sees Janice as—an old wreck who, just "yesterday, it seems to him, stopped being pretty" (8). The discord between his idea of himself and the reality of his scratching key testifies to the domestic discord between his idea of what their marriage should be and the reality of what it is. All too aware of the gap between what he heard on the radio running from Janice and the irritating scratch that keeps him locked in with her, he tells the Reverend Eccles in *Rabbit, Run* that their relationship is "decidedly second-rate." Rabbit explains, "I once did something right. I played first-rate basketball. I really did. And after you're first-rate at something, no matter what, it kind of takes the kick out of being second-rate. And that little thing Janice and I had going, boy, it was really second rate" (*Rabbit Angstrom* 92).

The sound bothers him, then, not only because it makes him feel ungraceful; it makes him feel trapped in something "second-rate" and, faintly, guilty for the failure. This guilt becomes evident and is even shared when the two hear the name of God. Having come into their apartment and begun to badger Janice with his resentments, he is interrupted by the sound of the TV. She is watching the Mouseketeers, and Jimmie, the "big Mouseketeer" warbles, "proverbs tell us what to do" (10). He continues, "'Know Thyself, a wise old Greek once said. Know Thyself. Now what does this mean, boys and girls? It means be what you are. [. . .] God doesn't want a tree to be a waterfall or a flower a stone. God gives to each one of us a special talent.' Janice and Rabbit become unnaturally still; both are Christians. God's name makes them feel guilty" (10). Hearing the name of God, like scratching metal, grates at their conscience. They feel guilty—toward each other as much as before God. They know their relationship is, as Rabbit says, "second-rate." Sin, in the Augustinian sense of privation (addressed in chapter 2), is second-rate—it's the degradation of the purposes of a good, first-rate creation. It *is* uncoordination, of a kind. Rabbit and Janice's marriage is second-rate for a variety of reasons, but the context in which those reasons become intelligible in *Rabbit Angstrom* is that their marriage is meant to be first-rate, to be an expression of humanity's essential gladness, and their failure to experience it as such is because of sin's grip on them. The problem is not in the institution of marriage or in the pleasures of sex; it's in their long-built-up habits of settling for the second-rate happiness that Christianity calls sin.

The domestic dissonance of the key's grating sound in the lock is repeated throughout the novels. At the beginning of the sequel, *Rabbit Redux,* it appears again, but this time from the other side of the door in a different house. Janice has left Rabbit this time, and Rabbit is momentarily caught in an embrace with the mother of his son's friend. She wants the kiss more than he, however, and he can only feel that "she has wrapped them in a clumsy large ball of darkness" (*Rabbit Angstrom* 361). Then: "Something scratches on the ball. A key in a lock" (361). Again, it's a dissonant sound associated with domestic fracture. Here, however, it separates Rabbit from an unwanted kiss, and it is his son and his son's friend who enter and interrupt with their whining, adding a whole other layer of aural anxiety to the scene. Like the name of God spoken by the television, here again guilt has a sound. Later, it comes after returning home from a former lover's funeral in *Rabbit at Rest.* "He works the key in the lock—maddening, the scratchy way the key doesn't fit in the lock instantly, it reminds him of something from way back, something unpleasant that hollows his stomach, but what?—and shoves the door open with his shoulder and reaches the hall phone just as it's giving what he knows will be its dying ring" (*Rabbit Angstrom* 1426). The hollow in his stomach and the ringing phone: guilt. He recognizes the sound, but his consciousness shrinks from admitting to the guilt.

Guilt comes through the second-rateness of these dissonant sounds as much as grace comes through the harmony Rabbit hears in his instinctual athletic grace. It comes through phones and children's voices and duties that Rabbit cannot recognize as the disciplines just as necessary for a first-rate marriage as for a first-rate basketball game. He has an instinctual sensitivity to beauty but no accompanying ceremonies to instruct in its virtues. So when he first runs from Janice, phones represent to him the net his social world has cast in order to trap him, "a net of telephone calls and hasty trips, trails of tears and strings of words, white worried threads shuttled through the night and now faded but still existent, an invisible net overlaying the steep streets" (37). This net of phone wires still has him trapped near the end of *Rabbit at Rest*. His children, too, produce grating sounds that make him feel guilt, which are rendered as sounding a lot like a key in a lock. His newborn daughter, Rebecca, who will drown before the end of the novel, lies in her "crib all afternoon and makes an infuriating noise of strain, *Hnnnnnah ah ah nnnnh,* a persistent feeble scratching at some interior door" (208). The noise makes Nelson "whiny," too. And in fact, even the adult Nelson tends to whine when talking to Rabbit (1417, 1488). Yet these dissonant sounds never produce enough guilt in Rabbit for him to see in their occasions a path toward becoming a better husband or father. After Janice confronts him for having slept with their daughter-in-law and tells him she will never forgive him, he responds with a disbelieving, "Really?" (1443). The callous, infuriating response is only one of many reasons readers find Rabbit so morally repulsive and Updike's style of narration lacking in a moral center. The way Updike uses dissonant sounds to elicit ultimately ineffectual guilt poses the problem of *Rabbit Angstrom*'s lack of ethical resolution and its disregard of novelistic empathy.

Martha Nussbaum has distinguished herself as the most prominent—and prolific—proponent of the novel genre's empathetic experiences. Yet it must also be noted that her work has tended to fall squarely in the secular humanist corner of Taylor's three-cornered picture. *Love's Knowledge* (1990) and *Poetic Justice* (1995) argued for the unique habits of thinking that literature—especially the novel—cultivate in order to achieve an imminent human good. According to Nussbaum, "literary works" are defined as such according to the degree to which "they promote identification and sympathy in the reader" (*Poetic Justice* 5). To be literary, for Nussbaum, a novel creates a certain level of identification in the reader with the characters. Nussbaum thinks that the novel "leads [readers] into certain postures of the mind and heart and not others" through those experiences of identification, particularly the kinds of empathetic "postures" peculiar to the health of democratic society (2). And the novel promotes them above all other forms of either education or entertainment: "The novel is a living form and in fact still the central morally serious yet popularly engaging fictional form of our culture" (6). That sentence was published a quarter-century ago, but Nussbaum has continued to insist on this in recent work, as exemplified in her reading of *Cry, the Beloved Country* (Paton 1948) in her *Anger and Forgiveness* (2016). With Updike's reputation for patriotic causes (from his support for the postal service to the Vietnam War to the election of our first black president), it seems like this vision of novel reading is precisely what he would endorse for his readers, where the novel can cultivate the empathetic virtues a diverse democracy needs. Rabbit would have appreciated being a part of such a patriotic cause, no doubt.

It is difficult to make such a case, however. To Updike, such projects break faith not only with his aesthetic principles (literary modernism's suspicion of reducing aesthetics to ethics) but also with his religious conviction that such moralistic thinking ultimately misses the mark on both the novel's social value and the values that define a good society. No novel will save the world. In an essay on how Updike draws on the Lutheran tradition in his fiction, Darrell Jodock observes that "the Lutheran tradition, for better or worse, has been non-moralistic. According to its diagnosis of the human condition, the fundamental problem is not human behavior in the sense that changing behavior alone will accomplish much" (127). Sin is the problem, and only grace can solve it. "We're all trash, really," Rabbit reflects at one point. "Without God to lift us up and make us into angels we're all trash" (*Rabbit Angstrom* 1362). The novels in *Rabbit Angstrom* make more of recognizing God's role in the redemption of his creation than affirming any specific set of moral norms.

Yet this isn't simply a question of Updike's Lutheran view of the fallen will's capacities. Updike doesn't eschew ethics for heartfelt evangelism; far from it. Furthermore, he would likely agree with Nussbaum that novels are "the central morally serious yet popularly engaging fictional form in our culture." Updike once characterized his writing as staging "moral debates with the reader," and I think *Rabbit Angstrom* morally serious (Plath 50). Rather than asserting that Updike has no interest in morality, or even the importance of empathy in the novel, it is a question of the human good that morally serious novels celebrate. Nussbaum assumes that ultimate human good is to be fostered by democratic feelings and that novels foster those feelings. The fact that the Rabbit novels offer a different answer—that grace is the preeminent good—should not disqualify them from moral seriousness.

For instance, Rabbit has a strong sense of duty and moral obligation toward his country. He launches patriotic, even nationalistic, sallies at other characters throughout *Rabbit Redux* and *Rabbit Is Rich*. Some of the sounds Rabbit hears in those novels remind him of the tensions pulling at that beloved country's social fabric. The sound of hammering he hears throughout *Rabbit Is Rich* is an example. It is a persistent background noise that, like the scratch in the lock, grates at Rabbit (*Rabbit Angstrom* 710, 765). Keeping in line with the spiritual resonance that sound carries, the hammering makes him think of the biblical allusion in Oliver Wendell Holmes's line, "Build thee more stately mansions, O my soul." At the same time, however, it unsettles him insofar as a lesbian couple owns the neighboring house that is its source. After Rabbit and Janice come back from their son Nelson's wedding, Rabbit announces to the neighbor who has been hammering, "My son got married today."

> His butch neighbor blinks and then calls back, "Good luck to her."
> "Him."
> "I meant the bride."
> "O.K. I'll tell her."
> [. . .] What he can't figure out about these butch ladies is not why they don't like him but why he wants them to, why just the distant

> sound of their hammering has the power to hurt him, to make him feel excluded. (845)

Does the sound of industrious women make him feel excluded? Or is it the sexual exclusion he feels from lesbian desire, as if his strongest asset—his insatiable sexual appetite—is suddenly no longer relevant? More likely it is simply that he cannot conceive of himself as anything but innately lovable, a quality that probably inspires his neighbor's arch comment on the new bride's undertaking. He can only imagine a country with him and his own sense of normalcy at its heart. So he responds to their presence by feeling excluded, threatened.

Would a different response to "these butch ladies" be more productive of democratic feelings? Or, for that matter, a better model of the ethical work of the novel? Would Updike be a more responsible novelist if he gave the reader access to the thoughts and feelings of the woman hammering rather than only the white, heterosexual, male Rabbit's thoughts? The fact is that it is questionable to what extent novels actually do increase one's ability to empathize in the way that Nussbaum suggests. As inspiring as "the widely promulgated 'empathy-altruism' hypothesis" may be, Suzanne Keen finds "the case for altruism stemming from novel reading inconclusive at best and nearly always exaggerated in favor of the beneficial effects of novel reading" (vii). In *Empathy and the Novel* Keen examines Nussbaum's claims in light of recent work in neuroscience and psychological testing and finds little evidence for concluding that novel reading directly translates into the kinds of political empathy Nussbaum celebrates. Critics who have taken issue with this "empathy-altruism hypothesis" fall into two different categories for Keen: "While *failed empathy* critics lament the inefficiency of shared feelings in provoking action that would lead to positive social or political change, *false empathy* critics emphasize the self-congratulatory delusions of those who incorrectly believe that they have caught the feelings of suffering others from a different culture, gender, race, or class" (159). There are more reasons why the empathy-altruism hypothesis might be misguided, to which I'll turn eventually, but suffice it to say that Updike's

Rabbit novels include pieces of both the failed and false empathy critiques. Their Lutheran roots offer little hope for moral engineering, and the scene with the lesbian neighbor exemplifies their wariness to cross the lines of genuine difference. While Updike is suspicious of fiction's ability to cultivate empathy through its representational content, his contemporary Patricia Highsmith offers an even more thoroughgoing critique of empathy and the promise of reader-identification in her series of novels about Tom Ripley.

Highsmith's Tom Ripley is nothing less than a criminal and a murder. Yet he is a sane, refined, and socially successful one who resents the tasteless vulgarity of the Mafia. Though Rabbit never commits outright murder, Ripley shares Rabbit's constitutional disregard for ethical responsibility. Yet he is perhaps most unlike Rabbit in that sexual desires have nothing to do with this disregard. Ripley seems to lack sexual desire altogether. This lack, which Slavoj Žižek has found especially provocative, is aptly foiled by Rabbit's excessive, uncontrolled desires. Žižek once began a book review effusing over Patricia Highsmith: "For me, the name 'Patricia Highsmith' designates a sacred territory: she is the One whose place among writers is that which Spinoza held for Gilles Deleuze (a 'Christ among philosophers')" (13). This sacred status is largely due to the "inhuman core" that Žižek finds in Highsmith's most famous and professed favorite character (13). Ripley casually sidesteps all humanist ethical expectations about what it means to be morally responsible. According to Žižek, "What is so disturbing about him is that he seems to lack even an elementary moral sense: in daily life, he is mostly friendly and considerate, and when he commits a murder, he does it with regret, quickly and as painlessly as possible, in the way one performs any unpleasant but necessary task" (14). Ripley is not evil. To call him evil would place him within the moral spectrum of good and evil, which Highsmith assiduously avoids doing. Instead, this inhuman void at the center of Ripley's character is, for Žižek, yet another parable of the antihumanist subject in its Lacanian guise. His Highsmith lays bare the abyss at the heart of modern subjectivity, sneering at the idea of a self as the stable locus of sentiment, truth, meaning, or morality. Highsmith herself once reported to a friend, "If I were to relax and become human," which for her means to stop writing, "I should not be able to bear my life" (Schenkar 343). Ripley is not immoral but inhuman.

Other characters complain that Rabbit has an "uncontrolled excess" of feeling, but Highsmith's barely human Ripley is clearly guilty of lacking much feeling at all. "All right, he may not be queer," a character in *The Talented Mr. Ripley* quips about Tom. "He's just a nothing, which is worse. He isn't normal enough to have any kind of sex life" (*Talented* 118). Ripley's lack of sexual desire repulses easy identification as much as Rabbit's excess of it does. This lack of reader-identification was intentional on Updike's part, who claims in his introduction to the tetralogy that "my intention was never to make him—or any character—lovable" (*Rabbit Angstrom* xx). Highsmith, too, thought little of the idea. "If there must be reader-identification, a term I am rather tired of," she once wrote in a manual on how to write for plot, "then provide the reader with a lesser character or two (preferably one who is not murdered by the hero-psychopath) with whom he can identify" (*Plotting* 47). Highsmith makes little effort to hide her contempt for the expectation that novels should school their readers in empathetic identification.

Ripley offers very few moments for reader-identification. Though he is prone toward self-pity in the first novel, Ripley rarely feels any genuine affection for anyone else and quickly dismisses feelings of pity for himself—or anyone—as foolish. In the later novels he respects and enjoys his wife's company, but it would be a stretch to say he ever expresses genuine love for her. As a murderer, however, he seems to neither take devilish pleasure in the killings nor feel anything like guilt about them. He is not hideous villain. He is charming and polite but far from calculating. In general, his approach is to wing it, waiting to see if violence will be necessary. Like Rabbit's need to play it by ear, Ripley relies on instinct. "Something always turned up. That was Tom's philosophy," as Highsmith lets her readers know early in the first of the five novels (*Talented* 17). Calculation is a failure in taste for Tom; it lacks the spontaneity of creativity.

Above all, music prompts Ripley's creative impulses but never occasions feelings of religious longing. Ripley listens to music for the moods and ideas its formal structure suggests to him. He listens not to set his soul ajingle but to bathe himself in its soothing or strengthening qualities. If Rabbit listens for the grace of his essential "gladly," Ripley listens for yet one more chance of asserting himself, of enjoying recreation, and so on. Where Rabbit hears grace in the created order, Ripley hears an order to create. In the second novel of the *Ripliad—Ripley Under Ground—*Ripley begins an underground operation that forges the paintings of the recently deceased painter, Derwatt. When he needs to find the presence of mind and courage to see his forgery scheme through, Ripley turns to music (not the paintings he so loves) to inspire him for another impersonation. This time it's the artist Derwatt (not the previous novel's Dickie Greenleaf). When Ripley arrives to impersonate Derwatt for a police investigator, Ripley immediately asks for his friend Jeff to shut off whatever it was he was playing and put Mendelssohn's *A Midsummer Night's Dream* on the record player instead. Jeff confesses to not having a recording of it, and Ripley sends him out to buy one: "Can you get it? That's what I'm in the mood for. It inspires me, and I need inspiration" (*Under Ground* 214). Once Jeff returns, the "music began—rather loud. Tom smiled. It was his music. An audacious thought, but this was the time for audacity" (214). Ripley's response to the music is to feel it and to turn its power toward his own creative ends. Unlike Rabbit, desire plays no part in his response to the music. While the magical transfigurations at the heart of Shakespeare's play are apropos for Tom's impending impersonation, it is the music that inspires him. Something bold in the romance of it all prompts his commensurate audacity.

In addition to audacity, Ripley also values the sense of wholeness that Barth found in Mozart. There is a rigor in its order. Earlier in the novel, Tom

> put on some music. He chose jazz. It was not good, not bad jazz, and, as he had noticed in other crucial moments in his life, the jazz did nothing for him. Only classical music did something—it soothed or it bored, gave confidence or took confidence quite away, because it had order, and one either accepted that order or rejected it. (*Under Ground* 188)

How different this is to Rabbit's reaction to "Without a Song." The music does not enter Ripley as it does Rabbit. It doesn't inspire a longing for transcendence. No deeper authenticity or freedom hides in the jazz. To the contrary, the classical order inspires Ripley to respond more precisely to the needs of the moment. Visiting the Mozart Museum in Salzburg later in *Ripley Under Ground,* Tom cannot help but, "as always," being "awed by Mozart" (245). Mozart's pure affirmation of life—that "obligation to live"—inspires in Ripley an obligation to create.

Ripley is driven by a belief that life should be spontaneous, creative. Whatever seeks to drain life of its risks drains life of its essential vitality and thereby enervates human experience. For Ripley, the ultimate good is reached not through cultivating democratic emotions but through creating new experiences (which democratic feelings can foster, but not necessarily). Highsmith does not write novels to offer moments of recognition. The empathetic experiences of a novel are subservient to its creative ends. As with Updike, the question is not whether a character or even a narrative structure is empathetic or not; at issue is what the novel values as good. As Tom values the possibilities music inspires, so Highsmith values the forms of life that her novels imagine.

POLYPHONY

I close this chapter showing how the narrative structure of the Rabbit novels points toward an ethics of peace. What Rabbit hears stirs up a sense of longing for a fuller contentment. Whether what he hears makes him feel graceful or guilty, excluded or excited, it puts him into motion on a quest for fulfillment. He is a sinner in search of grace, not a bad person in need of self-betterment through novelistic empathy. His spiritual quest has an internal dialectic to it in which both trying to escape to a better life and feeling overwhelmed at the blessing of his own life are experiences of spiritual longing. Yet that longing is not a purely private experience, since his leaving and staying is bound up in a net of social relations. Recall the net of telephone wires. His community is connected at the ear, weaving a net that, unlike the basketball net's ladylike whisper, is full of anxiety. Others, however, like Ruth Leonard, the prostitute he moves in with, have voices that reach out and draw him on. Rabbit feels how her "using his own name enters his ears with unsettling warmth" (*Rabbit Angstrom* 60). That warmth unsettles him into motion in his quest for the pleasure it promises. Rabbit's relationship with others is always tinged with an awareness of their ability either to enhance that feeling of fullness that basketball was for him, or to hamper it. The novels point toward how those relationships might be thought of in ways other than obligation—namely, as fulfillment and peace.

Take, for example, Rabbit's attitude toward the black characters of *Rabbit Redux*. That novel is about Rabbit staying put while Janice runs out on him. Yet it is also a novel about learning to listen to the other side of the culture war. Rabbit invites a young, white, liberal waif (Jill) and her black, Fanon-quoting friend (Skeeter) to live with him. Much of the novel consists of Rabbit sitting and listening to Skeeter pontificate; what he hears on the news also arouses a certain level of guilt in him. In one of the novel's more poignant scenes, Rabbit decides to meet a black coworker for drinks one evening. The white, patriotic Rabbit listens closely to the sounds around him on his walk over to the bar, "through the dulling summer light and the sounds of distant games, of dishes rattled in kitchen sinks, of television muffled to a murmur mechanically laced with laughter and applause, of cars driven by teenagers laying rubber and shifting down" (363). As if the all-American pastiche were not enough, he stops into "Burger Bliss" and orders a "double cheeseburger with an American flag stuck into the bun" (363).

Once he enters the bar, he hears echoes of all this in the songs from the thirties and forties that his coworker's friend Babe sings, "lyrics born in some distant smoke, decades ago when Americans moved within the American dream, laughing at it, starving on it, but living it, humming it, the national anthem everywhere [. . .] Here it all still was, in the music Babe played, the little stairways she climbed and came tap-dancing down, twinkling in black, and there is no other music, not really" (372). For Rabbit, even though he is a white man uncomfortably trying to listen to a black man's account of their very different experiences of American prosperity, this music is cast as music itself, music's purest expression. All other forms of music he's experienced flow from these primal melodies stashed away in his deepest sense of self. Whether it is Babe's skills, or the joint he's just taken a few hits from, or the music itself, "Rabbit is lost" in the music (373). Rabbit's ears connect him to his neighborhood, to his country, and even let him lose himself in this bar full of people so different from himself. The sounds he hears shape his sense of belonging just like the sound of the key in the lock makes him feel unappreciated or the hammering makes him feel excluded. Yet with Babe's music there is also something else: fear.

> Into the mike that is there no bigger than a lollipop she begins to sing, sings in a voice that is no woman's voice at all and no man's, is merely human, the words of Ecclesiastes. A time to be born, a time to die. A time to gather up stones, a time to cast stones away. Yes. The Lord's last word. There is no other word, not really. Her singing opens up, grows enormous, frightens Rabbit with its enormous black maw of truth yet makes him overjoyed that he is here; he brims with joy, to be here with these black others, he wants to shout love through the darkness of Babe's noise to the sullen brother [across from him]. He brims with this itch but does not spill. (373)

We see here again Szalay's point that Rabbit hears something truly authentic in her black voice. So authentic that it becomes "merely human." Yet whatever joy and love he now feels while *hearing* her sing, when Rabbit first entered the bar, he felt quite differently *seeing* so many black faces. It was not a "black maw of truth" he feared but black bodies. "Black to him is just a political word but these people really are, their faces shine of blackness turning as he enters, a large soft white man in a sticky gray suit. Fear travels up and down his skin, but the music of the great green-and-mauve-glowing jukebox [. . .] slides on, and the liquid of laughter and tickled muttering resumes flowing; his entrance was merely a snag" (364). As connected as he might feel to the music he hears, the stark visual difference of skin color makes him self-conscious and afraid. The voice may *sound* merely human, but Rabbit *sees* the stark differences between them.

This representation of racial difference is inseparable from Rabbit's spiritual quest insofar as Babe's singing represents the promise of an authentic experience of life, of fulfillment, but the black bodies he sees are a guilty reminder of how far he is from having it. The fear their bodies inspire is also a species of guilt that nags at Rabbit's sense of self-assurance and white privilege. *Rabbit, Run* establishes Rabbit's self-centeredness, both by his actions and by other characters' observations—such as Eccles telling Rabbit, "You're monstrously selfish. You're a coward. You don't care about right or wrong; you worship nothing except your own worst instincts" (115). But Rabbit's response in that novel was "If you have the guts to be yourself [. . .] other people'll pay your price" (129). There is in *Rabbit Redux,* however, a more explicit framing of Rabbit's selfishness against the background of racial politics. Rabbit begins to realize that not just someone but a whole group of people have been paying the price for the privileges of his whiteness. In the moment he enters the bar he sees what he didn't want to hear, and he spends much of the rest of the novel listening to others and trying to reckon with that fear he feels. Indeed, late in life, in *Rabbit at Rest,* he comes to the realization, "There's more to being a human being than having your own way. Fact is, it has come to Rabbit this late in life, you don't have a way apart from what other people tell you [. . .] Your life derives, and has to give" (1460).

None of these realizations, however, promotes any truly empathetic identification with the other characters or even opens the reader up to such an experience of them. Instead, Updike incorporates those real differences into a single song, a single word: "There is no other music, not really" and there "is no other word, not really." Yet the racial difference is far from erased; the visual description of black and white is still present, and the reader has access only to Rabbit's thoughts. Yet in the sounds of the song Rabbit hears something graceful, the "Lord's last word," that he feels connects him with everyone else at the table. The aural pleasure to be had, the feelings of fear and joy incited, are part of a spiritual longing for a fuller friendship that the scene enshrines at the center of it.

The correlation of the visual differences of color with the shared aural space of the song is no coincidence. The sounds of *Rabbit Ang-*

strom offer something different from an ethical perspective. Perspective is a visual experience, but sound opens up a different kind of shared experience. What if we think of Rabbit's selfish need for freedom in terms of the experience of sound this scene opens? Instead of the perspectival switch that empathy implies, does the shared sound-space of the ears offer another way of thinking about ethics? The preponderance of visual metaphors for ethical thought is something that Updike's aural attunement can help ameliorate: in particular, how the novel posits the sense of creaturely purpose that the experience of music represents for Rabbit—the grace that differentiates Christianity's version of the good—as an alternative to the ethics of empathy. For instance, remember that when Rabbit walks into the bar, he hears the music, the laughter, and the muttering all at once. Several distinctly different sounds occupy the same moment in time, whereas inside the bar the different bodies occupy their own discrete space. We can hear distinct sounds at the same time that do not cancel each other out but remain distinct. Perspective, on the other hand, implies a single place in space, which is much more difficult for three-dimensional bodies to share (Begbie 160–61). It is this distinct aural coexistence, particularly in its use of dissonance and harmony, that *Rabbit Angstrom* demonstrates—not only in its attention to hearing but also in the layering of its narrative context within the narrative of divine comedy. The social space inside the bar is defined more by this simultaneous layering of sound than by visual perspectives.

When Rabbit listens to Babe's music, for instance, the novel provides for us several different layers of context. First, there is the racial tension. Second, we know Rabbit is there because his wife has left him and his coworker is trying to provide a distraction. Both of these points are key to the story. But then we also know that *Rabbit, Run* has a passage about another black woman singing and that it, too, has a deeply spiritual effect on him. Another novel is being repeated in this narrative context. I am not making yet another point about literature and intertextuality here. Rather, the narrative context I've been tracing throughout this chapter is that when Rabbit is moved by music, he is drawn into a spiritual longing that the novel makes sense of through its theology of sense. It draws on the Christian story, which asserts that the good creation has fallen, was then saved, and will be fully restored in a new creation—a divine comedy where the final scene enshrines peace. The way in which the novel bears witness to the good of human life is intelligible only in light of that story—neither the secular ethics of empathy nor the Nietzschean celebration of life as a vital force can explain the ethical framework of the novel, because neither of them makes use of the unique conception of the good on which Updike is drawing.

This insistence on the validity of its extratextual religious narratives is *Rabbit Angstrom*'s key contribution to any conversation about the ethics of the novel in postsecular studies. The novels it collects provide a powerful answer to the question lurking behind much of the celebration of the ethics of empathy of the novel: Why bother reading novels at all? Why study them? This book proposes that Updike's theology of sense offers a way of thinking about reading as offering styles and patterns for conceiving aesthetic experience. I doubt Updike's books will make you more empathetic, but they're still worth reading. Why? Because of how they encourage their reader to fall in love with the goodness of creation and to reflect on the meaning of beauty for human life. Reading *Rabbit Angstrom* may not make readers more empathetic people, but it can renew one's attention to the senses and it can help us rethink the overarching narratives that inform how we think about bodies. It provides models for thinking about genuine, peaceful social relations grounded in fulfilled gratitude. Moreover, as I argue in the next chapter, reading through the catalog of vivid sense experiences Updike describes can make us aware of the multitude of good things that much of American culture seeks to stifle.

CHAPTER 5

Smelling

"THE ACT OF SEEING is itself glorious, and of hearing," Updike pauses to reflect in *Self-Consciousness,* only to finish with "and feeling, and tasting" (247). It is a typical celebration of the senses for Updike, but he only names four. On the next page, he recounts how he went to his wife to ask which one he was forgetting.

> "Smell," she said, when I had named my four. She was in the bathtub, up to her neck in bubbles, and though the bathroom smelled nicely of vitamin-enhanced soap I was not sorry I had suppressed "smell," since of the five senses it delivers most unpleasantness to us, and least well illustrates the point I was trying to make. When I stopped smoking, a whole unwelcome new world of odors came upon me, of dead rats in the wall and what people had eaten for lunch hours before. When I get out of bed in the morning, my own smell surprises me: stale flesh, warmed over. (248)

Smell is not glorious; the other senses may channel praiseworthy experiences, but smell, for Updike, seems to deal mostly in death.

Even the scent of "vitamin-enhanced soap" is little more than an attempt to cover over that other scent of "stale flesh." Rarely does Updike's work register a scent outside of this duality of pleasantly artificial or naturally unpleasant. In Updike's *Seek My Face,* the painter Hope Chafetz likens genuine artistic creativity with the ability to sense a certain "*rottenness* in things" (41). The true artist must have a good nose as well as good eyes. "It's this nose for the rotten," she ventures, "that takes the sensitivity, and the courage" (42). Smell, however, is key to Updike's theology of sense insofar as his writing has the sensitivity and the courage to think about why living bodies, and especially aging bodies, often smell bad.

In traditional aesthetic discourse, smell, one of the "lower" haptic senses, is not considered open to beauty. Smell may immediately please or repel, but it does not teach us like other sense experiences of the beautiful. Yet for Updike, smells—like any other experiences of beauty—help to cultivate desire and disgust. In Updike's writing, one of the ways we fail to appreciate the beauty of the human body, even feel contempt for it, is in our disdain for its smell. His representations of American mass-produced goods often contain a muted repugnance at their sterility. The early period of his work saw an enormous shift in how Americans thought of personal hygiene—the innovations of germ theory receded to new forms of marketing goods meant to increase personal health and beauty. The body was not so much cleaned as embalmed with increasingly potent new deodorants and mouthwashes. One of Updike's characters in his 1978 novel, *The Coup,* bemoans how Americans "make deodorants to mask their God-given body scents" (253). Another character in that same novel, a drugstore salesman, wryly observes while encouraging the purchase of some deodorant and mouthwash, "God sees the soul; men smell the flesh" (240). While critical questions about the human body are now being asked in new ways with the advances of biotechnology and the various theoretical discourses circulating around the term "posthuman," Updike was prescient in probing how the postwar economy's emerging consumer culture stoked an implicit contempt for the body's limitations.

Yet he was also apt to show how American Christianity participated in this subtle scorn for the living body through its spiritual alliance with new sales strategies for selling hygiene products. At one point in *A Month of Sundays* the Episcopal priest Tom Marshfield exclaims with exasperation to a colleague, "The biggest sales force in the world selling empty calories—Jesus Christ. What is it, Frankie? A detergent? A deodorant? What does it do, Frankie? This invisible odorless thing?" (156). American Protestant Christianity, Marshfield implies throughout the novel, wants too deeply to become pure spirit, an odorless ideal disconnected from embodied sense experience. How could this odorless Jesus create converts and change people's lives when he seems so ethereally spiritual? And why would a stinky Jesus be better? Because we belong in our bodies; or rather, we have no sense of home outside of our five senses. In denigrating the body and its constraints or smothering it in the artificial scents of purchased products, human creatures lose contact with a vital source of self-knowledge. Our sense of smell brings us back to the dirty earth and our human membership with the rest of creation.

One reason smell has been thought of as unrelated to beauty is precisely this: It reminds us of our animality. Yet for Updike the smell of death is not only a fact of embodiment but also a lesson about what it means to be a creature in God's good creation. There is a moment in *Rabbit Is Rich* when the middle-aged Rabbit Angstrom begins to smell on himself what he associated with his aging high school basketball coach, "an old man's sour sad body smell," an "odor like a corpse just beginning to sweeten" (*Rabbit Angstrom* 830). Though Rabbit at this moment has little of the sense of God's presence that he had in younger years, the awful whiff becomes God's "calling card left in the pit of the stomach, a bit of lead true as a plumb bob pulling Harry down toward all those leaden dead in the hollow earth below" (830). There is something true, perhaps life's deepest truth, in the faintly sour smell of aging. Could an invisible odorless Christianity speak to Harry's harrowing smell? Such a religion would, like vitamin-enhanced soap, foster a desire either to hide or to foolishly ignore the body's creaturely limitations.

In this chapter I begin by comparing Updike's treatment of smell with the agrarian writer Wendell Berry. Berry's work provides a useful foil for Updike's own interest in the forms of local community and what Berry calls "home economics." Almost an exact contemporary of Updike's, Berry writes with a substantially different pace and gravity. Additionally, Berry's novels consistently present powerful arguments for staying on the farm while Updike just as often revisits his triumph in leaving it. Yet Berry, like Updike, raises love for the familiar to the level of theological conviction. Berry believes that the "real infinitude of experience is in familiarity," and, accordingly, he shares Updike's interest in domestic life (*Life Is a Miracle* 139). For both, it is in the concrete and local world of a particular place and time that we learn to pay attention, to seek knowledge, and to know the real infinitude of experience.

In comparing Updike with Berry I hope to reveal their common understanding of creation and how representations of the sense of smell in their work reveal their theological understanding of the human body. After briefly sketching how the sense of smell works in Berry's embrace of creaturely embodiment and his rejection of popular notions of heaven, I turn to how Updike does something similar with his representation of the smell of sex in his novel *Villages*. Yet Updike's most sustained treatment of smell comes from two sources that are often treated as outliers in his oeuvre—his African novel *The Coup* and his stories about the Jewish writer and New York intellectual Henry Bech. In that novel and those stories, Updike develops an affirmation of life's less pleasant smells as worth smelling and provides reasons why the sense of smell deserves a place in postsecular aesthetics' accounts of the beautiful.

GNOSTIC NOSES

Wendell Berry's characters, like Updike's Tom Marshfield, are suspicious of an odorless Christianity. In one of Berry's early novels, *A Place on Earth* (1967), Burley Coulter writes to his nephew, Nathan Coulter, about the time the pastor of the town's Baptist church came to give his condolences after hearing that Nathan's brother Tom had been killed in the war. Unlike Burley and his nephews, Brother Preston is not a hardworking farmer, which has something to do with why the preacher manages the visit so poorly. The knowledge he gains from books and from his education is of an entirely different sort from the knowledge Burley and his nephews cultivate, sustain, and share. Burley and the boys have built up a fund of knowledge in their familiarity with one another, their embodied familiarity, to which the scholarly preacher has no access. Burley recalls feeling frustrated at their gap in knowledge: "Preacher, who are you to speak of Tom to me, who knew him, and knew the very smell of him?" (*A Place on Earth* 104). Smell provides access to a unique kind of knowledge. Burley knew Tom so well that he knew his smell—it is a knowledge based on consistent embodied proximity. Brother Preston's callow promise of a heavenly reunion, however, can offer little more than "thin comfort" to Burley's strong sense memory. For Burley, life is lived *and known* in the needs of daily farm work: "Surely the talk of a reunion in Heaven is thin comfort to people who need each other here as much as we do." Burley continues, however, with a clarification: "I ain't saying I don't believe there's a Heaven [. . .] Even while I hope for it, I've got to admit I'd rather go to Port William" (105). The Coulters' hometown, Port William, offers its own infinitude of experience.

Brother Preston's heaven lacks Tom's reality, even demeans it. Port William is not a place they want to leave for a spiritual ideal. Burley loves the town for its concrete familiarities—including the very smell of its inhabitants. It is, after all, *A Place on Earth.* Earlier in the novel Berry attests to the problem of the preacher's otherworldly perspective from the preacher's own point of view, as Brother Preston confesses, "The Word, in his speaking it, fails to be made flesh" (101). For a Christian preacher, that is a serious failure—it's a failure to convey the deepest mystery of his faith, Christ's incarnation. All too aware of his inadequacy, Brother Preston rues the fact that he is "the bringer of the Word preserved from flesh" (101). Preserving the Word from anything that might feel like an embodied reality sells his faith short and threatens it with irrelevance as much as heresy. Instead of bringing comfort to the bereaved, Brother Preston feels "they are offering to *him,* out of some kind of hospitality, the safe abstraction of his belief. They are releasing him from the particularity of the time and place, and of the life he is talking about" (99). Berry's theology of the earth as our human home condemns "heaven" as a subtle form of contempt for humans' creaturely status as embodied beings.

In offering this critique of Brother Preston's odorless comfort, Berry dramatizes the heavenly escapism present in American Christianity. In Updike's *A Month of Sundays,* Tom Marshfield's "invisible odorless" Jesus deliberately invokes the Gnostic heresies Brother Preston fears he unintentionally propagates. Marshfield updates the Gnostic strain of American Christian culture—the Gnosticism Harold Bloom simply calls the "American Religion"—in light of postwar America's mass-produced hygienic products. Berry rues the way such Gnosticism degrades the value of farm work, its forms of knowledge, and the way of life it represents. In different ways, both Berry and Updike portray fully embodied desires as having a particular smell. According to the theologian Norman Wirzba, Berry teaches us "to recognize that disembodied desire, desire cut off from the natural and social webs of interdependence, eventually leads to our own homelessness" ("Introduction" xiii). This sense of feeling at home in the world, of knowing particular people and places in it well enough to know their smells, is vital to both Updike's and Berry's sense of the writer's vocation.

A Christian writer risks making the same mistake Brother Preston made: offering abstract comforts. Hence, according to Berry, "A good artist is one who applies knowledge skillfully and sensitively to the particular creatures and places of the world" (*Life* 148). A writer's words cannot be persevered from flesh, but they should serve its particularity. Undoubtedly, the series of novels and stories Berry has written about Port William, a thinly guised version of his own Port Royal, Kentucky, demonstrate that Berry attempts to apply his own knowledge of words and the world to "the particular creatures" and place in the world he knows best. Describing them *as creatures* at home in creation is part of the work such a task involves. To read *A Place on Earth* is not the same as knowing a particular place on earth, but it does encourage such knowledge and does portray ways to achieve and protect it. The words on the novel's pages are there as a kind of stewardship, where Berry has written to apply his knowledge with skill and sensitivity "to the particular creatures and places of the world."

Moreover, success in fiction writing, like in the act of farming, depends on understanding one's creaturely relation to God and the rest of God's creation. In his essay "Christianity and the Survival of Creation," Berry exhorts respect for the work of good fiction as part of a Christian's understanding of the holiness of creation: "The Bible leaves no doubt at all about the sanctity of the act of world-making, or of the world that was made, or of creaturely or bodily life in this world. We are holy creatures living among other holy creatures in a world that is holy" (*The Art of the Commonplace* 308). This is not, however, the cultural norm within either American Christianity or the consumer society it has played no small part in building. Instead of declaring the sanctity of bodily life Berry thinks American Christians too often shames it with a belief in a disembodied soul. Writing on the Gnostic duality that plagues American life, Berry counters,

> The breath of God is only one of the divine gifts that make us living souls; the other is the dust. Most of our modern troubles come from our misunderstanding and misevaluation of this dust. Forgetting that the dust, too, is a creature of the Creator, made by the sending forth of His spirit, we have presumed to decide that the dust is "low." We have presumed to say that we are made of two parts: a body and a soul, the body being "low" because made of dust, and the soul "high." [. . .] And the predictable result has been a human creature able to appreciate or tolerate only the "spiritual" (or mental) part of Creation and full of semiconscious hatred of the "physical" or "natural" part, which it is ready and willing to destroy for "salvation," for profit, for "victory," or for fun. (314)

To forget the value of dust, that it too is "a creature of the Creator," can lead to a deep self-hatred—a hatred that Updike's Tom Marshfield rightly equates with the combined sales force of Christianity and capitalism. The work of writing, on the other hand, includes pushing back against such Gnostic tendencies with sensitivity for the particularity of bodies in place and time.

Updike's 2004 novel *Villages* seeks to render the sanctity of the created world in the fullness of its unique bodies. In several respects, *Villages* is a rewriting of Updike's earlier bestseller, the 1968 bestseller

Couples. *Couples* sought to define a new sociological phenomenon but is perhaps more celebrated for its graphic sexual descriptions and blunt reportage of the sexual revolution: "Welcome," one character famously enjoins just before consummating an affair, "to the post-pill paradise" (63). Coming nearly four decades later, *Villages* does not shock in the same way but takes an even more naturalistic view of the coupling that keeps *Couples* going. Using the development of personal computers and touch screens as its backdrop, the novel unfolds the sexual escapades of its narrator, Owen Mackenzie, from childhood to old age. While Updike's 1986 novel *Roger's Version* explored mechanized computation and its implications (or lack thereof) for how we think about the knowledge of God, *Villages* incorporates computers into its story as fully physical things: They are products in circulation just like the sex circulating through its villages. The computer is portrayed as a mechanized body more than a metaphor for disembodied knowledge. "In a materialist age," the novel confides, "matter must be trusted" (57). Trusting matter takes the form of two different but interlinked smells in *Villages*. "Sex and religion," the narrator prepares us, "had distinct, ancient odors" (17).

Sex, for Owen, is hard to separate from sin. His first sight of a girl's pubic hair is a "sin" (33), and the idea of sin is in itself both tactile and nasal: "As he grew, he discovered more places in [his hometown of] Willow where sin cast its shadow, which did not slide away like most shadows but had a sticky, pungent quality" (32). Later, with his high school girlfriend, that pungency became even stronger. Afraid of intercourse and the entanglements it suggested, Owen said, "It had become their way in the car for him to bend over and kiss the silky warm inner sides of her thighs and then press his mouth as far up as he could into the warmth, her warmth, its aroma at times like the tang his mother gave off on a summer day and at others of the musky mash bins in the back of her father's store" (69). Musk and tang are not the coded data Owen would eventually learn to harness and transfer in computing, but they are nevertheless a form of vital knowledge. Yet flirting with this ancient odor of sin, Owen is unsure just what form of knowledge he is seeking. He knows only that the "pleasure was his, in being this close to a secret, in having her yield it up to him, even her fragrance, which was strong enough at times to exert a counterforce, a wish to pull his face away" (69). It is a counterforce he describes in less than erotic terms as the "low-tide smell of cunt" in *Couples* (318). However crude or offensive such descriptions are, forbidden sex carries not only the promised pleasures of a body but also an unignorable olfactory surprise.

When Owen's girlfriend, "for the first time ever, begins fumbling at his belt buckle," it exposes his "prick aching behind his fly," only "to release it, its imperious pressure, its closeted sour smell" (74). Instead of some enticing fantasy, both the male and female genitals carry a sour scent of rot. And then again, not much later in the novel, when Owen loses his virginity on his wedding night, he cannot help noticing again how his penis emits "an anxious little stink" (109). In his first adulterous encounter, too, he registers "the faintest gust of genital scent" before they begin (152). Why are these genital descriptions so unabashedly rank? Perhaps the smell of the genitals reveals something important about the body's relation to death. Updike certainly links these sex scenes with Owen's innocent childhood sense memory of the "wet-paper smell of old bodies" in his live-in grandparents' room (48).

In a review of A. S. Byatt's *The Biographer's Tale,* published a few years prior to *Villages,* Updike noted that the novel's titular biographer's writing "comes most alive when he describes, in generous olfactory detail, making love to Vera and Fulla, and Byatt's novel quickens with it" (*Due Considerations* 314). The smell of sex propelled the life of the novel in Updike's estimation, and *Villages* capitalizes on the insight. For Updike, the smell of the genitals is a truth that pulls prose back into the specificity of living things—things that, like plots, tend to move toward death. He deliberately associates the delights of desire with the dread of death in the very smell of those life-giving parts. However central their location on the body and in the novel's plot, sex is inseparable from the physical reality of the genitals. It is a bizarre contradiction that *Villages* muses on later in the novel: "These hair-adorned nether parts, closely fitted into the sites of urination and defecation, were seats of being, ugly and odorous in external contemplation but in sensation exquisite" (*Villages* 203). Ugly and odorous, but in sensation exquisite. It is an aesthetic judgment, as well as a theological conviction about embodiment. It is a creaturely truth that some of its most transcendent feelings come from the body's basest parts.

The association of bodies with the process of dying is what makes Owen squirm when his first wife tells him, "You're very tied to your senses" (131). It is an obvious observation to the reader of Owen's sexual reminisces, but nonetheless he "hated to hear this, since having children had reawakened in him his childhood premonitions of dying, and one clear thing about the event was the unlikelihood of taking your senses with you. MIT had shown him the universe swept clean not only of Heavenly furniture but of endless energy—of endlessness in any measureable form. Every form of order, even the proton, ended: he preferred in practical life to forget this fatal thermodynamic pinch" (131). After MIT the senses are less the glorious teachers that reveal the ancient secrets of sex and religion and instead perpetual reminders of the all-too-conspicuous fact of embodiment: death. To be tied to his senses is to know that he will die. Owen's breakthrough invention, DigitEyes, "a method of drawing with a light pen on a computer screen," is a computational achievement that only confirms his understanding of the limited universe (132). DigitEyes' revolutionary technology of pixel plotting suggests "an abyss of calculation, of electronic information—as if every atom in the universe were an individual, with its own private story" (133). That every atom might have its own private story is one way of understanding Updike's attention to detail in his prose. Contemporary American Christianity's callous treatment of those precious atoms, however, becomes an increasingly irksome problem for the aging Owen.

The novel's penultimate chapter, "You Don't Want to Know," begins, "In Haskells Crossing, people die" (269). Haskells Crossing is the village Owen has come to at the end of his life, where he, too, will die. It is also where he and his second wife, Julia, regularly attend their local Episcopalian parish church. There they hear the Prayers of the People read out from the *Book of Common Prayer* and listen as the names of the ill, the dying, and the dead are read out loud. "The congregation responds, in entreaty to the huge hypothetical entity that hangs over these village proceedings, *Lord, have mercy,* or, of the departed, secure in their coffins and urns, *Let light perpetual shine upon them*" (271). This prayer makes Owen think back to the lessons he learned at MIT about the expanding universe. He rues American liberal Christianity's emphasis on individual spirituality and its avoidance of cosmological claims: "The church in strategic retreat abandons the cosmos to physics, and takes refuge in the personal—the cosmos of fragile, evanescent consciousness" (271). Updike, however, does not. In his writing, the cosmos is creation; fragile, evanescent consciousness is the human creature's way of being a part of it. Paying attention to the smells involved in sex is one way of keeping them there.

For *Villages* is finally about what keeps us here. "It is a mad thing, to be alive," it concludes; villages "exist to moderate this madness," to "protect us from the darkness without and the darkness within" (321). The villages of the novel, beginning with Willow and ending with Haskells Crossing, gave Owen a place to be; they kept him interested and curious about the paradoxes his sense experiences presented. As he reflects, the villages in which he had sex gave him "the happiness of orientation, of his position being plotted on a specific cartography, of being *somewhere*. There are fewer and fewer somewheres in America, and more and more anywheres, strung out along numbered highways" (309). The smell of sex is one of the ways that Updike's fiction insists on the somewhere-ness of life.

In fact, Updike makes a case for his attention to the odors of sex as precisely the kind of literary product that grates against consumer habits. "Capitalism," one character in the novel asserts, "asks only one thing of us: that we consume. The stupider we are, the better consumers we are, not just of that sliced pap called bread and of dishwasher detergents that kill fish in the river, but of canned entertainment. The less friction it makes going in our ears and eyes, the more we can take in and pay for" (196). I think it fair to assume that Updike writes the way he does about sex to create a form of aesthetic friction, to increase the reader's attention to the body and to produce the knowledge of living things rather than consumer habits—and, furthermore, to plant Christianity's claims firmly within the cosmos of matter and material experience.

FOLLOW YOUR NOSE

Updike left the local environs of his American shore for the first time in *The Coup*. It is narrated by Colonel Hakim Félix Ellelloû, the black dictator of a Marxist Islamic regime in the fictional African country of Kush. Such a character and location are pretty far from Owen Mackenzie in *Villages*. Moreover, Ellelloû hates all things American. Or at least, so he says. Ellelloû's critiques of the nation in which he was educated and married his second wife are often comically hypocritical. Nevertheless, Ellelloû's attempt to, as one character admonishes him, "follow your nose" through the geopolitical machinations of American foreign aid makes a pungent case for what the nose knows.

The novel opens with Ellelloû narrating an encyclopedialike description of Kush, noting its geography and agriculture, in which *The Coup*'s political and sensual theme is introduced with its principal export, peanuts. Peanut oil is made into "soaps designed not for my naturally fragrant and affectionate countrymen but for the antiseptic lavatories of America—America, that fountainhead of obscenity and glut" (3). The artificial fragrances of these soaps lurk just beneath Ellelloû's nose throughout the rest of the novel, and in some respects what there is of a plot moves forward through Ellelloû's attempts to discover the source of that antiseptic scent. Is it real or imagined? Has that "fountainhead of obscenity and glut," despite his strict legislation and ferocious anticapitalist rhetoric, found a way into his native Kush?

Updike lampoons the misguided humanitarianism and ulterior motives of American aid in *The Coup*, as well as Ellelloû's authoritarian attempts to secure national borders from Western capitalism. Neither Ellelloû nor the American agents in the novel have a keen grasp of the complexities of political maneuvering. Ellelloû has come to power through a military coup that deposed King Edumu IV, Kush's constitutional monarch, as well as the king's friendships with imperialist Europe and the United States. As the new military leader of the country, Ellelloû has completely severed what remained of those friendships. Having heard of a US attempt to provide aid to his drought-plagued, starving country, Ellelloû comes to the border to discover a consonant mound of cereal boxes, "*Kix Trix Chex Pops*," a "mountain of fetchingly packaged pap" (36). Curious what Ellelloû will do, a hungry crowd has gathered. But it is not the crowd that vexes Ellelloû. "From out of the anxious mob behind me," he pauses to trace, "out of the stench of dung fires and stale sweat and the bad breath that goes with empty stomachs, there came, sharp as a honed sword, a sweet and vivid whiff, alcoholic and innocent, of hair tonic such as would blow from the open doorway of a barbershop in Wisconsin. It came, and went" (35). The scent comes and goes throughout the novel, but it is here linked to something more than a geopolitical farce. The stench of dung fires and stale sweat and bad breath are all products of the body, whereas hair tonic is applied to enhance and beautify the body. The novel carries this distinction throughout less as a way to interrogate the role of capitalism in geopolitics than as a way to trace how American Gnosticism propels its capitalism.

Ellelloû makes a show of refusing this "packaged pap," however, telling the American official in front of the gathered crowd, "The people of Kush reject capitalist intervention in all its guises. They have no place in their stomachs for the table scraps of a society both godless and oppressive. Offer your own blacks freedom before you pile boxes of carcinogenic trash on the holy soil of Kush!" (40). While his tirade is a suspicious dictator's rant, it opens up one of the novel's latent questions: If American mass-produced goods are bad, what is bad about them? The people of Kush have more than enough room for some extra food, as their starving bodies suggest. Obviously, there is something good in the aid, and Ellelloû's nose tells him as much after the entire pile of it goes up in blazing flames, for then their "nostrils acknowledged the quantity of grain our triumphant gesture had consumed, for the scorched air was bathed in the benevolent aroma of baking bread" (44).

Yet there is something else, a spiritual despair, lurking in these smells as well. When first confronted with the American, Ellelloû puts his nose back to work, sensing a whole life's desperate trajectory. "I could smell on the victim, under the sweat of his long stale wait and the bland, oysterish odor of his earnestness, the house of his childhood, the musty halls, the cozy bathroom soaps, the glue of his adolescent hobbies, the aura of his alcoholic and sexually innocent parents, the ashtray scent of dissatisfaction" (43). Americans smell like the goods they consume, but the smell is disquieting. Is that "ashtray scent of dissatisfaction" unique to a "society both godless and oppressive?" Ellelloû seems to think so. Does Updike?

While the novel never explicitly endorses such a reductionist suggestion, it nonetheless offers a telling contrast to the "cosmetic odor" of Americans "mired in materialism and its swinish extinction of spirit" (115). When Ellelloû falls in love with a peasant woman while traveling incognito with a group of well diggers, her "rank smell grew sweet to me" (30). An otherwise unappealing scent, "her fragrance of musk and dung, of smoke and hunger, of Kush" grew sweetly familiar (48). The familiarity of the smell only makes it more desirable. Similarly, when he returns to his tribal homeland, the "smells of rancid butter, roasted peanuts, pounded millet, salted fish, and human eliminations mixed in an airy porridge that Ellelloû's nostrils, after a minute of adjustment, found delicious: the smell of being Salu" (92). This airy porridge is food for Ellelloû's soul. It reveals that what bothers him most about America is not its meddling attempts to open new markets but the contempt for embodied human life that its marketed goods convey. As Wendell Berry's Burley Coulter complained of the preacher's lack of knowledge since he did not have Burley's familiarity with Tom's smell, Ellelloû celebrates the smell in this woman's body and in the food of his childhood for their familiarity. Yet note, too, how those smells are strong, sour smells more than fragrant or delicate.

Compare Ellelloû's experience of smelling what it means to be Salu to the olfactory experience he has while a student in the United States, inside his American girlfriend's childhood home. Its opulent appearance is due not to an overwhelming sense of life's abundance but to a sterile fantasy of plenty. What Ellelloû smells is a half-hearted attempt at covering smells, insofar as the "living-room had puddles of cosmetic odor here and there" (151). When he repositions himself in the room, he becomes "freshly overwhelmed by its *exotisme,* its fantasy, the false flowers and fires, the melting-iceberg shapes of its furniture, its whiteness and coldness and magnificent sterility; the emptiness, in short, of its lavish fullness, besprinkled with those inexplicable cork coins" (157). This American living room feels empty in its parody of fullness, and, with its cork coasters, it smells too strongly of a manufactured effrontery to living things. According to Updike's adjectives, there's something vaguely malevolent in its false flowers and fires, its sterile furniture, its cosmetic odors.

Ellelloû suspects a twisted politics of desire at work in the US panoply of sanitizing smells. To long for such smells implies that one longs for the death of one's own familiar smells. Ellelloû tells his peasant lover, once she has become a wealthy, self-serving political advisor, "You have lost the good smell of dirt you had in the ditches of the north. Now you stink of French soap" (80). The scent of soap and body odor is a favorite theme of Ellelloû's. His political, spiritual, economic, and physical concerns often return to it. Even while declaiming the corruption of such soaps, he scents the hint of them in mid speech. At an American business's new and unauthorized oil well, where Ellelloû despairs that he can no longer "smell the desert" in the industrial fumes (243), Ellelloû ineffectually tries to stir up the listless crowd into mob revolt against American intervention. As he speechifies, something piquant but initially unidentifiable wafts in the midst of the strong industrial fumes.

> Of your blood they make deodorants to mask their God-given body scents and wax for the matches to ignite their death-dealing cigarettes and more wax to shine their shoes while the people of Kush tread upon the burning sands barefoot!
>
> A new scent, also sweet but astringent, had arisen: he groped to identify it, while returning to larger more spiritual themes. (253)

It only takes a moment to develop his spiritual themes, however, before he is back to his nose: "Ellelloû identified the odor that had intruded: it was of the pink, 'sanitizing' cake of soaplike substance that reposed within the bottom lip of urinals in men's 'rest' rooms of some American service stations and restaurants" (254). Ah, the political stink of soap again!

Much of this is, no doubt, Updike having fun with Ellelloû's posturing; the notion that American living rooms are false, sterile, and empty is a hackneyed critique of the consumerist family of the postwar boom. One could argue that Ellelloû's harangue is merely to embellish his character as an anti-American dictator with a bit of caricatured bluster. Yet there is more in this opposition of the rank smells of life against the obtuse, ornamental odors of manufactured goods than simply fodder for Ellelloû's tirades. Updike is dramatizing olfactory prejudices about the goodness of creation. Both the smells of Ellelloû's Salu village and the smells of his American girlfriend's living room are perceived in terms of warmth and belonging. Yet in addition to the experiences of exoticism, the smell of rank pungency is construed as positive, and cosmetic cleanliness as repulsive. Underneath Ellelloû's association of Kush with the smell of living things and the sterility of the United States is one of Updike's abiding questions: What does it mean to love *a body*? Especially, when the human body is so good at making bad smells? Do our olfactory prejudices teach us to despise our bodies?

The Coup makes us aware of our suspicious regard for our own bodies and cleanses our noses of such prejudices: first, in its reflexive awareness of its attention to smells; and second, in its reflexive awareness about its own lyrical playfulness. Updike has one character indirectly explain the novel's nostril-cleaning experiment.

> The channels of the mind, it may be, like those of our nostrils, have small hairs—cilia, is that the word? If we think always one way, these lie down and grow stiff and cease to perform their cleansing function. The essence of sanity, it has often been my reflection, is the entertainment of opposite possibilities: to think the contrary of what has been customarily thought, and thus to raise these little—cilia, am I wrong?—on end, so they can perform again in unimpeachable fashion their cleansing function. (228)

To "think the contrary of what has been customarily thought" is no easy calling; it requires the work of imagination. In its complete change of location and its attention to odors more than visual impressions, *The Coup* certainly cleanses the cilia of Updike's prose. It is important to note here that the smells we grow familiar with we quickly cease to register. It is precisely those familiar smells, though, that tell us who we are and what we love. To cleanse the gates of perception, as William Blake had it, is to raise the cilia back to their cleansing function and reveal the beauty of embodied experience. That's in part what Updike is trying to do in *The Coup*—to rethink consumer culture from the body's perspective—or, rather, its nose.

The novel's attempt to brush back the cilia of sense experience often takes on a playfully recursive style, and *The Coup* self-consciously nods toward its own lyrical bloat. A sentence describing a government official's escape from prison doubles as an arch reflection on the novel's prose style.

> Rather than risk confrontation with the soldiers and their doxies quartered in the fourth-floor corridor, who, if not fully alerted to the *nuancé* shifts of inner-circle leadership in Kush, certainly had caught the smoky whiff of *tabu* that now attached to Ezana, he, by a series of ripping, knotting, and measuring actions that like certain of these sentences were maddeningly distended by seemingly imperative refinements and elaborations in the middle, constructed a rope of caftans and agals and descended, through the silver kiss of the last moon of Safar, down the wall, in his terrified descent accompanied by his indifferent shadow, a faint large bat-shape whose feet touched his abrasively. (165)

The cartoonish escape route—sheets tied together and thrown out the window—becomes a confession that commits the very sin it confesses: the single sentence expands to mirror the distention it concedes, delights in the refined diction of "caftans and agals," and elaborates its phrases to include the useless detail of his shadow's indifference. Updike's performance is not meant only as a performance, however, but as a cilia-cleansing exercise, for it is through the novel's lyrical flourishes that it breathes deepest.

If America is a "land of obscenity and glut," as Ellelloû calls it at the novel's opening, then this is a gluttonous American novel. Updike's descriptions of obscene content and the "maddeningly distended" sentences parallel much of Ellelloû's critique of capitalism. As I have argued in previous chapters, Updike is fascinated by the productivity of natural processes and human culture. Such productivity is not *necessarily* good. There are cultural forms that denigrate the givenness of the world, and one would think that the postmodern novel, whose hermetic reflexivity Updike dallies with in this novel, is a prime specimen of such artistic disrespect. Such a style does bear resemblance to Ellelloû's critique of the artificiality of American consumer culture. Yet Ellelloû is not merely the narrator of *The Coup*: He actually writes the novel. It is his manuscript we are reading. While this could be nothing more than the playful icing of a postmodern cake, it more crucially gives the act of writing a primary role in learning to smell well. The familiar world becomes more familiar—in the sense of becoming more fully sensed—through the literary representation of the sense experience. In the end, the novel is less about foreign government than about the senses in which sense experiences come alive. Peculiarly swollen sentences can play a part in refining sense.

A HAIRY-NOSTRILLED GOD

The critiques of American capitalism and American Christianity leveled in *Villages* and *The Coup* are also arguments for how the concrete particularities of literature can combat their Gnostic abstractions. Both novels assume that a two-way street exists between literature and life. Yet more than any of Updike's other work, his Henry Bech stories raise consistent sallies against the too-neat distinction between literature and life. While writing is a vocation for the Protestant Updike, a way to praise the Creator through a good day's work, for Bech literature is not only life's highest calling—it *is* life. The Bech stories, begun after Updike's visit to the Eastern Bloc nations of the Soviet Union as a cultural ambassador for the United States, offered Updike a Jewish alter ego, a chance to write about a writer—something Updike had hitherto consciously avoided doing. Like Ellelloû's African Islam, the milieu of a secular Jew is foreign to Updike. Such novelty seems to realign Updike's imaginative cilia, however, insofar as Bech and his "hairy-nostrilled God" (*The Complete Henry Bech* 245) put writing in direct relationship with "the garbagy smells of life" (455). In the Bech stories, life smells a lot like death.

Alice and Kenneth Hamilton have noted how crucial the link between literature and life—biological life—is in Updike's first book-length collection of Bech stories, *Bech: A Book,* singling out Paul Valéry's notion of "biological metamorphosis" as its central conceit (Hamilton and Hamilton 120). For the Hamiltons, Bech is a literary character utterly different from Updike but, like Updike, concerned with the transformative relationship between life experiences and literary production. Several of Updike's characters seem like mere stand-ins for his own experience, but Bech became Updike's only major character to make his money by writing fiction. Perhaps it was their differences that allowed Updike to use the Bech stories to meditate so explicitly on his own artistic ends and purposes. For both Updike and Bech, writing and reading open the body to the world. Moreover, both aver that literary representations of life should focus not on sentimental feelings but on fear and desire, that surfaces are deeper than ideas, that particularities are the good. While the Bech stories are unquestionably concerned with the transformation of life into literature, they are just as much concerned with the transformation of literature into new modes of life.

In fact, the Bech stories begin with a covert toast to the way life can become literature. Ward Briggs and Biljana Dojčinović have shown in detail not only the several ways that the first Bech story, "The Bulgarian Poetess," was inspired by real-life events but also how the story itself crossed over from the realm of fiction and into real life. The story closes with a tribute to an impossible love affair—a love affair that ended before it even began, leaving little but a work of fiction in its wake. Briggs and Dojčinović contend the story is "essentially a love letter written by John Updike and delivered by the *New Yorker*" to Blaga Dimitrova, the remarkable poet he met in Sofia during his travels in the Eastern Bloc nations (2). "The Bulgarian Poetess" ends with a dedication from Bech to Vera, the poet he falls in love with during the course of the story. But Bech does not sign the dedication in the original *New Yorker* version. Instead, the final line of the story signs the story's fictional dedication with the actual author's name, "John Updike." The first Bech story begins as a lover's experiment with the pliability of literature for life.

This intimate context—where one writer unabashedly admires another's dedication to her art in thinly disguised fiction—sets the stage for the candor of the following Bech stories. The way that Updike portrays Bech's writing reveals as much about Updike's own writing as do his comments in interviews. For instance, the mere titles of Bech's books portray important aspects of Updike's. While Bech's first novel, *Travel Light,* is an obvious play on Updike's early success, *Rabbit, Run,* his second novel, *Brother Pig,* is named after "St. Bernard's expression for the body" (*The Complete Henry Bech* 45). Beyond the oblique allusion to *The Centaur,* here we see something of how Updike frames his own preoccupation with the body. It's a wonderfully Christian phrase: the body as an unruly seat of appetites, but as unruly as a *brother,* and thus also a source of comfort and even identity.

Yet his affinity for surfaces, for the movements of bodies in space, make Bech's aesthetic pronouncements particularly insightful. As if to answer his own critics, Updike has Bech defend another writer's (Vera, the Bulgarian poet) shallow lack of ideas: "Shallowness can be a kind of honesty" (49). This shrugging maxim captures Updike's theology of sense: We are our bodies, and metaphors of depth can skew our self-knowledge. Later in the story Updike writes that Bech's writing had "sought to show people skimming the surface of things with their lives, taking tints from things the way that objects in a still life color one another" (53). People are not only defined by their bodies in Updike's writing, but, as I argued in the first chapter, so are the objects they touch. Bech's shallowness, his insistence on a brotherly camaraderie with the body and its sensory responses, his attention to the surface of life, from which living things take their colors—this is Updike's own theology of sense. The meaning of life is not beneath those surfaces but right there on the surface, in the contact between bodies and objects in space.

In "Bech Panics" life doesn't have meaning, however, so much as smell. And it smells pretty bad, at least to Bech. Having arrived at a women's college in a pastoral setting in Virginia to make an appearance as a literary celebrity, "the powerful smell of horse manure" rampages in his "citified nostrils" (80). He seems to be the only one who notices it, however, and he feels "as if one of his senses had short-circuited to another channel" (81). The disconnect between the idyllic view and the malodorous smell is too much: "Along with the sun's reddening rays and the fecal stench a devastating sadness swept in. He knew that he was going to die" (81). When asked, he confides to the English professor who had invited him, "*Angst.* I'm afraid of dying. Everything is so implacable. Maybe it's all these earth-smells so suddenly" (92). Death is in the smell of the earth for Bech, since "inhaling the strenuous odors, being witness to myriad thrusts of new growth through the woodland's floor of mulching leaves" gives him an overwhelming sense of the circularity of it all: "Life chasing its own tail" (93). Bech cringes from the smells he is confronted with, but his despairing panic is testament to how *good* it is for him to smell these smells. Registering those "earth-smells" has much more to with his openness to them as a writer than their foreignness to his "citified nostrils."

The smell of decay is a good smell, not because Bech finds it particularly pleasant but because the emotional response it elicits is a spiritual realization. The good is not always immediately pleasant, and the goodness of creation is not immediately evident. The reason the smell of all this death—life "chasing its own tail"—is good is that it occasions a spiritual realization derived from the knowledge of the senses. Bech confesses to an earnest young interviewer that the ideal reader he had always envisioned does not exist. On top of this disillusionment, "one loses heart in the discovery that one is not being read. That the ability to read, and therefore to write, is being lost, along with the abilities to listen, to see, to smell, and to breath. That all the windows of the spirit are being nailed shut" (105–6). It may be difficult to extricate any one sense from the others, but notice how intimately linked the ability to read, write, and sense are for Bech. Bech seems more interested in *creating* the ideal reader than in finding her. The ability to sense depends, in this case, on the ability to read and write. Is Bech's sensitivity to the smell of the horse manure due to his citified nostrils, the fact that he is in a panic, or the fact that he's a writer who believes in the honesty of shallowness? The senses, and the written word, are the windows of the spirit. In this case, what's good about the "fecal stench" Bech smells is precisely this spiritual relationship: that life has an unsavory scent is a literary and spiritual insight. The specificity of the literary scenario meets the specificity of the smell that Updike's words strive to convey.

In "Bech Swings," the next story in *Bech: A Book,* Bech picks up on that specificity and tells an interviewer that it is from "particular, concrete realities, whence all goodness and effectiveness derive" (116). All goodness derives from detail? There's a fascinating contradiction here: How does goodness, such a general and abstract concept, derive from details? What inductive contortions of logic can discover in the diversity of concrete realities a blanket affirmation of goodness? Yet the human spirit, not the devil, is in the details for Bech. Any definition of goodness must begin with the variety of its "particular, concrete realities," and the work of literature is to reveal them. To do so is to open the windows of the spirit. Knowing the "garbagy smells of life" (455) is the spiritual wisdom Bech's (and Updike's) writing offers, but the Bech stories also go so far as to associate this wisdom with the Bible and the Bible's "hairy-nostrilled God" (245).

Associating Bech's literary "windows of the spirit" with biblical spirituality might seem a duplicitous subterfuge on my part. Is not Bech a quintessential New York intellectual in that he is both Jewish and completely secular? Is not his insistence on "concrete realities" the most secular aesthetic available? At this point in my argument I hope it is clear that equating the material world with the secular world is a wrong-headed assumption about the relationship between religion and secularity in postsecular aesthetics, but especially in the case of Updike. Bech's hairy-nostrilled God might seem quite different from Updike's Protestant one. And indeed, the passage that employs that hirsute appellation is creating a distinction between the Jewish God and the Protestant God. According to Bech, the "bizarre, Christmassy religion" of "these Wasps" "lacked organic festiveness"; "their God, for all of His colorful history and spangled attributes, lay above Earth like a whisper of icy cirrus, a tenuous and diffident Other Whose tendrils failed to entwine with fibrous blood and muscle" (245). The Wasps whom Bech knows—his girlfriend's family—worship a spiritual God who has little contact with the world of "particular, concrete realities." He is too far removed from it. Bech's "irrepressible Jewish God, the riddle of joking rabbis, playing His practical jokes upon Job and Abraham and leading His chosen into millennia of mire without so much as the promise of an afterlife," however, is a "hairy-nostrilled God beside Whom even the many-armed deities of the Hindus appeared sleek and plausible" but who "nevertheless entered into the daily grind and kibitzed at all transactions" (245). For Bech, unlike that angelic God of the Wasps, the Jewish God is involved in everyday concrete realities.

Of course, Updike is playing with stereotypes about Wasp culture and Protestantism's emphasis on private, individual belief. Yet Bech's hairy-nostrilled God sounds a lot like the "big-bellied Lutheran God" Updike describes growing-up with in *Self-Consciousness* (226). Updike notes that the God of his childhood affirmed creation's goodness: "The world is good, our intuition is, confirming its Creator's appraisal as reported in the first chapter of Genesis" (230). Updike then further explains, "God is the God of the living, though His priests and executors, to keep order and to force the world into a convenient mould, will always want to make Him the God of the dead, the God who chastises life and forbids and says No. What I felt, in that basement Sunday school of Grace Lutheran Church in Shillington, was a clumsy attempt to extend a Yes, a blessing, and I accepted that blessing" (231). Updike never thought of himself as a Wasp—his rural Shillington upbringing and his Pennsylvania Dutch roots offered little sense of ethnic identity with that group (Plath 56). And his own understanding of God's relation to creation is quite different from Bech's caricature of Protestantism. Updike's God says Yes to creation.

What does it mean to say that writing opens the windows of the spirit, the senses, up to God's Yes? It requires a view of both literature and life that affirms the goodness of death. The letter kills, but the spirit brings life; yet the life of the spirit fulfills the letter's promise (2 Cor. 3:6). The smell of death is the smell of life in the Bech stories because life is made anew in dying. As the Gospel of John has it, "Except a corn of wheat fall into the ground and die, it abideth alone: but if it die, it bringeth forth much fruit" (Jn. 12:24). This mystery includes the process of dying that is writing, where living things apparently die on the page in order to become the sense of some idea, only to give new forms of life to the senses. Having discussed this aspect of Updike's work in the chapter on tasting, I will not belabor the point again here. In the Bech stories, however, the garbagy smells of life are affirmed by both Bech's hairy-nostrilled God *and* the ostensibly life-denying, cloistered routines of his urban intellectual life. The bad smell of living things dying is in fact a good smell to know— it is a smell that knows that the death that is life slain on the page, and the death that is the body in the grave, can both lead to new life.

EPILOGUE

The Aesthetics of Easter

THIS BOOK has been about postsecular aesthetics and how Updike's theology of sense inspires his attention to the human sensorium. His work should challenge the notion that sense perception is purely secular simply because it is concerned with material reality. When Updike writes, as he does in *Endpoint and Other Poems* (2009), "In the beginning Culture does beguile us / but Nature gets us in the end," it is not to confess a materialist's fatalism about the work of culture but to submit the human creature to its place in the created order. Updike's religious convictions were not opposed to such a high view of nature. People are bodies, and however hard the work of culture might try to transcend that fact, doing so forfeits the grateful praise and love that makes being human, in Updike's rendering, "glorious" (*Self-Consciousness* 247). Aesthetics, insofar as it is the study of sense perception's judgments, is not more exact by the subtraction of theological concepts. Religious conviction—even Updike's Protestant penchant for "secular parables"—can enhance the willingness to receive whatever lessons the experience of embodiment teaches.

Yet this book has also been a tour through the various ways that literature portrays perception as more than a question of sense experience and instead as a whole constellation of assumptions about the meaning of embodiment. Updike's writing illustrates how writing about touch opens up new ways of being touched. It can show us how looking closely requires love, how physical tasting can prompt a more creaturely account of beauty, that hearing elicits spiritual longing just as smell prompts acutely physical experiences of spiritual insight. Reading and writing, for Updike, are not only ways to imagine or create but ways to more fully participate in creation: to know and feel the given world as worth loving. According to his theology of sense, beauty begins with bodies, and the writer's task is to reveal it.

I conclude these arguments by taking up the thematic concern of the previous chapter—how a genuine affirmation of embodied life entails accepting that even death contains its own good blessing— and trace how Updike's poetry deals with the life and death of bodies. Updike's poems, even up till the last month of his life, represent death as playing a part in creation's goodness. As Katie Roiphe tells in her moving study of Updike and other writers at the end of their lives, *The Violet Hour: Great Writers at the End,* "One of the great draws and challenges of Updike is that horrible truths are happily reported, reveled in, celebrated, and aging is no exception" (130)— including his last poems about aging into the painful clutches of chemotherapy, and eventually death itself.

Updike is rarely considered a poet since he wrote so much successful fiction. Yet not only did he write a quantity of light verse at the start of his career; he also worked at writing poetry his entire life. Indeed, he took it quite seriously. In the preface to his *Collected Poems* (1993), Updike distinguishes his light verse from his poetry with a telling distinction: "My principle for segregation has been that a poem derives from the real (the given, substantial) world and light verse from the man-made world of information—books, newspapers, words, signs. If a set of lines brought back to me something I actually saw or felt, it was not light verse" (xxiii). What distinguishes poetry as poetry, for Updike, is its singular address to the "given, substantial" world of embodied experience. Poetry is not about poems; poetry is about what "I actually saw or felt." Unlike the reflexive playfulness of light verse, Updike's poetry playfully registers the body's perceptions. Brad Leithauser calls it "naked poetry" for this reason: "You could say he offered us his body" (xvii).

I would emphasize the playfulness as well as the nakedness, since even his poetry has the bawdy wit of his light verse. From "The Beautiful Bowel Movement" and "Cunts" to "To a Waterbed" and "To Two of My Characters," (*Americana*) Updike's poetry wallows in farce, rarely suppressing its need to wink. There are, however, plenty of serious, even moving, poems, too, such as "My Children at the Dump" or "In the Cemetery High above Shillington" (*Americana*). However, regardless of their tone, the poems can feel like a kind of sideshow or a series of footnotes to the fiction. For instance, while the pre-Rabbit poem "Ex-Basketball Player" is poignantly elegiac and unquestionably stands on its own as a poem, would it be nearly as interesting to read if we didn't see Rabbit twitching in its shadow? Updike is a novelist and short story writer first, an essayist and reviewer next, and a poet last (some might say playwright, too, but I must confess his lone play, *Buchanan Dying*, was too stilted for me). I argue against the impression that poetry was Updike's literary form of playful recreation, however, and show how his poetry expresses the aesthetic purport of his belief in the resurrection of the body. The quip Updike made to Charlie Rose over a quarter-century ago, about publishing his *Collected Poems*, puts them squarely in the context of a man confronting death: "Well, why would you collect your poems unless you were getting ready to go on a journey?" (qtd. in Pritchard 253).

ROTTING BODIES

Updike's belief in Christianity's teaching about the resurrection of the dead does not rest at his recitation of the creed during Sunday morning worship services. As I have argued throughout the book, his religious sensibility is inextricable from his aesthetics. His poetry is no exception; rather, it is prototypical. For example, "Seven Odes to Natural Processes" is both a feat of scientific terminology turned poetry and a series of observations on the fate of physical bodies (though not necessarily human). While each of the seven odes addresses the natural side of their respective processes, they also reflect on the meaning of process itself and what it means for Christian faith. The odes begin with the "Ode to Rot" and end with the "Ode to Healing," and, according to their trajectory, decomposition is only a hairsbreadth from recomposition (*Collected Poems*). Healing is every bit as messy as rotting.

Rotting, however, is where it all begins. The first of the seven odes opens, "*Der gute Herr Gott* / said, "Let there be rot" (191). The rewriting of the famous line from Genesis, and its Germanic (Lutheran!) rendering, announces right from the start the theological context that frames Updike's theology of sense: Creation is good. Even the rotting body of a woodchuck:

> Pure rot
> is not
> but benign; without it, how
> would the forest digest its fallen timber,
> the woodchuck corpse
> vanish to leave behind the poem? (192)

Benign, pure rot makes space—not only for new trees, but, a few stages later in the process of decomposition, a poem. As I argued in the first chapter, Updike refuses to separate language, even writing, from the processes of living bodies. The dead letter is, in his work, a momentary transition moving from life to life or, as the *Book of Common Prayer* has it, "from strength to strength" (qtd. in *Villages* 270). Moreover, even words themselves can come to life in new ways, as Updike attests by exploiting the iambic pentameter "of carbohydrates photosynthesis" and the dactyls of "nitrogen, phosphorus, gallium" to turn the textbook terms into rhythmic chant (*Collected Poems* 191,192). Rotting is not a reprehensible loss but a new kind of fullness: "The world, reshuffled, rolls to renewed fullness" (192). While such calm assurance seems at odds with the number of characters Updike has given sweats and terrors at the prospect of dying and rotting in the ground, it confidently rests in the "counterplot" to which "rot" points: resurrection.

> All process is reprocessing;
> give thanks for gradual ceaseless rot
> gnawing gross Creation fine,
> the lightning-forged organic conspiracy's
> merciful counterplot. (193)

The "Ode to Rot" ends, not in pure decomposition and the dissolution of order, but with creation's "reprocessing." All the poem's rotting suggests a "merciful counterplot" where the dying will soon enough produce another, as yet unknown, form of living.

An element of mystery lurks behind the counterplot of this organic conspiracy. In the "Ode to Evaporation," the simple process of water evaporating into the air attests to a faithfully persistent, numinous order hiding in the unseen: "Molecular to global, the kinetic order rules / unseen and omnipresent / merciful and laughingly subtle like the breathing of naiads" (193, 194). The consistency of nature does not lessen its mystery but instead inspires exaltation at the bizarre confluence of infinitesimal changes and ethereal space: "I exulted / in the sensation of delivery / of vapor carrying skyward" (195). That exaltation is muted, though the mystery remains, only when he turns to the body's aging growths in "Ode to Growth." Though the eye suffers "irreversible presbyopia," the skin "goes keratinous," and "the epiphyses of the long bones unite with the shaft," nevertheless our "aging's a mystery, as is our sleep": "The protean codes" keep "their smuggling secrets still" (196). The baffling biochemistry does not hold him back from philosophizing that "death and surrender / are part of growth's package" (196). Growth teaches us that our death is merely yet another form of surrender to life. Not knowing the secrets behind these changes, Updike admonishes "let us die / rejoicing,"

> as around us uncountable husks
> are split and shed by the jungle push of green
> and the swell of fresh bone
> echoes the engendering tumescence. (196)

Sex's "echoes," and what the poets of the English Renaissance called a little death, provide the final lesson that growth gives us. To die mid-orgasm is to die rejoicing, yet Updike's imagery suggests that any and all forms of rejoicing involve some kind of affirmation of the death that orgasm prefigures.

"Ode to Fragmentation" derives similar lessons from natural processes but on a geological scale, reminding the reader that the human imagination is itself, when one reaches far enough back, the product of crumbling bedrock.

> had not Earth's aboriginal rock
> submitted to fragmentations lash,
> no regolith would have seasoned into soil,
> and the imaginary
> would never have taken root. (198)

Yet when the next ode takes up entropy, it is not keen on following such time scales too far forward into the future. "Entropy!" it moans, "thou seal on extinction / thou curse on Creation" (199). Here Updike refuses to allow entropy the role of a philosophical natural process. It cannot teach us about the most basic laws of matter because it defies the imagination that has taken root in the soil of an ancient regolith. Entropy's "future voids are scrims of the mind, / as academic as blackboards" (200). Against them, Updike asserts another law of mismatched energy, a law that begins with the body, is part of the imagination, and looks to the stars. Nature does not love balance, Updike suggests, and even if its processes do seek equilibrium, they are too many and too byzantine to end. I quote the final stanza in its entirety:

> Did you know
> that four-fifths of the body's intake goes merely
> to maintain our temperature of 98.6°?
> Or that Karl Barth, addressing prisoners, said
> the prayer for stronger faith is the one prayer
> that has never been denied?
> Death exists nowhere in nature, not
> in the minds of birds or the consciousness of flowers,
> not even in the numb brain of the wildebeest calf

> gone under to the grinning crocodile, nowhere
> in the woods or the tons of sea, only
> in our forebodings, our formulae.
> There is still enough energy in one overlooked star
> to power all the heavens madmen have ever proposed. (200)

For Updike, who poses questions much more than he answers them, and who tends to keep things jocular in his poetry, it's a strikingly confident and earnest ending. It seems, in a small way, the poem has suddenly taken the tone of the pulpit. Yet do not miss that the sermon's lesson is not, finally, about the human spirit but how the natural world dwarfs the human world in its vast capacity for creative energy. Do not be fooled by the bit about Barth and prayer, as if Updike were establishing an opposition between the spiritual and physical. "Ode to Entropy" puts the spiritual and natural along the same continuum, praising their processes' ability to progress in spite of their apparent regress. Though it does little to stem the fear of one's own individual death, it is perhaps easier to conceive of something like a resurrected body if one believes, as Updike puts it, "Death exists nowhere in nature." And it helps illuminate the theology of sense motivating lines like the one near the end of Updike's novel *Brazil* (1994), where he writes: "The spirit is strong, but blind matter is stronger still" (260). For Updike, matter is the very material of God's good plan for His creation and cannot be separated from His redemptive plan.

The juxtaposition of—but refusal to conclusively oppose—nature and culture continues in "Ode to Crystallization." The compression involved in the process of crystallization, and the inferred past to which it witnesses, necessarily suggests that "there is *something else*" (202). What else? "Ode to Healing" begins with something like an answer.

> A scab
> is a beautiful thing—a coin
> the body has minted, with an invisible motto:
> In God We Trust.
> Our body loves us

> and, even while the spirit drifts dreaming,
> works at mending the damage that we do. (202)

A scab is beautiful? As a witness to God's goodness, yes! This is what it means to take the body as the starting point for thinking about aesthetics, for scabs proclaim that wounds heal; that, if "In God We Trust," then we can rest assured that the "body loves us." Inverting Jesus' maxim that the spirit is willing but the flesh is weak, here the body is at work willing to heal while the spirit weakly "drifts dreaming" (Matt. 26:41). Note, too, how the body works unnoticed by that drifting, dreamy spirit. Updike closes the last of the odes by invoking faith's role in these processes, insisting, "Faith is health's requisite." Healing is a natural process whose relation to time requires trusting the body. Such faith is, after all the natural processes the odes recount, the closest proof we have that "*Herr Gott* is *gute*." Faith in the fact of healing ends the odes right where they began: "We have this fact in lieu / of better proof of *le bon Dieu*" (204).

RISING BODIES

Updike's faith is remarkably evident in his last poems. It is fitting, and poignantly moving, that the last two poems he wrote addressed his hope in the resurrection of the body. *Endpoint,* his posthumously published collection of poems, contains a series of ten autobiographically connected poems that give the book its title (a title that deliberately echoes his long autobiographical poem from 1969, *Midpoint*). The last of the ten poems tracing Updike's final years and months is titled "Fine Point." The poem is dated a month before his death, and its title is a pun on both the fine point of argument dealt with in the poem's content and the very fine point his life is nearing. It is a sonnet that simply, with sober candor, reaffirms his Sunday school belief in the resurrection of the dead. To listen to someone's last words, whoever they are, is a moving experience, yet especially so when it is a prolific writer addressing the existential crisis so many of his characters faced, now with the tender bravado of one who sees his own imminent death. Here it is in full:

> *Fine Point 12/22/08*
> Why go to Sunday school, though surlily,
> and not believe a bit of what was taught?
> The desert shepherds in their scratchy robes
> undoubtedly existed, and Israel's defeats—
> the Temple in its sacredness destroyed
> by Babylon and Rome. Yet Jews kept faith
> and passed the prayers, the crabbed rites,
> from table to table as Christians mocked.
> We mocked, but took. The timbrel creed of praise
> gives spirit to the daily; blood tinges lips.
> The tongue reposes in papyrus pleas,
> saying, *Surely*—magnificent, that "surely"—
> *goodness and mercy shall follow me all
> the days of my life,* my life, forever. (*Endpoint* 29)

The poem opens by acknowledging the void that sometimes opens up between practice and belief, but questions it. Why go to Sunday school, even when forced by your parents, and not believe what was taught? Yet another question is implied here: Why write day in and day out as a form of praise and not believe in the Creator and that Creator's promises? To do so would betray the value of the very daily life Updike's art sought to value, for the poem is a celebration of the daily reality of religious practice and the reality of its quotidian truths. The "desert shepherds" wore "scratchy robes," and that little adjective, "scratchy," brings their reality home to us in the specificity of its sense experience. Why write with such care for reality if that reality is not of infinite value? In the daily practice of their prayers the Jews provided the example that the Christians "took" and continued to recite in the Psalms. It is not only the worshipping Christians, however, but the Christian writer who "gives spirit to the daily" in his writing. The "magnificent" "surely" of Psalm 23 should again be read reflexively: for Updike's own daily practice of writing sought to do just that, to remind and show his readers how utterly sure they should be that "goodness and mercy" were there to be found in the experiences of their five senses. To the readers who wondered if Updike was losing his faith he responds with befuddlement: Why else participate in the Eucharist, a rite in which "blood tinges lips," with such regularity? And why write in praise of daily goodness and affirm the goodness of physical experience over and over again without believing in the promise behind it: that matter is good, that God is good, that his mercy is "forever."

The poem that precedes "Fine Point" is an equally confident statement of faith insofar as it not only affirms the goodness of creation and faith in its Creator; it goes so far as to affirm the goodness of death. While "Creeper" is stylistically far from "Seven Odes to Natural Processes," it too sees in death something good. The difference, however, is the difference of a writer in the prime of life versus one who sees his death coming in a matter of days. In "Creeper" Updike makes the astounding confession that he can see in his own impending death something good. Again, the poem is short and I quote it in full:

> *Creeper*
> With what stoic delicacy does
> Virginia creeper let go:
> the feeblest tug brings down
> a sheaf of leaves kite-high,
> as if to say, *To live is good*
> *but not to live—to be pulled down*
> *with scarce a ripping sound,*
> *still flourishing, still*
> *stretching toward the sun—*
> *is good also, all photosynthesis*
> *abandoned*, quite quits. Next spring
> the hairy rootlets left unpulled
> snake out a leafy afterlife
> up that same smooth-barked oak. (28)

"*To live is good / but not to live*": Can this truly be "*good also*"? How does someone as in love with life as Updike was ever come to that conclusion? As this poem testifies, for Updike, it is the hope of the resurrection that brings him there. That hope, however, was nothing new. It was with him throughout his life and invigorates his work's view of embodiment and its style.

In conclusion, I want to show how Updike's best-known poem about resurrected bodies, "Seven Stanzas at Easter," is not only a testament to his faith but his most succinct aesthetic manifesto. In this poem we find the single conviction imbuing everything else Updike writes. Furthermore, it adds an essential fact to the development of postsecular aesthetics—that a prominent Protestant American writer is invested not merely in spirituality but in making matter matter. For Updike, matter matters even more than how you sense matter, which is to say, even more than aesthetics. Or, to put it another way, aesthetics draws its value from the material world. For Updike, aesthetics is a special form of knowledge, not because it knows how the arts determine the beautiful but because it shows us how to know the world *as beautiful*.

"Seven Stanzas at Easter" cautions against the symbols, metaphors, and story-making that serve preconceived notions of beauty instead of material facts. A key component to his aesthetic is that Updike refused to endorse twentieth-century liberal theology and the idea that modern methods of scientific research and humanistic inquiry required revising traditional Christian doctrines. He saw no conflict between science and religion. For Updike, the truths of science do not require us to reinterpret the Scriptures; the Scriptures, for Updike, require us to think scientifically. Updike's "Seven Odes to Natural Processes" needs to be read alongside his "Seven Stanzas at Easter" as twin declarations that all of matter is God's and all hope of an afterlife depends on the truth of this claim.

The first of the seven stanzas does not begin with the symbolism of the sacrificial Lamb of God or the inspirational hope of new life, but by invoking Christ's amino acids.

> Make no mistake: if he rose at all
> it was as His body;
> if the cell's dissolution did not reverse, the molecules reknit,
>   the amino acids rekindle,
> the Church will fall. (*Collected Poems* 20)

"Make no mistake," the poem begins, laying down an imperative that is, crucially, an either/or that depends on an if/then conditional. *Either* he rose "as His body," *or* Christianity is meaningless and the

Church, an institution that has lasted hundreds of years, will crumble soon enough. *If* he rose, and we really don't know if he did, but *if* he rose, *then* "it was as His body." Either the Church makes it clear that they take their identity from a resurrected body, or they should (and will) shut up. Such a high-stakes beginning poses two different problems for the rest of the poem. (1) The resurrection is more about the physical fact of "amino acids" than beauty or inspiration, and (2) any beauty or inspiration that this poem will achieve as an aesthetic object is entirely in the service of this fidelity to the possibility of such a physical fact.

This physical fact does not translate into a natural process. No, Updike's point here is that bodies are what really matter, but that bodies are not only known through scientific disciplines. Christianity, too, is about belief in the truth of physical facts.

> It was not as the flowers,
> each soft spring recurrent;
> it was not as His Spirit in the mouths and fuddled eyes of the
>   eleven apostles;
> it was as His flesh; ours. (21)

Yet there is an attendant insight here: If words begin in the mouth of a real human body and go out toward another real human body, then words are for bodies. Bodies do not exist in order to create words; words serve as one way in which the body can praise its Creator. One of the lasting consequences of the idealism this book opened by critiquing is the assumption that words and ideas are not only longer-lasting but more ontologically substantial than bodies. Bodies age and decay; the ideas that words convey don't. Yet notice how explicitly this stanza rejects the notion that the words of the apostles are in any way more important than the fact that it was Christ's body that was raised. The words serve the physical event.

The fourth stanza continues down this road, clarifying that what might be poetry's greatest tool, metaphor, is a way of understanding reality, not demeaning it. If metaphor in any way subtracts from the physical truth of God's embodied relation to creation, it is being misused.

> Let us not mock God with metaphor,
> analogy, sidestepping, transcendence,
> making of the event a parable, a sign painted in the faded
>   credulity of earlier ages:
> let us walk through the door. (21)

Literature, for Updike, could too easily betray the physical truth of the risen Christ's body in service of its own metaphor-making. Literary tropes thus deployed further support the "easy Humanism" Updike warns against in *Midpoint,* when he writes, "An easy Humanism plagues the land; / I choose to take an otherworldly stand" (38). Curiously, that "otherworldly stand" requires an absolute affirmation of matter—not an analogical flourish but a robust belief that requires a body to make that stand and to walk through that door.

The last three stanzas further clarify that both the imaginative world of literature and the spiritual world of angels are only true insofar as they speak toward God's role in the physical world. The stone of Christ's tomb is not the stone of a story but the "rock of materiality"; the angel at that tomb is no spiritual being but "weighty" and "opaque"; Christ's body, nothing less than a monstrous offense.

> The stone is rolled back, not papier-mache,
> not a stone in a story,
> but the vast rock of materiality that in the slow grinding of
>   time will eclipse for each of us
> the wide light of day.
>
> And if we have an angel at the tomb,
> make it a real angel,
> weighty with Max Planck's quanta, vivid with hair, opaque in
>   the dawn light, robed in real linen
> spun on a definite loom.
>
> Let us not seek to make it less monstrous,
> for our own convenience, our own sense of beauty,
> lest, awakened in one unthinkable hour, we are embarrassed
>   by the miracle,
> and crushed by remonstrance. (*Collected Poems* 21)

This last stanza is an aesthetic mandate as much as a confession of belief. The believer cannot fix his belief on what he thinks likely or pleasing. Neither can the writer fix his art on what he thinks likely or pleasing. Updike did not attempt to make any aspects of either his religion or the created world any less monstrous. For the risen body of Christ asserts a revolutionary aesthetic: that each body—not a formal ideal, but the uniqueness of each body, "His flesh; ours"—contains its own goodness, and its own beauty, and its own truth. Each body offers its own "remonstrance" at the shallow, inattentive callousness of "our own sense of beauty." As much as an affirmation of faith, "Seven Stanzas at Easter" offers an aesthetic derived from the event of Easter: that the concept of beauty is not a presumed ideal or an abstract form but derives from the God-given gift that is *this* body.

WORKS CITED

Asad, Talal. *Formations of the Secular: Christianity, Islam, Modernity.* Stanford: Stanford UP, 2003.

Augustine. *The City of God: XI–XXII.* Trans. William Babcock. New York: New City Press, 2013.

———. *Confessions.* Trans. Henry Chadwick. New York: Oxford UP, 1991.

———. *The Retractions.* Trans. Mary Inez Bogan. Washington, DC: Catholic U of America P, 1968.

Bailey, Peter J. "'The Bright Island of Make-Believe': Updike's Misgivings about the Movies." *John Updike Review* 1, no. 1 (2011): 69–87.

———. *Rabbit (Un)redeemed: The Drama of Belief in John Updike's Fiction.* Madison, NJ: Fairleigh Dickinson UP, 2006.

Balthasar, Hans Urs von. *The Glory of the Lord: A Theological Aesthetics. Volume I: Seeing the Form.* Trans. Erasmo Leiva-Merikakis. Ed. Joseph Fessio, SJ, and John Riches. 2nd ed. San Francisco: Ignatius Press, 2009.

———. *Love Alone Is Credible.* Trans. D. C. Schindler. San Francisco: Ignatius Press, 2004.

Barrett, Laura. "Don DeLillo." *The Cambridge Companion to American Literature after 1945.* Ed. John Duval. Cambridge: Cambridge UP, 2012. 244–54.

Barth, John. "The Literature of Exhaustion." *The Friday Book: Essays and Other Non-Fiction.* London: John Hopkins UP, 1984.

Barth, Karl. *Church Dogmatics*. Trans. G. W. Bromiley. Ed. G. W. Bromiley and T. F. Torrance. Edinburgh: T&T Clark, 1956–77.

Barthes, Roland. *The Rustle of Language*. Trans. Richard Howard. Berkeley: U California P, 1989.

Batchelor, Robert. *John Updike: A Critical Biography*. Santa Barbara: Praeger, 2013.

Begbie, Jeremy. *Music, Modernity, and God: Essays in Listening*. New York: Oxford UP, 2014.

Begley, Adam. *Updike: A Life*. New York: Harper, 2014.

Berlant, Lauren. *Cruel Optimism*. Durham: Duke UP, 2011.

Berry, Wendell. *The Art of the Commonplace*. Ed. Norman Wirzba. Berkeley: Counterpoint, 2003.

———. *Life Is a Miracle: An Essay against Modern Superstition*. Washington, DC: Counterpoint, 2000.

———. *A Place on Earth*. 1967. Washington, DC: Counterpoint, 2001.

Blanchot, Maurice. *The Work of Fire*. Trans. Charlotte Mandell. Stanford: Stanford UP, 1995.

Bloom, Harold. *The American Religion*. 1992. New York: Chu Hartley, 2006.

Boswell, Marshall. *John Updike's Rabbit Tetralogy: Mastered Irony in Motion*. Columbia: U of Missouri P, 2001.

———. "Review: Rabbit (Un)Redeemed: The Drama of Belief in John Updike's Fiction." *Modern Fiction Studies* 53, no. 1 (2007): 191–94.

Branch, Lori. "The Rituals of Our Re-Secularization: Literature between Faith and Knowledge." *Religion & Literature* 46, no. 2–3 (2014): 9–33.

Briggs, Ward and Biljana Dojčinović. "The Bulgarian Poetess: John and Blaga." *John Updike Review* 3, no. 2 (2015): 1–36.

Brown, Bill. *Other Things*. Chicago: U of Chicago P, 2015.

Buell, Lawrence. *The Dream of the Great American Novel*. Cambridge: Belknap, 2014.

Burchard, Rachel. *John Updike: Yea Sayings*. Carbondale: Southern Illinois UP, 1971.

Burnett, Whit, ed. *America's 85 Greatest Living Authors Present: This Is My Best in the Third Quarter of the Century*. New York: Doubleday, 1970.

Byatt, A. S. *The Biographer's Tale*. New York: Knopf, 2001.

Coviello, Peter and Jared Hickman, eds. "Introduction: After the Postsecular." *American Literature* 86, no. 4 (2014): 645–54.

Crowe, David. *Cosmic Defiance: Updike's Kierkegaard and the Maple Stories*. Macon, GA: Mercer UP, 2014.

De Bellis, Jack. "'It Captivates . . . It Hypnotizes': Updike Goes to the Movies." *Literature/Film Quarterly* 23 (1995): 169–87.

———. *The John Updike Encyclopedia*. Westport, CT: Greenwood Press, 2000.

DeLillo, Don. *The Body Artist*. New York: Scribner, 2001.

———. *Underworld*. New York: Scribner, 1997.

———. *Zero K*. New York: Scribner, 2016.

Detweiler, Robert. *John Updike*. New York: Twayne Publishers, 1972.

Dewey, John. *Art as Experience*. 1932. New York: Perigree Books, 2005.

Dombech, Kristin. *The Selfishness of Others: An Essay on the Fear of Narcissism*. New York: Farrar, Straus and Giroux, 2016.

Edwards, Jonathan. *The Religious Affections*. Carlisle, PA: Banner of Truth Trust, 1961.

Farmer, Michial. *Imagination and Idealism in John Updike's Fiction*. Rochester, NY: Camden House, 2017.

Felski, Rita. *The Limits of Critique*. Chicago: U of Chicago P, 2015.

Fessenden, Tracy. "The Problem of the Postsecular." *American Literary History* 26, no. 1 (2014): 154–67.

Fromer, Yoav. "'The Insider-Outsider': John Updike as a New York Intellectual—From Shillington, Pennsylvania." *John Updike Review* 4, no. 4 (2016): 29–55.

Gabriel, Markus. *Why the World Does Not Exist*. Trans. Gregory Moss. Malden, MA: Polity Press, 2015.

Greiner, Donald. "John Updike and the Film Version of *Rabbit, Run*: Novel, Script, Movie." *Critique: Studies in Contemporary Fiction* 53, no. 2 (2012): 174–84.

———. "John Updike: The Literary Vermeer." *Critique: Studies in Contemporary Fiction* 51, no. 2 (2010): 177–84.

Haddox, Thomas F. *Hard Sayings: The Rhetoric of Christian Orthodoxy in Late Modern Fiction*. Columbus: The Ohio State UP, 2013.

Hale, Dorothy. "Aesthetics and the New Ethics: Theorizing the Novel in the Twenty-First Century." *PMLA* 124, no. 3 (2009): 896–905.

Hamilton, Alice and Kenneth Hamilton. *The Elements of John Updike*. Grand Rapids: Eerdmans, 1970.

Haque, Danielle. "The Postsecular Turn and Muslim American Literature." *American Literature* 86, no. 4 (2015): 799–829.

Harman, Graham. *Towards Speculative Realism: Essays and Lectures*. Washington: Zero Books, 2010.

Hart, David Bentley. *The Beauty of the Infinite: The Aesthetics of Christian Truth*. Grand Rapids: Eerdmans, 2003.

Hauerwas, Stanley. *The Hauerwas Reader*. Durham: Duke UP, 2001.

Hewitt, Avis. "The Obligation to Live: Duty and Desire in John Updike's *Self-Consciousness*." *John Updike and Religion: The Sense of the Sacred and the Motions of Grace*. Ed. James Yerkes. Grand Rapids: Eerdmans, 1999. 31–49.

Highsmith, Patricia. *Plotting and Writing Suspense Fiction*. New York: Poplar Press, 1983.

———. *Ripley Underground*. 1970. New York: Norton, 2008.

———. *The Talented Mr. Ripley*. 1955. New York: Norton, 2008.

Hungerford, Amy. *Postmodern Belief: American Literature and Religion since 1960*. Princeton: Princeton UP, 2010.

Hunsinger, George. *How to Read Karl Barth: The Shape of His Theology*. New York: Oxford UP, 1991.

Hunt, Gorge. *John Updike and the Three Great Secret Things: Sex, Religion, and Art*. Grand Rapids: Eerdmans, 1980.

Jamison, Leslie. *The Empathy Exams: Essays*. Minneapolis: Graywolf Press, 2014.

Jodock, D. "What Is Goodness? The Influence of Updike's Lutheran Roots." *John Updike and Religion: The Sense of the Sacred and the Motions of Grace*. Ed. James Yerkes. Grand Rapids: Eerdmans, 1999.

Jüngel, Eberhard. *God as the Mystery of the World: On the Foundation of the Theology of the Crucified One in the Dispute between Theism and Atheism*. Grand Rapids: Eerdmans, 1983.

Keen, Suzanne. *Empathy and the Novel*. New York: Oxford UP, 2007.

Lake, Christina Bieber. *The Incarnational Art of Flannery O'Connor*. Macon, GA: Mercer UP, 2005.

———. *Prophets of the Posthuman: American Fiction, Biotechnology, and the Ethics of Personhood*. Notre Dame: U of Notre Dame P, 2013.

Leithart, Peter. "Painter of Surfaces." *First Things* (September 10, 2014). www.firstthings.com/blogs/leithart/2014/09/painter-of-surfaces.

Leithauser, Brad. "Introduction." *Selected Poems*. By John Updike. Ed. Christopher Carduff. New York: Knopf, 2015.

Lovejoy, Arthur O. *The Great Chain of Being: A Study of the History of an Idea*. 1936. Cambridge: Harvard UP, 1976.

Lukács, Georg. *The Theory of the Novel: A Historical-Philosophical Essay on the Forms of Great Epic Literature*. Trans. Anna Bostock. Cambridge, MA: MIT Press, 1971.

MacIntyre, Alastair C. *Three Rival Versions of Moral Enquiry: Encyclopedia, Genealogy, and Tradition: Being Gifford Lectures Delivered in the University of Edinburgh in 1988*. Notre Dame: U of Notre Dame P, 1990.

———. *Whose Justice? Which Rationality?* Notre Dame: U of Notre Dame P, 1988.

Marcuse, Herbert. *Eros and Civilization*. 1955. Boston: Beacon Press, 1974.

Marion, Jean-Luc. *The Erotic Phenomenon*. Trans. Stephen Lewis. Chicago: U Chicago P, 2008.

McClure, John. *Partial Faiths: Postsecular Fiction in the Age of Pynchon and Morrison*. Athens: U of Georgia P, 2007.

McTavish, John. *Myth and Gospel in the Fiction of John Updike*. Eugene, OR: Cascade Books, 2016.

Miller, D. Quentin. "Updike, Middles, and the Spell of 'Subjective Geography.'" Ed. Stacy Michele Olster. *The Cambridge Companion to John Updike*. New York: Cambridge UP, 2006. 15–28.

Miller, Perry. *Errand into the Wilderness*. Cambridge: Harvard UP, 1956.

Nancy, Jean-Luc. *Corpus*. Trans. Richard A. Rand. New York: Fordham UP, 2008.

———. *The Sense of the World*. Trans. Jeffrey S. Librett. Minneapolis: U of Minnesota P, 1997.

Naydan, Liliana. "Justification by Temperate Faith Alone: Fundamentalism, Fanaticism, and Modernity in John Updike's *In the Beauty of the Lilies*." *John Updike Review* 1, no. 1 (2011): 89–106.

Newman, Judie. "Updike's Golden Oldies: Rabbit as Spectacular Man." *Literature and the Visual Media*. Ed. David Seed. Cambridge: Cambridge UP, 2006. 123–41.

Novak, Barbara. *American Painting of the Nineteenth Century: Realism, Idealism and the American Experience*. 3rd ed. Oxford: Oxford UP, 2007.

Novak, Michael. "Updike's Quest for Liturgy." *John Updike: A Collection of Critical Essays*. Ed. David Thorburn and Howard Eiland. Englewood Cliffs: Prentice-Hall, 1979. 192–95.

Nussbaum, Martha Craven. *Anger and Forgiveness: Resentment, Generosity, Justice*. New York: Oxford UP, 2016.

———. *Love's Knowledge: Essays on Philosophy and Literature*. New York: Oxford UP, 1990.

———. *Poetic Justice: The Literary Imagination and Public Life*. Boston: Beacon Press, 1995.

O'Connor, Flannery. *Collected Works*. New York: Library of America, 1988.

Percy, Walker. *Love in the Ruins*. 1971. New York: Picador, 1999.

———. *The Moviegoer*. 1961. New York: Vintage, 1998.

Perrin, Tom. *The Aesthetics of Middlebrow Fiction: Popular US Novels, Modernism, and Form, 1945–75*. New York: Palgrave Macmillan, 2015.

Plath, James, ed. *Conversations with John Updike*. Jackson: UP of Mississippi, 1994.

Pritchard, William H. *Updike: America's Man of Letters*. South Royalton, VT: Steerforth Press, 2000.

Proust, Marcel. *In Search of Lost Time, Volume 4*. 1981. Trans. Terrence Kilmartin and Scott Moncrieff. New York: Everyman's Library, 2001.

Rebora, Carrie. "Copley and Art History: The Study of America's First Old Master." *John Singleton Copley in America*. Ed. Carrie Rebora et al. New York: Metropolitan Museum of Art, 1995.

Roiphe, Katie. *The Violet Hour: Great Writers at the End*. New York: Dial Press, 2016.

Schaefer, Donovan O. *Religious Affects: Animality, Evolution, and Power*. Durham: Duke UP, 2015.

Schenkar, Joan. *The Talented Miss Highsmith: The Secret Life and Serious Art of Patricia Highsmith*. New York: St. Martin's, 2009.

Schiff, James. "Updike, Film, and American Popular Culture." *The Cambridge Companion to John Updike*. Ed. Stacey Olster. Cambridge: Cambridge UP, 2006. 134–48.

———. *Updike's Version: Rewriting* The Scarlet Letter. Columbia: U of Missouri P, 1992.

Sedgwick, Eve Kosofsky. *Touching Feeling: Affect, Pedagogy, Performativity*. Durham: Duke UP, 2003.

Sengupta, Pradipta. "Engendering Pleasure: Sringara Rasa in John Updike's *S*." *John Updike Review* 3, no. 3 (2015): 83–99.

Smith, Christian. *Moral Believing Animals: Human Personhood and Culture*. New York: Oxford UP, 2003.

Smith, James K. A. *Desiring the Kingdom: Worship, Worldview, and Cultural Formation*. Grand Rapids: Baker Academic, 2003.

Smith, Rachel Greenwald. *Affect and American Literature in the Age of Neoliberalism*. New York: Cambridge UP, 2015.

Sontag, Susan. *Against Interpretation, and Other Essays*. 1966. New York: Picador, 2001.

———. *At the Same Time: Essays and Speeches*. New York: Farrar, Straus and Giroux, 2007.

Stewart, Kathleen. *Ordinary Affects*. Durham: Duke UP, 2007.

Szalay, Michael. *Hip Figures: A Literary History of the Democratic Party*. Stanford: Stanford UP, 2012.

Tanenhaus, Sam. "John Updike's Archive: A Great Artist at Work." *New York Times*. June 20, 2010. http://www.nytimes.com/2010/06/21/books/21updike.html.

Tate, Andrew. *Contemporary Fiction and Christianity*. New York: Continuum, 2008.

Taylor, Charles. *A Secular Age*. Cambridge, MA: Belknap Press, 2007.

———. *Sources of the Self: The Making of the Modern Identity*. Cambridge: Cambridge UP, 1992.

Tournier, Michel. *Friday*. Trans. Norman Denny. 1985. Baltimore: Johns Hopkins UP, 1997.

Updike, John. *Always Looking: Essays on Art*. New York: Knopf, 2012.

———. *Americana and Other Poems*. New York: Knopf, 2001.

———. *Assorted Prose*. New York: Knopf, 1965.

———. *Bech: A Book*. Fawcett Columbine, 1998.

———. *In the Beauty of the Lilies*. New York: Knopf, 1996.

———. *Brazil*. New York: Knopf, 1993.

———. *The Centaur*. New York: Knopf, 1963.

———. *Collected Poems: 1953–1993*. New York: Knopf, 1993.

———. *The Complete Henry Bech*. New York: Knopf, 2001.

———. *The Coup*. New York: Knopf, 1978.

———. *Couples*. New York: Knopf, 1968.

———. *Due Considerations*. New York: Knopf, 2007.

———. *The Early Stories*. New York: Knopf, 2003.

———. *Endpoint and Other Poems*. New York: Knopf, 2009.

———. "Foreword." *Wolfgang Amadeus Mozart*. 1956/1986. Karl Barth. Trans. Clarence K. Pott. Eugene, OR: Wipf and Stock, 2003.

———. *Gertrude and Claudius*. New York: Knopf, 2000.

———. *Higher Gossip*. New York: Knopf, 2011.

———. *John Updike: The Collected Early Stories*. Ed. Christopher Carduff. New York: Literary Classics of the United States, 2013.

———. *John Updike: The Collected Later Stories*. Ed. Christopher Carduff. New York: Literary Classics of the United States, 2013.

———. *Just Looking: Essays on Art*. New York: Knopf, 1989.

———. *Licks of Love: Short Stories and a Sequel, Rabbit Remembered*. New York: Knopf, 2000.

———. *The Maples Stories*. New York: Everyman's Library, 2009.

———. *Memories of the Ford Administration*. New York: Knopf, 1992.

———. *Midpoint and Other Poems*. New York: Knopf, 1969.

———. *A Month of Sundays*. New York: Knopf, 1975.

———. *Of the Farm*. New York: Knopf, 1965.

———. *Olinger Stories*. New York: Everyman's Library, 2014.

———. *Picked Up Pieces*. New York: Knopf, 1975.

———. *The Poorhouse Fair*. 1959. New York: Knopf, 1977.

———. *Rabbit Angstrom: The Four Novels*. New York: Everyman's Library, 1995.

———. "Remarks on Receiving the Campion Medal." *John Updike and Religion: The Sense of the Sacred and the Motions of Grace*. Ed. James Yerkes. Grand Rapids: Eerdmans, 1999.

———. *Roger's Version*. New York: Knopf, 1986.

———. *S*. New York: Knopf, 1988.

———. *Seek My Face*. New York: Knopf, 2002.

———. *Self-Consciousness*. New York: Knopf, 1989.

———. *Still Looking: Essays on American Art*. New York: Knopf, 2005.

———. *Terrorist*. New York: Knopf, 2006.

———. *Toward the End of Time.* New York: Knopf, 1997.

———. *Villages.* New York: Knopf, 2004.

———. *The Widows of Eastwick.* New York: Knopf, 2008.

———. *The Witches of Eastwick.* New York: Knopf, 1984.

Verduin, Kathleen. "Imprinting Mortality: Updike Reading Books." *Modern Language Quarterly* 71, no. 3 (2010): 329–66.

Versluys, Kristiaan. "'Nakedness' or Realism in Updike's Early Short Stories." Ed. Stacy Michele Olster. *The Cambridge Companion to John Updike.* New York: Cambridge UP, 2006. 29–42.

Viladesau, Richard. *Theological Aesthetics: God in Imagination, Beauty, and Art.* New York: Oxford UP, 1999.

Wallace, David Foster. "John Updike, Champion Literary Phallocrat, Drops One; Is This Finally the End for Magnificent Narcissists?" *New York Observer,* October 13, 1997. www.observer.com/1997/10/john-updike-champion-literary-phallocrat-drops-one-is-this-finally-the-end-for-magnificent-narcissists/.

Webb, Stephen. "Writing as a Reader of Karl Barth: What Kind of Religious Writer Is John Updike Not?" *John Updike and Religion: The Sense of the Sacred and the Motions of Grace.* Grand Rapids: Eerdmans, 1999. 145–61.

What Makes Rabbit Run? A Profile of John Updike. Dir. David Cheshire. British Broadcasting Corporation, 1982.

Williams, Rowan. *The Edge of Words: God and the Habits of Language.* New York: Bloomsbury, 2014.

Wirzba, Norman. "Introduction: The Challenge of Berry's Agrarian Vision." *The Art of the Commonplace: The Agrarian Essays of Wendell Berry.* Ed. Norman Wirzba. Berkeley: Counterpoint, 2002. vii–xx.

Wood, James. *The Broken Estate: Essays on Literature and Belief.* New York: Picador, 2010.

Wood, Ralph. *The Comedy of Redemption: Christian Faith and Comic Vision in Four American Novelists.* South Bend: U Notre Dame P, 1988.

Words and Pictures. Dir. Fred Schepisi. Perf. Juliette Binoche, Clive Owen. Latitude Productions, 2013.

Yerkes, James. *John Updike and Religion: The Sense of the Sacred and the Motions of Grace.* Grand Rapids: W. B. Eerdmans, 1999.

Žižek, Slavoj. "Not a Desire to Have Him, but to Be like Him." *London Review of Books* 25, no. 16 (2003): 13–14.

INDEX

"A&P" (Updike), 35
adjectives, 8, 9, 21, 36, 51, 52, 65, 162, 181
aesthetic experience, 56, 58, 103, 147
aesthetics, 5–6, 9, 30, 33, 37, 55, 58, 62, 67, 69, 87, 92, 111, 116, 157, 159, 175, 180, 183, 184, 186; creaturely, 95–102; ethics and, 136; hedonistic, 89; history of, 27; postsecular, 2, 3, 23, 25, 59, 91–92, 122, 152, 170, 173; theological, 27, 93–94, 108
affective theory, 32, 42, 60, 73, 75, 87; theology of sense and, 51–52
Against Interpretation (Sontag), 87
Alden, Felicia, 35
alienation, 18, 20, 21, 44
American Literary History, 24
American Literature, 24
American Painting in the Nineteenth Century (Novak), 70
angelism, 21

Anger and Forgiveness (Nussbaum), 136
Angstrom, Harry "Rabbit": character of, 132; desires of, 118, 123; freedom for, 146; grace and, 134–35, 136; Janice and, 14–15, 31, 133, 134, 135, 137, 143; music and, 127, 129, 131, 142; narcissism of, 130; patriotism of, 137, 143; Ripley and, 125, 139, 140–41, 142; as sinner, 132; spirituality of, 121, 128, 145
Angstrom, Janice: Rabbit and, 14–15, 31, 133, 134, 135, 137, 143
Angstrom, Nelson, 127, 130, 135, 137
Angstrom, Rebecca, 135
anthropology, theological, 27, 29, 93–94
Aristotle, 8, 104
ars erotica, 16, 89
art: criticism, 63–65, 73; erotics of, 86; performance, 45
Art as Experience (Dewey), 33, 55, 56

Augustine: concubine and, 17, 19, 20; God and, 18; love and, 63; *ordo amoris* and, 16; psychology of, 18, 20; theology of love and, 17
"Augustine's Concubine" (Updike), 17, 20
autobiographical writing, 7–8, 33, 48–49
awareness, 2, 49, 54, 72, 88, 102, 143, 164

Babe, 143, 144, 145, 146
Bailey, Peter J., 30, 74, 75
Balthasar, Hans Urs von, 27, 108, 129
Barrett, Laura, 44
Barth, Karl, 9, 29, 52, 85, 123, 178, 179; gratitude and, 8, 101; influence of, 124; Mozart and, 128, 129, 131, 141; music and, 128, 130; secular humanism and, 131; secular parables and, 25; theology of, 30, 101, 102; Updike and, 25, 30, 101
Barthes, Roland, 62, 87
basketball, memory of, 126, 128, 132–33, 135, 143
"Beautiful Bowel Movement, The" (Updike), 175
beauty, 19, 74–89, 93, 94, 102, 108, 117, 150, 174; aesthetic, 88, 129; in-sight of, 103; mathematical, 107; nature and, 89; representations of, 129; sacred experiences of, 114; singular bodies of, 107; smell and, 151; theology of, 109
Bech, Henry, 152, 168–69; stories, 166, 167, 169, 170–71
Bech: A Book (Updike), 166–67, 168, 169
"Bech Panics" (Updike), 168
"Bech Swings" (Updike), 169
Begley, Adam, 97
belonging, 164; sense of, 48, 62, 75, 144
Berlant, Lauren, 40
Bernhard, Martha Ruggles, 17

Berry, Wendell, 152, 155, 162; home economics and, 151; theology of, 153–54
bestialism, 21
bias: conceptual, 69, 70, 86; teleological, 12
Biographer's Tale, The (Byatt), 157
black characters, 143–44, 145
Blake, William, 164
Blanchot, Maurice, 98
"Blessed Man of Boston, My Grandmother's Thimble, and Fanning Island, The" (Updike), 26, 111
Bloom, Harold, 154
bodies, 16, 93; aesthetics of, 87; affirmation of, 7, 128; black, 120–21, 145; change of, 46; fetishization of, 120–21; identity and, 50; living, 150; physical, 15, 176; resurrected, 183, 184, 185, 186; rising, 180–86; rotting, 175–80; self and, 50–51; theological understanding of, 152; three-dimensional, 146; violence and, 15
Body Artist, The (DeLillo), 44, 45
Bogart, Humphrey, 83
Book of Common Prayer, 35, 103, 158, 176
Book of Nature, 26
Borges, Jorge Luis, 52
Boswell, Marshall, 30
Bourdieu, Pierre, 117
Boy in a Windsor Chair (Limner), 68
Boy with a Flying Squirrel (Copley), 68
boyhood, 47; childhood and, 43
Boys in a Pasture (Homer), 64
Branch, Lori, 24
Brazil (Updike), 179
Briggs, Ward, 167
Brown, Bill, 66, 67
Buchanan Dying (Updike), 175
Buell, Lawrence, 1–2
"Bulgarian Poetess, The" (Updike), 167

Burchard, Rachael, 57
Burk, Edmund, 92
Byatt, A. S., 157
Byrd, Admiral, 12

Caldwell, Phoebe, 42, 66
Campbell, Jeff, 5
"Can Genitals Be Beautiful?" (Updike), 15
capitalism, 155, 159, 161, 165
Centaur, The (Updike), 38, 66, 94, 97, 168
ceremonies, 18, 111–18
Cezanne, Paul, 65, 66
Chafetz, Hope, 150
Cheshire, David, 98
chewing, 93, 104, 106, 107, 116; taste and, 103, 108
Christ, 33, 34, 108, 151, 153; body of, 107; literature and, 25; Mary and, 34; Paul and, 35; touch of, 36, 38
Christianity, 2, 21, 22, 53, 85, 92, 99, 109, 123, 124, 134, 154, 175, 176, 183–84; American, 155, 158, 166; good and, 146; Protestant, 5, 86–87, 150–51; world-frame of, 5
"Christianity and the Survival of Creation" (Berry), 155
Church Dogmatics (Barth), 101
cinema, 61, 80; church and, 74; responses to, 63
City of God, The (Augustine), 19
"Clarity of Things, The" (Updike), 67, 70, 75
Clark, 83, 84; fantasy of, 85–86
Clayton, Alfred, 16
Collected Poems (Updike), 174, 175
Comedy of Redemption, The (Wood), 30
communion, 103, 104; liturgy of, 106
concubine, 17, 19, 20
confessions, 20, 24, 27, 104, 106, 165, 182, 186

Confessions (Augustine), 17, 18, 19, 20
"Conscience of Words, The" (Sontag), 88
Contemporary Fiction and Christianity (Tate), 30
Copley, John Singleton, 71, 73, 86; aesthetics and, 69; lininess and, 72, 73, 82; realism of, 70; Updike and, 67–68; West and, 68
"Copley and Art History" (Rebora), 70
Coulter, Burley, 152, 153, 162
Coulter, Nathan, 152
Coulter, Tom, 152, 153, 162
Coup, The (Updike), 6, 150, 152, 159–60, 164, 165, 166
Couples (Updike), 3, 16, 94, 156, 157
creation, 5, 18, 32, 37, 38, 58, 71, 117, 176, 178, 184; degradation of, 134; doctrine of, 41, 101, 131; giftedness of, 66, 93; goodness of, 147, 182; harmony of, 131, 132; holiness of, 155; redemption of, 136; theology of, 3
Creator, 32, 38, 108, 118, 155, 166, 181, 184; God's role of, 36; praise for, 5
"Creature, The" (Barth), 101
creatures, 23, 51, 128, 151, 154, 155
"Creeper" (Updike), text of, 182
"Crop, The" (O'Connor), 109, 110, 111
Crowe, David, 30
Crusoe, Robinson, 53, 54, 55
Cry, the Beloved Country (Paton), 136
culture, 24, 88, 125, 138, 173, 179; American, 76, 86, 147; Christian, 118, 154; human, 29, 113, 165; literature and, 94; religion and, 94; visual, 74; Wasp, 170
"Cunts" (Updike), 175

Dalai Lama, 130
Dante, 128
Day, Doris, 74, 81
De Bellis, Jack, 74
De Rougement, Denis, 16

death, 158, 174, 177, 178, 179, 180; smell and, 149–50, 168, 169
Defoe, Daniel, 53
Deleuze, Gilles, 27, 53, 54, 139
DeLillo, Don, 8, 43–44, 45; language of, 33; touch and, 47
DeMott, Alma (Essie Wilmot), 82
Descartes, Rene, 23
desire, 3, 102, 118, 123; cultural foundations of, 116; erotic, 84; sexual, 140; transformative pedagogy of, 11
Detweiler, Robert, 52
Dewey, John, 33, 55, 56, 57, 58
Dickinson, Emily, 7
Dimitrova, Blaga, 167
Dimmesdale, Arthur, 86
dissonance, 125, 132–42, 146
Divine Comedy (Dante), 128
Dogmatics (Barth), 131
"Dogwood Tree: A Boyhood, The" (Updike), 39, 43, 48–49, 50
Dojčinović, Biljana, 167
Dombech, Kristen, 123

Eccles, Lucy, 129–30
Eccles, Reverend, 119, 120, 128, 133, 145
Ecclesiastes, 144
Edumu IV, King, 160
Edwards, Jonathan, 82, 86; on God/soul, 71–72; theory of sensational rhetoric and, 72; Updike and, 69–70, 70–71
Either/Or (Kierkegaard), 9
Ellellôu, Hakim Félix, 6, 159–60, 161, 166; capitalism and, 165; smelling and, 162, 163–64
embodiment, 2, 21, 22, 27, 44, 94, 151, 152, 157, 158, 173, 182; aesthetics of, 30, 87; meaning of, 174; theology of, 3
emotion, 8, 28, 51, 71, 73, 76; democratic, 142; seeing/hearing and, 57

empathy, 125, 135, 139, 147; ethics of, 122, 146, 147; narcissism and, 123; political, 138; self-betterment and, 142
Empathy and the Novel (Keen), 138
Empathy Exams, The (Jamison), 123
Endpoint and Other Poems (Updike), 94, 173
Errand into the Wilderness (Miller), 70
ethics, 9, 123, 135, 139, 147; aesthetics and, 136; evangelism and, 137; Kantian, 124; literary, 122, 125; theological, 124; thinking about, 146
Eucharist, 21, 103, 107, 111
"Ex-Basketball Player" (Updike), 175
existentialism, 30, 108, 124, 131

Fall, 5, 42
fantasy, 14, 21, 85–86
Farmer, Michial, 30
Felicia, Jane, 35
Fessenden, Tracy, 24
"Fine Point 12/22/08" (Updike), 180, 182; text of, 181
Flaubert, Gustave, 62
forgiveness, 38, 41, 42, 103
Friday (Tournier), 53
friendship, 8, 19, 98, 145, 160
"Full Glass, The" (Updike), 94, 112, 113, 115–16
full glass feeling, 113, 114, 115, 118

Gabriel, Christopher, 16
Gabriel, Markus, 66
García Márquez, Gabriel, 6
gastronomy, reconciliation and, 102–11
Genesis, 171, 176
Gertrude and Claudius (Updike), 26
Glory of the Lord, The (Balthasar), 27, 108
Gnosticism, 20, 154, 155, 161, 166
God, 37, 39, 76, 156, 163, 170; belief in, 77; creation of, 38, 117; forgive-

ness of, 41; as God of the living, 5; goodness of, 4, 29, 118, 180; loss of, 77, 78; lovers and, 129; as objective truth, 12; proof of, 29; redemption and, 136; sense of, 4, 151; soul and, 71–72; speech about, 42; touch of, 46

God as the Mystery of the World (Jüngel), 29

Good, 2, 74–89, 146

Good Samaritan, 123

Gospel of John, 41, 171

grace, 72, 107, 130, 134–35; athletic, 119, 120, 135; rebellion against, 132; signs of, 104–5; sin and, 136

"Grandparenting" (Maple), 79

gratitude, 9, 10, 93, 116; creaturely, 8, 52, 101, 102; social relations and, 147; style and, 11

Great Chain of Being, The (Lovejoy), 65

Greenleaf, Dickie, 141

Greiner, Donald, 62, 74

Griffith, D. W., 76

guilt, 17, 18, 20, 103, 105, 106, 107, 111, 133, 134–35, 140, 142, 143, 145

"Gun Shop, The" (Updike), 94, 95–96, 98, 100–103, 113

Gurley, Ben: death of, 105

Haddox, Thomas, 30, 93

Hadot, Pierre, 117

Hale, Dorothy, 121, 122

Hamilton, Alice, 6, 166

Hamilton, Kenneth, 6, 166

Hamlet (Shakespeare), 25, 26

hands, arranging, 51–60

"Happiest I've Been, The" (Updike), 7

Haque, Danielle, 24

Harbor—Great Spruce Head, The (Porter), 64

Hard Sayings: The Rhetoric of Christian Orthodoxy in Late Modern Fiction (Haddox), 30

Harman, Graham, 66

harmony, 125, 126–32, 146

Hart, David Bentley, 7, 102, 109

Hartke, Lauren, 45, 46

Hauerwas, Stanley, 123, 124

Hawthorne, Nathaniel, 86

hearing, 57, 119, 120, 121, 149

heart: ear and, 119; inclination of, 72

Hewitt, Avis, 129

Highsmith, Patricia, 124, 125, 139, 140, 142

Holbein, Hans, 69

Holmes, Oliver Wendell, 137

Homer, Winslow, 64, 72–73

Hoyer, Linda Grace, 38

human being, meaning of, 65

human experience, animal aspects of, 41

humanism, 122, 131, 185

Hume, David, 23

Hungerford, Amy, 23, 24, 30

Hunt, George, 30, 85, 86

idealism, 1, 67, 184

identity, 46, 78, 169; body and, 50; religious, 76

images, 7, 51, 62, 63, 69, 74, 75, 76, 77, 78, 81, 83, 111, 112; affective ontology of, 86; idealized, 82; objectifying, 13; visual, 87

In the Beauty of the Lilies (Updike), 63, 74, 75, 76, 77, 86, 94

"In the Cemetery High above Shillington" (Updike), 175

Incarnation, 41, 104, 153; theology of, 108

Infinite Jest (Wallace), 11

Jamison, Leslie, 123

Jefferson Lecture in the Humanities, 67

Jerusalem Prize, 88

Jodock, Darrell, 136
John Singleton Copley in America (Rebora), 70
John, son of Zebedee, 34
John Updike: Yea Sayings (Burchard), 57
Joyce, James, 22
Jüngel, Eberhard, 29
Justin Martyr, 103

Kant, Immanuel, 92, 116, 123
Keen, Suzanne, 121–22, 138
Kern, David, 35, 37, 40, 58; Christ's touch for, 36, 38; study by, 56–57
Kierkegaard, Søren, 9, 21, 30

Lake, Christina Bieber, 3
Lambert, Roger, 29
Leithart, Peter, 6
Leithauser, Brad, 175
Leonard, Ruth, 143
Limner, Beardsley, 68
lininess, 69, 72, 73, 82
literalism, lavish, 69, 72, 85, 86
literature, 56, 57, 135, 146; culture and, 94; religion and, 23–24
"Literature of Exhaustion, The" (Barth), 52
"Long-Legged Fly" (Yeats), 130
love, 20, 108, 128; Christian teaching on, 123; forgiving, 10–11; free, 15; seeing and, 63; sexuality and, 16; theology of, 17
Love in the Ruins (More), 21
Love in the Western World (de Rougement), 16
Lovejoy, Arthur O., 65–66
lovers: God and, 129; knowers and, 16
Love's Knowledge (Nussbaum), 135
Lukács, Georg, 76

MacIntyre, Alasdair, 122

Mackenzie, Julie, 158
Mackenzie, Owen, 156, 157, 158, 159, 160
Maple, Joan, 15
Maple, Richard, 15, 79
Marcuse, Herbert, 14
Marion, Jean-Luc, 27
Marshfield, Tom, 13, 14, 151, 152, 154, 155; on ethical passion, 9; gratitude and, 9; objects and, 12; sexual gratification and, 9
Mary, Christ and, 18, 34
Mary Magdalene, 33, 34, 35, 40
McClure, John, 23, 24, 30
McTavish, John, 30
meaning: construction of, 25; sense of, 47, 93; superabundance of, 52
memories, 47–48, 49, 58, 59, 107
Memories of the Ford Administration (Updike), 16
Mendelssohn, Felix, 141
Merleau-Ponty, Maurice, 27
Midpoint (Updike), 185
Midsummer Night's Dream, A (Mendelssohn), 141
Miller, D. Quentin, 7
Miller, Perry, 70, 71, 72
Miscellanies (Edwards), 70
Month of Sundays, A (Updike), 9, 10, 14, 25, 53, 151, 154; passage from, 11–12
morality, 66, 84, 85, 86, 137
More, Thomas, 21
Morrison, Toni, 2
Motes, Hazel, 110
Motun, Lot, 110
Moviegoer, The (Updike), 21
Mozart, Wolfgang Amadeus, 132, 142; Barth and, 128, 129, 131, 141
music, 56, 127, 131, 132, 141, 142, 143–44, 145–46

"Music School, The" (Updike), 94, 102–3, 105, 107, 109, 111, 113
"My Children at the Dump" (Updike), 175

Nancy, Jean-Luc, 27–28, 40
narcissism, 16, 93, 123, 126, 130, 132
nature, 88, 91, 178, 179; beauty and, 89; dictates of, 67–68
Naydan, Liliana, 75
New Testament, 10
New York Times Book Review, 44
New Yorker, 4, 13, 167
Newman, Judie, 74
Nietzsche, Friedrich, 57
Novak, Barbara, 69, 70, 86
Novak, Michael, 117
Nussbaum, Martha, 135, 136, 137, 138

O. Henry, 12
O'Connor, Flannery, 7, 109, 110, 111
"Ode to Crystallization" (Updike), 179
"Ode to Entropy" (Updike), 179
"Ode to Evaporation" (Updike), 177
"Ode to Fragmentation" (Updike), 178
"Ode to Growth" (Updike), 177
"Ode to Healing" (Updike), 176, 179
"Ode to Rot" (Updike), 176, 177
Of the Farm (Updike), 38, 61, 94
"On Being a Self Forever" (Updike), 50, 51, 52
ontology, 65, 71, 83, 88, 104; aesthetic, 82; affective, 63, 75, 86, 87; realist, 67
ordo amoris, 13–22, 89
Owen, Clive, 61

"Packed Dirt, Churchgoing, a Dying Cat, a Traded Car" (Updike), 111, 112, 114
Partial Faiths (McClure), 23
Pascal, 72, 120

patriotism, 129, 136, 137, 143
Paul, Christ and, 35
Pennington, Mary, 15, 18
perceptions, 11, 53–54, 56, 57, 58
Percy, Walker, 2, 20–21, 22
philosophy, 2, 4; continental, 27; modern, 29
photography, 62–63, 88
Pickford, Mary, 76
Picturing America (NEH program), 67
"Pigeon Feathers" (Updike), 35, 38, 51
pigeons, 36, 37, 56–57
Pines and Rocks (Cezanne), 65, 66
Place on Earth, A (Berry), 152, 154
Planck, Max, 185
Plato, 1, 2, 38, 65
Platonism, 65
pleasure principle, reality principle and, 36
plentitude, 63–69, 75, 81, 89
Plotinus, 65
Poetic Justice (Nussbaum), 135
poetry, 33; educational use of, 11; writing, 174–75, 180
politics, 44, 138, 163; racial, 145
Poorhouse Fair, The (Updike), 2
pornography, 16, 85
Porter, Fairfield, 64
Portrait of Master Bunbury (Reynolds), 68
Postmodern Belief (Hungerford), 23
postmodernism, 24, 57, 165
postsecularism, 23, 24, 40
Prayers of the People, 158
Preston, Brother, 152, 153, 154
Protestantism, 5, 29, 86–87, 150–51, 170, 171
Proust, Marcel, 2, 22, 112
Psalm 23: 112, 181
purpose, 37, 57, 72, 77, 81, 134, 146, 167; higher, 18, 20; loss of, 78; sexual, 15

Pynchon, Thomas, 2, 8

Rabbit Angstrom: The Four Novels (Updike), 44, 122, 126, 128, 129, 130, 131, 132, 134, 135, 136, 137, 145–46, 147
Rabbit at Rest (Updike), 94, 127, 132, 134, 135, 145
Rabbit Is Rich (Updike), 14, 126, 130, 137, 151
Rabbit Redux (Updike), 134, 137, 143, 145
"Rabbit Remembered" (Updike), 130
Rabbit, Run (Updike), 21, 72, 120, 126, 127, 128, 133, 146, 168; film adaptation of, 74; opening of, 119
race, 138; representation of, 144–45
racism, 121, 146
realism, 1, 12, 27, 29, 52, 66, 70, 74, 98, 101; affect, 62; concrete, 170; mimetic, 75; photographic, 75; pleasure principle and, 36; sense of, 43–44
Rebora, Carrie, 70
reconciliation, 70, 93, 95, 99, 100; doctrine of, 101; gastronomy and, 102–11
Redemption, 5, 42, 136
Reid, Thomas, 23
religion, 21, 42; culture and, 94; literature and, 23–24; postsecularity and, 24; sex and, 156
Religion and Literature, 24
Religious Affections, The (Edwards), 71, 72
Religious Affects: Animality, Evolution, and Power (Schaefer), 40
representation: literary, 58, 100, 166; morality of, 67, 73, 74, 82, 88
resurrection, 176, 182, 183, 184, 185, 186
Reynolds, Joshua, 68
Rimbaud, Arthur, 53

Ripley, Tom, 124; Rabbit and, 125, 139, 140–41, 142
Ripley Under Ground (Highsmith), 42, 141
rituals, 21, 24, 26, 41, 105, 113, 116, 128
Robbe-Grillet, Alain, 12, 13, 53, 57
Robinson, Joey, 38, 39, 42
Robinson, Peggy, 38, 39
Robinson Crusoe (Defoe), 53
Robles, Rey, 45
Roger's Version (Updike), 9, 29, 156
Roiphe, Katie, 17
Rose, Charlie, 175
Roth, Philip, 8

S. (Updike), 9, 16
"Savages" (Schaefer), 41
Scarlet Letter, The (Hawthorne), 9
Schaefer, Donovan, 40, 41, 42
Schiff, James, 9, 74
Schweigen, Alfred, 104, 105, 106, 107, 108–9
"Sea's Green Sameness, The" (Updike), 63
Secular Age, A (Taylor), 122
secular humanism, 122, 123, 131
secular parables, 3, 25, 29, 30, 173
secularism, 2, 24
Sedgwick, Eve Kosofsky, 40
"Seducer's Diary" (Kierkegaard), 9
seeing: act of, 149; emotion and, 57
Seek My Face (Updike), 150
self, 47; body and, 50–51; construction of, 25
self-consciousness, 18, 49, 51
Self-Consciousness (Updike), 5, 38, 41, 53, 58, 80, 94, 129, 149, 171; body and, 50
Selfishness of Others, The (Dombech), 123
Sengupta, Prendita, 16

sensational rhetoric, 69–73
sense, 48, 76, 93, 104, 166; descriptions of, 20–21; senses of, 22–30; theology of, 2, 3, 4, 8, 12, 118, 174
Sense of the World, The (Nancy), 27
"Seven Odes to Natural Processes" (Updike), 175–76, 182, 183
"Seven Stanzas at Easter" (Updike), 94, 183, 186
sex, 10, 121, 140; little death and, 177; religion and, 156; sin and, 156; smell of, 152, 159
sex scenes, 13, 14–16, 61–62, 157
Shakespeare, William, 22, 25, 141
shallowness, 3, 5, 168, 169
"Shillington" (Updike), 58
Sidney, Sir Philip, 11
similes, 8, 48
sin, 132, 134; grace and, 120, 136; sex and, 156
Skeeter, 143
Smart, Jane, 35
smell, 152; bad, 157, 162, 164; beauty and, 151; death and, 149–50, 168, 169; sanitizing, 163; treatment of, 151, 152
Smith, James K. A., 116, 117
Smith, Rachel Greenwald: neoliberal novel and, 32
soap, vitamin-enhanced, 149, 150, 151
social relations, 142, 147
"Soft Spring Night in Shillington, A" (Updike), 49
Sontag, Susan, 63, 86–87, 88
soul, God and, 71–72
Sources of the Self (Taylor), 26
Spinoza, Baruch, 139
spiritual longing, 127, 142, 145, 146, 174
spiritual world, 6, 113, 185
spirituality, 6, 28, 105, 121, 128, 146, 151, 161, 163, 169, 174; ethics and, 122; individual, 159

Stewart, Kathleen, 31, 32
style, 1, 55–56, 126; gratitude and, 11; limner, 68–69; lyrical, 37; visual, 61–62
subjectivity, 1, 26, 52, 55–56, 126
Symposium (Plato), 38
Szalay, Michael, 120, 121, 144

Talented Mr. Ripley, The (Highsmith), 140
taste, 89, 92, 104, 120; aesthetic problem of, 91; chewing and, 103, 108; language of, 102; learning, 95; theology of, 93, 112; treatment of, 116; well-trained, 91
"Taste" (Updike), 91, 116
Tate, Andrew, 30
Taylor, Charles, 4, 26, 122, 135
teleology, 12, 13
"Telephone Poles" (Updike), 94
"Temple of the Holy Ghost, A" (O'Connor), 111
Terrorist (Updike), 6
themes, 43–44, 174
theology, 2, 8, 10, 11, 30, 92, 93, 124; Barthian, 129; Christian, 4, 7, 41, 42, 86, 94, 130; concepts, 5–6, 51, 132, 157, 173; liberal, 183; natural, 29, 42, 131; superficial, 12–13
3rd Biennial Conference of the John Updike Society, 97
This Is My Best (Updike), 111
Three Rival Versions of Moral Inquiry (MacIntyre), 122
Time, 13, 124
"To a Waterbed" (Updike), 175
"To Two of My Characters" (Updike), 175
Tothero, Marty, 118, 121
touch, 31, 32, 51–60, 104; Christ's, 36, 38; orienting, 43–51; words, 33–43
Touching Feeling (Sedgwick), 40

Tournier, Michel, 53, 54, 55, 56, 58
Toward the End of Time (Updike), 33
transformation, 10, 55, 78, 167
Travel Light (Bech), 167
Trump, Donald, 123
Trupp, Ben, 95–96, 98, 100; Murray and, 96, 97, 99; reconciliation and, 101
Trupp, Murray, 95, 100, 101–2; Ben and, 96, 97, 99
truth, 5, 109, 111; aesthetic, 108; secular parables of, 25; theological, 22
Tunis, John, 12
Turnbull, Ben, 33, 34, 35
"Twin Beds in Rome" (Updike), 15

Undertow (Homer), 72–73
Underworld (DeLillo), 44
Updike, David, 97, 98
Updike, Wesley Russell, 38

Valéry, Paul, 166
Van Eyck, Jan, 69
Vendredi ou les limbes du Pacifique (Tournier), 53
Verdi, Giuseppi, 78
Verduin, Kathleen, 49
Versluys, Kristiaan, 52
Villages (Updike), 27, 94, 152, 155–56, 157, 159, 160, 166
violence, 73, 96, 99, 102, 124, 140; bodies and, 15; redemptive, 100
Violet Hour: Great Writers at the End, The (Roiphe), 174
visual arts, 56, 63
visual experience, 63, 74
visual metaphors, 125, 146

Waco siege (1993), 76
Wallace, David Foster, 11, 123
Webb, Stephen, 30, 85
Weber, Max, 26
West, Benjamin, 68
What Makes Rabbit Run? A Profile of John Updike (Cheshire), 98
White Noise (DeLillo), 44
whiteness, privileges of, 145, 162
Whose Justice? Which Rationality? (MacIntyre), 122
Widows of Eastwick, The (Updike), 16, 16–17
Willerton, Miss, 109, 110, 111
William James Lectures, 56
Williams, Rowan, 42, 43
Wilmot, Clarence, 76, 77, 79, 81, 86; movies and, 80; purpose/identity and, 78
Wilmot, Essie, 81, 82, 83
Wilmot, Teddy, 77, 79, 80, 81, 83
Wirzba, Norman, 154
Wise Blood (O'Connor), 110
Witches of Eastwick, The (Updike), 15, 35, 94
"Without a Song," 120, 142
Wood, James, 7
Wood, Ralph C., 7, 30
Word of God, 23, 153
Words and Pictures (film), 61
Work of Fire, The (Updike), 98
Wyeth, Andrew, 1

Zero K (DeLillo), 44
Žižek, Slavoj, 125, 139

LITERATURE, RELIGION, AND POSTSECULAR STUDIES
LORI BRANCH, SERIES EDITOR

Literature, Religion, and Postsecular Studies publishes scholarship on the influence of religion on literature and of literature on religion from the sixteenth century onward. Books in the series include studies of religious rhetoric or allegory; of the secularization of religion, ritual, and religious life; and of the emerging identity of postsecular studies and literary criticism.

A Theology of Sense: John Updike, Embodiment, and Late Twentieth-Century American Literature
  SCOTT DILL

Walker Percy, Fyodor Dostoevsky, and the Search for Influence
  JESSICA HOOTEN WILSON

The Religion of Empire: Political Theology in Blake's Prophetic Symbolism
  G. A. ROSSO

Clashing Convictions: Science and Religion in American Fiction
  ALBERT H. TRICOMI

Female Piety and the Invention of American Puritanism
  BRYCE TRAISTER

Secular Scriptures: Modern Theological Poetics in the Wake of Dante
  WILLIAM FRANKE

Imagined Spiritual Communities in Britain's Age of Print
  JOSHUA KING

Conspicuous Bodies: Provincial Belief and the Making of Joyce and Rushdie
  JEAN KANE

Victorian Sacrifice: Ethics and Economics in Mid-Century Novels
  ILANA M. BLUMBERG

Lake Methodism: Polite Literature and Popular Religion in England, 1780–1830
  JASPER CRAGWALL

Hard Sayings: The Rhetoric of Christian Orthodoxy in Late Modern Fiction
  THOMAS F. HADDOX

Preaching and the Rise of the American Novel
  DAWN COLEMAN

Victorian Women Writers, Radical Grandmothers, and the Gendering of God
  GAIL TURLEY HOUSTON

Apocalypse South: Judgment, Cataclysm, and Resistance in the Regional Imaginary
  ANTHONY DYER HOEFER

www.ingramcontent.com/pod-product-compliance
Lightning Source LLC
Chambersburg PA
CBHW020946230426
43666CB00005B/200